Historically the encounter between Christianity and Islam has been primarily defined either by confrontation and war or by the subjugation of Christians as *dhimmis* in Muslim territories. Khee-Vun Lin writes out of his existential struggles as a Chinese Christian living in Malaysia, a Muslim-majority state. Against this background he courageously asks the question: Is there a third way which avoids either extreme of confrontation or subjugation and which allows Christians simultaneously to play a meaningful citizenship role in the nation and to be faithful in Christ's mission? He believes that it would be possible if Christians embrace the practice of incarnational mission which empowers them to actively engage with the socio-political challenges of the nation rather than passively withdraw from it. Lin's bold thesis needs to be taken seriously especially today when both the historical confrontational and dhimmitude models are slowly but certainly being challenged and broken down under the impact of modernity and globalization. I recommend this book heartily.

Bishop Emeritus Hwa Yung
The Methodist Church in Malaysia

Khee-Vun Lin offers a theologically reflective and engaging book providing a guide for followers of Jesus to engage their context in order to be an incarnational presence which continues the mission of the triune God. Incarnational engagement does not abandon a culture, nor accommodate to a culture. Rather, through "being with" a culture in dialogue and action, this new missionally informed politic is present to and serves within a local context demonstrating and sharing the transformative power of the gospel. *Dialogue of Life* is an important contribution to the missional church literature. The theological premise of this book, and its outworking in a specific context, will be of benefit to those who seek to be a faithful presence in other settings.

Kurt N. Fredrickson, PhD
Associate Dean of Professional Doctoral Programs,
Associate Professor of Pastoral Ministry,
Fuller Theological Seminary, Pasadena, California, USA

This is a significant work which takes serious consideration of the condition of minority Christians in a challenging multicultural context. This is a work that promotes understanding, peace, and dialogue, yet at the same time provides a theological basis and practical suggestions for minority Christians to remain faithful to God's mission. It is particularly meaningful and important to the Chinese Christians in Sabah who are close to my heart, and relevant to those who are in similar situation. This is a book that speaks to the church. I gladly recommend this book to church leaders and those who are responsible to church policymaking.

The Most Revd. Datuk Melter J. Tais
Bishop of Sabah
Archbishop and Primate, Province of the Anglican Church in South East Asia
President, Council of Churches of Malaysia

This is an important work on incarnational mission for minority Christians in the non-Western world. It shows how deep and critical theological reflections of the incarnation produce not only good practical theology, but a model of mission that integrates evangelism in the realm of social engagement amidst a challenging religious and ethnonationalistic context. It deserves to be read by ministers, missionaries, and scholars as an example of how missional theology, social analysis, and public theology come together in service of the church to not only help believers survive but thrive in hope as courageous vessels of Christ that seek to make the good news truly good for all people.

John Cheong
Research Associate at-Large, Asian Centre for Mission

Dr. Khee-Vun Lin observes that the Chinese Christians in Sabah (CCS) have a dualistic theology of mission which lacks being rooted in our Malaysian soil and so fails to take cognizance of the present Malay-Muslim hegemony. He attempts to provide a way forward beyond the present constitutionalism and cultural rights approach of the CCS to one of social engagement ("being-with") that is based on an incarnational mission (as in Immanuel, God-with-us) – a "being with" and serving others in meeting their needs, spiritual and material. This allows the CCS to make space for Christian witness without being accused of being a threat. I strongly recommend this book for Christians to reflect and to act, based on an incarnational mission of social engagement which is in process.

Tan Kong-Beng
Executive Secretary, Christian Federation of Malaysia
Former Lecturer in Theology, Malaysia Bible Seminary, Kuang, Malaysia

Sensitive to the cultural tensions impacted by religious and ethnic identities of both the majority and minority populations in Malaysia, Lin offers insight into the challenges that Chinese Christians in Sabah encounter. Rather than a confrontational approach as a solution, Lin invites us to a practical theology approach to Christian witness that applies to the grassroot level through social engagement. Recovering the theological significance of terms such as "missional" and "incarnational," he revisits the concepts of "mission," "kingdom of God," and "Christ's presence" reflexively from a Christian minority perspective informed by perceptions of dominance and conquest that contradict the gospel. Lin's offer of dialogue and social engagement as necessary expressions of God's mission and kingdom ethics needs to be seriously considered, especially in social-cultural contexts plagued by divisive politics, religious suspicion, and social hostility. It is not only relevant but is fundamentally faithful to the gospel and to Jesus's call to be peacemakers.

Rev. Sivin Kit, PhD
Program Executive for Public Theology and Interreligious Relations,
The Lutheran World Federation

Dialogue of Life

Social Engagement as the Preferred Means to
Incarnational Mission in the Context of Malay Hegemony

Khee-Vun Lin

MONOGRAPHS

© 2020 Khee-Vun Lin (Lin Khee Vun)

Published 2020 by Langham Monographs
An imprint of Langham Publishing
www.langhampublishing.org

Langham Publishing and its imprints are a ministry of Langham Partnership

Langham Partnership
PO Box 296, Carlisle, Cumbria, CA3 9WZ, UK
www.langham.org

ISBNs:
978-1-83973-217-1 Print
978-1-83973-453-3 ePub
978-1-83973-454-0 Mobi
978-1-83973-455-7 PDF

Khee-Vun Lin has asserted his right under the Copyright, Designs and Patents Act, 1988 to be identified as the Author of this work.

All rights reserved. No part of this publication may be reproduced, stored in a retrieval system or transmitted, in any form or by any means, electronic, mechanical, photocopying, recording or otherwise, without the prior written permission of the publisher or the Copyright Licensing Agency.

Requests to reuse content from Langham Publishing are processed through PLSclear. Please visit www.plsclear.com to complete your request.

Scriptures taken from the Holy Bible, New International Version®, NIV®. Copyright © 1973, 1978, 1984, 2011 by Biblica, Inc.™ Used by permission of Zondervan.

British Library Cataloguing-in-Publication Data
A catalogue record for this book is available from the British Library.

ISBN: 978-1-83973-217-1

Cover & Book Design: projectluz.com

Langham Partnership actively supports theological dialogue and an author's right to publish but does not necessarily endorse the views and opinions set forth here or in works referenced within this publication, nor can we guarantee technical and grammatical correctness. Langham Partnership does not accept any responsibility or liability to persons or property as a consequence of the reading, use or interpretation of its published content.

Disclaimer: The content in this book is solely the author's personal views, thoughts, and opinions, and may not reflect the views of the author's employer, organization, committee, or other group or individual associated with the author.

In memory of my father, Lin Fen Chong,

and

to my mother, Ngui Moi Ching

Contents

Preface xiii

Acknowledgments xv

List of Abbreviations xvii

Introduction 1
    The Definition of Social Engagement...2
    The Definitions of Nation and State..3
    The Rationale of the Study...4
    The Need for Practical Theology 6
    Methodology and Scope 7
        Ministry Context..8
        Ministry Challenge 9
        Theological Reflection...10
        Proposed Application 11

Chapter 1 15
    Historical Context of Chinese Christians in Sabah
        Chinese Christians as Immigrants in North Borneo 15
        Chinese Immigrants in North Borneo..15
            Chinese in a Segregated Social Context................................17
            Chinese as Partners to the British Colonists 18
        The Formation of Malaysia 19
            The Malaysia Proposal 19
            Chinese Opposing the Formation of Malaysia as North
                Borneans...20
            The Chinese Conceded Defeat...22
        Summary: The Cultural Isolation of the CCS and Their
            Fondness for the British..23

Chapter 2 25
    The Rise of Malay Hegemony
        Malay Ethnogenesis, Immigrants' Threat, and Colonial Struggle........25
            The People (*Bangsa*) Movement 26
            The Islamic Influence..26
        Independence and the Formation of the "Malay Nation-State" 29
        The Rise of Malay Supremacy 32
        Islamization as a Political Necessity 34
            The Emergence of Islamic Revivalism (*Dakwah*) 34

  UMNO and PAS 35
 The Islamization to the Emergence of Malay Hegemony 37
  The Islamized Public Space 38
  The Irrepressible Malay Hegemony 41
  The Defeat of the Moderates 43
 Functional Dhimmitude as the Expression of Malay Hegemony 45
  Dhimmitude Explained 46
  Functional Dhimmitude in Malaysia Today 50
 Summary: From Malay Nationalism to Malay Hegemony 53

Chapter 3 57
 The Clash of Nationalisms and Social Withdrawal of the Sabah
 Chinese Christians
 The Clash of National Discourses 57
  The Cultural Nationalism of Malaysian Chinese 57
  The Malaysian Malaysia, Multiculturalism, and
   Constitutionalism 58
  Political Identity and Multiculturalism in Malaysia 59
 Malay Hegemony Alienated the Chinese Christians in Sabah 60
  Malay Nationalism and Islamization in Sabah 62
  Malay Hegemony a Betrayal to the Sabah Chinese 64
 Civil Negotiations by the Chinese Christians 65
  Chinese Civil Negotiation 65
  Christians' Civil Negotiation as a Response to Islamization 66
  Civil Negotiations of the Chinese Christians in Sabah 68
 The Limitations of Civil Negotiations 69
  The *Dakwah* Revivalists' Sentiment toward Civil Negotiation 70
  A Critical Assessment on Christian Civil Negotiation 72
 Summary: Unsettled "Malaysian" Identity, Detachment from
  Nation-Building 74
  Weakened Commitment of the Malaysian Chinese in
   Nation-Building 75
  The Detachment of the CCS from Nation-Building 75

Chapter 4 77
 Absence of Chinese Christians in Sabah's Mission Engagement
 with the Malay Muslims
 Early Mission Engagement in the Immigrant Church 77
  Pastoral Covering 77
  The Centripetal Mission Churches 78
  Mission Schools 80
 Chinese Christians in Sabah Losing Mission Engagement 80

  Losing the Mission Schools 80
  A Different Mission Field 81
  Breakthrough in Evangelism, Absence of Social Engagement 82
  The Limitations of Evangelism and Interfaith Dialogue 85
   The *Dakwah* Revivalists' Sentiment toward Christians 86
   Evangelism to the Malays 88
   Interfaith Dialogues 91
  Summary: Limited Missional Engagement with the Malays 93

Chapter 5 97
Incarnational Mission Defined
  Incarnation, "the Incarnation," and "Incarnational Mission" 98
   The Motives and Logic of Incarnation 99
   Incarnation as a Model for Mission 100
   Countering Criticisms of Incarnational Mission 103
  Incarnational Mission and the Missional Church 107
   The Missional Church and *Missio Dei* 107
   The Missional Church's Incarnational Mission 108
  The Missional Church Is Christ's Continuous Presence in
   the World 111
   The Church as the "Body" 111
   Imitation and Discipleship as Christ's Continuous Ministry 112
  The Missional Church Represents the Kingdom of God 113
   The Kingdom and New Humanity 113
   Kingdom Ethics Incarnated 115
  The Missional Church Identifies with the People 115
   Solidarity with Others and Their Situation 115
   Respect and Acceptance of Others' Culture 117
   The Practice of Identification 118
  Transformation and Human Flourishing 119
   Value and Transformation of Humanity 120
   Submission to God in Transformation 122
  Summary: The Shape of Incarnational Mission 123

Chapter 6 125
Restoring Incarnational Mission among the Chinese Christians in Sabah
  Embracing an Incarnational and Malaysian Identity 125
   The Absence of Missional and Incarnational Identity 126
   A Critique on Liberalism as the Basis for Christian Identity
    in Malaysia 127
   An Incarnational Political Theology 128

Restoring CCS's Incarnational Identity as Malaysians	131
Restoring the Missing Social Dimension of the Gospel among CCS	132
Eschatological and Soteriological Reductionisms	132
The Diminishing Public Presence of CCS	134
Embracing the Social Dimension of Incarnational Mission	136
Identification in Civil Negotiations	137
Restoring Incarnational Witnessing among the Chinese Christians in Sabah	137
Limited Evangelism and the Absence of Missional Strategy to the Malays	137
Incarnational Mission through Witnessing	138
Summary: Incarnational Identification	141

Chapter 7 145
Social Engagement as a Preferred Means for Incarnational Mission

Christian Social Engagement in Malaysia	145
An Incarnational Approach of Social Engagement	146
Approaches of Social Engagement	146
Social Engagement as an Outworking of Incarnational Mission	148
Sociopolitical Reasons for Social Engagement	148
Social Engagement as a Means to Identify with the Malay Muslims' Culture	148
An Alternative to Civil Negotiation in Nation-Building	151
Social Engagement as Witness to Muslims in Malaysian Legal Context	154
Dialogue as the Practice of Social Engagement	156
Summary: Incarnational Mission in Practice	164

Summary and Conclusion 165

Epilogue 171

Rejection of Multiculturalism	171
Rejection of Moderate Islam	173
Non-Muslims under Malay Hegemony	175
Conclusion	176

Bibliography 179

Preface

The date was September 15, 2019. Over lunch, I told a pastor friend from the UK, that the then prime minister-in-waiting, Anwar Ibrahim will not take the helm of the Malaysian government should he remain a moderate. In February 2020, a political coup effectively ended Anwar's prospect to be the next prime minister. Anwar has come a long way, from being a young radical to being the prime minister-designate prior to the 1998 financial crisis. He was then imprisoned, made a political comeback, and once again became prime minister-in-waiting for the second time. What has caused the one-time radical champion of Islamism to lose support in 2020? One of the reasons I believe, is his transformation to a moderate Islamist. There are obviously other factors involved, but there are many indications that a moderate Islamist stance is not popular anymore among the Muslim majority in Malaysia today, even though moderate Muslims in Malaysia maintain much, if not all, of the fundamental characteristics of Islamism.

I was able to predict the fate of Anwar because of a study I embarked on Malay hegemony through my doctoral dissertation. I learned how Malay politics dominated Malaysia's fortune, and the development of Malay hegemony – a term I intend to define as the new form of Malay Supremacy fueled and directed by Islamism. Blessed with a background that has various multicultural exposures and postgraduate studies in mission, I am sensitive to the various cultural signs of the people groups within Malaysia, and am able to differentiate a typical "Western" reading of the Asian situation from a genuine and local perspective. This is certainly helped by the fact that I am conversant in the Chinese, Malay, and English languages.

I was particularly concerned with the lack of in-depth theological reflection that engages the sociopolitical context in Malaysia through rigorous ethnographic studies. This deficiency has resulted in ineffective and defective Christian responses toward Malay hegemony. In other words, the lack of understanding of the context has led to the inability for Malaysian Christians to formulate a comprehensive response appropriate to their sociopolitical context. This is inevitably interconnected with the deficient understanding of the gospel's holistic nature, leading to the failure to remain faithful to God's mission. This work is a response to such shortcomings. I believe the proposed methodology used in this work would showcase how a theological response should be constructed through a more comprehensive study of the context and the meaning of mission.

An epilogue is added in this volume to respond to the changes which took place after the dissertation was completed in late 2018. Updated resources are added in a few places, and some improvements are also made in the original work. Particularly, there are some significant additions and revisions in chapter 2 and 5. Most Islamic terms used in this work are based on their Malaysian translations.

My prayer is for this book to be a blessing to those who face a similar plight like the Chinese Christians in Sabah (CCS) and Malaysia. Hopefully, this work would serve as a showcase for practical theology, and an example of how ecclesiology, missiology, and ethnography may integrate to form a Christian response in a difficult situation. After completing this work, I have been able to see the similarities between the situation of CCS and many Christian minorities in the world. I believe many will agree with me after reading this book.

Acknowledgments

I would like to express my gratitude to Scott W. Sunquist and Kurt Fredrickson who were the content readers for the dissertation which this book is based on. This work would not be possible without their guidance. I am thankful to the wonderful people associated with Fuller Theological Seminary who made the completion of the dissertation possible – the team at the Doctor of Ministry Program, Jim Gustafson, John Ng and Peter Chao of Eagles Communication, Singapore, and my fellow classmates. A special acknowledgment of the trust and confidence shown by the late Bishop Albert C. F. Vun in my academic pursuit.

I am grateful to my bishop, the Most Rev. Melter J. Tais, the bishop of Sabah, who is also the Anglican archbishop of Southeast Asia, for his care, support, and encouragement over the years. I am thankful for the Board of Governors and colleagues of the Anglican Training Institute (ATI). My church family, the Diocese of Sabah, through ATI, has provided me with various forms of aid and helped to complete this work.

With gratitude and love, I thank my wife Yee Shong, and my children Zhan Mao (Athanasius) and Yue (Eunice). I am indebted to their support and sacrifices.

I wish to acknowledge the help provided by: Jonathan Chan, Lee Soo-Tian, Sivin Kit, Hwa Yung, Tan Kong-Beng, and Kenneth Thien who helped to read the manuscript and provided valuable feedback; John Cheong for his inputs on incarnational mission and overall feedback; Bishop James Wong (Basel Church), President Hii Kong-Hock (Methodist Church), and many others for their willingness to share resources.

I am thankful for my tutors at Trinity College, Bristol, UK, whose guidance has helped formed the foundation for this work.

Finally, I would like to express my appreciation to Langham Partnership for publishing this work.

List of Abbreviations

ABIM	Angkatan Belia Islam Malaysia (Malaysian Muslim Youth)
Amanah	Parti Amanah Negara (National Trust Party)
CCS	Chinese Christians in Sabah
CCM	Council of Churches of Malaysia
CFM	Christian Federation of Malaysia
CGA	Chinese Guilds and Associations
CMS	Church Missionary Society
Company	British North Borneo Chartered Company
DAP	Democratic Action Party
GE	General Election
ICERD	International Convention on the Elimination of All Forms of Racial Discrimination
IFC	Interfaith Commission
IRC	Islamic Representative Council
IS	Islamic State
ISMA	Ikatan Siswazah Muslim Malaysia (Muslim Student Solidarity Front)
JAKIM	Department of Islamic Development Malaysia
KDM	Kadazandusuns and Muruts
MUIS	Majlis Ugama Islam Sabah (Sabah Islamic Council)
NCP	National Culture Policy
NECF	National Evangelical Christian Fellowship
NEP	New Economic Policy
PAS	Pan-Malaysian Islamic Party

PH	Pakatan Harapan (Alliance of Hope)
PN	Perikatan Nasional (National Alliance)
RC	Roman Catholic Church in Sabah
SCC	Sabah Council of Churches
SPG	Society of Propagation of the Gospel
Tunku	Tunku Abdul Rahman
UMNO	United Malay National Organization
USIA	United Sabah Islamic Association
WWII	The Second World War

Introduction

Churches in Malaysia today face aggressive Islamization resulting from Malay hegemony. Malay hegemony is a form of Malay nationalism galvanized by Islamism.[1] Under Malay hegemony, non-Malays, including Chinese Christians in the state of Sabah (CCS), have come under the predicament of functional "dhimmitude."[2] Meanwhile, CCS have their very own nationalism which is ideologically in conflict with Malay hegemony's version of nationalism, namely, the idea of Malaysia as a nation in the minds of CCS is different from the one upheld by the state that is dominated by Malay hegemony. This clash of nationalisms has detached the CCS from nation-building. It has also created much religious, cultural, and social tensions between CCS and the Malay Muslims.[3]

---

1. Islamism is defined as "the views of those Muslims who claim that Islam, or more specifically, the Islamic sharī'ah, provides guidance for all areas of human life, individual and social, and who therefore call for an 'Islamic State' or an 'Islamic Order.' Islamists focus primarily on political matters, but they are also concerned with economic, social, and moral issues." William E. Shepard, François Burgat, and Armando Salvatore, "Islamism," *The Oxford Encyclopedia of the Islamic World. Oxford Islamic Studies Online*, http://www.oxfordislamicstudies.com. fuller.idm.oclc.org/article/opr/t236/e0888. Mohamed Nawab Mohamed Osman, "The Islamic Conservative Turn in Malaysia: Impact and Future Trajectories," *Contemporary Islam* 11, no. 1 (2017): 1–20. The influence of globalized Islamism on Malaysia will be discussed in the subsequent sections.

2. Dhimmitude is "the totality of the characteristics developed in the long term by communities subjected in their own homeland to the laws and ideology imported through jihad." Bat Ye'or, *The Decline of Eastern Christianity under Islam: From Jihad to Dhimmitude: Seventh-Twentieth Century*, trans. Miriam Kochan and David G. Littman (Madison, NJ: Fairleigh Dickinson University Press, 1996), 221. It also refers to "the submission-protection condition of infidels obtained by surrendering their territory to the Islamic authority." Bat Ye'or, "Jews and Christians under Islam: Dhimmitude and Marcionism," trans. Nidra Poller, *Commentaire* 97 (2002): 2. See chapter 2 for a comprehensive deliberation on "dhimmitude," including the rationale of the sources used.

3. According to Malaysia's constitution, all Malays are Muslims. Muslims in Malaysia are a religious-cultural identity. This work uses "Malay" and "Muslims" interchangeably.

Consequently, CCS lack a sense of belonging to the country. They are constantly defending their cultural identity and their version of nationalism, negotiating with the state amidst the force of Malay hegemony. Yet, their negotiation yields little result. Meanwhile, they find themselves further detached from the Muslims, and wonder, with such social, cultural, and political distances, how might they bear witness for Christ among the Muslims faithfully. The struggles of the CCS expose the lack of a clear and comprehensive theological framework and corresponding course of action. The CCS need a practical theology that takes the Malaysian sociopolitical and cultural context seriously, while providing a practical solution resulting from deep theological reflection.

Taking the missional church perspective, this study argues that incarnational mission should be the theological and ministry framework of the CCS in the context of Malay hegemony.[4] Incarnational mission, an important theological premise of the missional church movement, is able to resolve the challenges faced by the CCS through providing a theological rationale and a framework for the proposed praxis. The concept of incarnational mission would reinvigorate the motivations of the CCS in active nation-building and social involvement. It would also guide CCS in their mission to the Malay Muslims. Considering their sociopolitical context that is dominated by Malay hegemony, social engagement in the form of "dialogue of life" is then argued as the preferred means to apply the incarnational mission of the CCS.

The Definition of Social Engagement

Social engagement involves "aiding the disadvantaged and seeking the public good," and in the process, going beyond transforming individual lives to change social structures if necessary, in order to seek justice.[5] Referring to the

---

4. The "missional church" in this book refers to the church envisioned by the missional church movement, most notably recorded in Darrell L. Guder, ed., *Missional Church: A Vision for the Sending of the Church in North America* (Grand Rapids, MI: Eerdmans, 1998). Other major works on the subject and detailed definition of "missional church" are discussed in chapter 5, where "incarnational mission" is also defined.

5. Brian Steensland and Philip Goff, eds., *The New Evangelical Social Engagement* (New York, NY: Oxford University Press, 2013), Kindle, "Introduction." Seeking "shalom" or welfare of the city is the most consistent biblical basis used for Christian social engagement. *Pilgrims and Citizens: Christian Engagement in Asia Today* (Adelaide: ATF Press, 2006). Social engagement

above as social responsibility, the Lausanne movement helpfully categorizes Christian social engagement into social service and social action.[6] Examples of social service include the acts of relieving human need, philanthropic activity, and works of mercy, with the aim of ministering to individuals and families. Social action includes the act of removing the cause of human need, political and economic activity, the quest for justice, and seeks to transform the structure of society.

While the term covers a wide range of meanings, this study differentiates social engagement from the forms of public or civil negotiations that are legalistic, political, and public. Here, social engagement focuses on the social aspects of a community. It concerns relationships, cultures, and emotions instead of official or formal negotiations, which are based on rules, regulations, or legal positions.

The Definitions of Nation and State

In the context of this study, the state is to be understood as the legal-political entity defined according to a set of objective criteria of a country. It is "a tangible phenomenon that can be defined in terms of territory, population, and government."[7] The nation, on the other hand, is understood as a cultural and subjective entity, a product of ethnogenesis.[8] A nation's essence is "psychological, a matter of attitude rather than of fact."[9] Most states consist of various ethnic groups and in such cases "nation state" which implies "a

---

is also an intrinsic part of practical theology. Mark L. Branson and Juan F. Martinez, *Churches, Cultures and Leadership: A Practical Theology of Congregations and Ethnicities* (Downers Grove, IL: IVP Academic, 2011), Kindle, chap. 1.

6. "LOP 21 – Evangelism and Social Responsibility: An Evangelical Commitment," *Lausanne Movement*, 25 June 1982, https://www.lausanne.org/content/lop/lop-21.

7. Walker Connor, "Ethnic Nationalism as a Political Force," *World Affairs* 133, no. 2 (1970): 91; Graeme Gill, *The Nature and Development of the Modern State* (New York: Palgrave Macmillan, 2003), 2–7.

8. The biblical concept of ἔθνος, is defined as "a body of persons united by kinship, culture, and common traditions, nation, people." Walter Bauer, *A Greek-English Lexicon of the New Testament and Other Early Christian Literature*, ed. Frederick William Danker, 3rd ed. (Chicago: University of Chicago Press, 2001), 276.

9. Connor, "Ethnic Nationalism as a Political Force," 91. The definition of "nation" is complex. Here, Connor's definition is preferred over Anthony D. Smith's. See Walker Connor, "The Timelessness of Nations," *Nations and Nationalism* 10, no. 1–2 (2004): 35–47; Anthony D. Smith, *Nationalism: Theory, Ideology, History*, 2nd ed. (Cambridge, UK: Polity, 2010).

coincidence between state and ethnic nation . . . is a misnomer."[10] Rather, it is more likely for various nations within a state to have their respective nation-of-intent.[11] Nation-of-intent is an intended ethno-nationalism not in exact correspondence to the politically defined state. It is "a more or less precisely defined idea of the form of a nation-state . . . that is its territory, population, language, culture, symbols, and institutions."[12] It is a nation's idea of a state, a foundational tenet for its very own nationalism.

The Rationale of the Study

The rationale of this study rests in the unique sociopolitical context of the CCS as a minority and the need for them to respond with a practical theology.[13] According to the latest census, 65.37 percent of the Sabah population identify themselves as Muslims while 26.62 percent are Christians.[14] Chinese Christians are only 11.29 percent of the total Christian population in Sabah; hence, they constitute only about 3 percent of the total population.[15] In contrast, the only Christian majority state in Malaysia, Sarawak, is 42.61 percent Christian in population, compared to 32.22 percent Muslims.[16] Sarawak, together with Sabah (then "North Borneo") and Singapore, joined Malaya to form the federation of Malaysia in 1963. Both the Bornean states of Sabah and Sarawak were promised equal status with Malaya. Although the autonomy of both states has been repressed over the years, Sarawak today retains greater autonomy compared to Sabah and remains a relatively isolated sociopolitical

---

10. Gill, *Nature and Development*, 6.

11. "Nations exist in the sense that a collective identity has been formed, but do not find institutional expression in the form of the creation of a coterminous state." Joseph Liow, *Religion and Nationalism in Southeast Asia* (Cambridge, UK: Cambridge University Press, 2016), 32.

12. A. B. Shamsul and Sity Daud, "Nation, Ethnicity, and Contending Discourse in the Malaysian State," in *State Making in Asia*, ed. Richard Boyd and Ngo Tak-Wing (London: Routledge, 2012), 136.

13. Another minority Christian group in Southeast Asia with their own nation-of-intent is the Karen. See Ananda Rajah, "A 'Nation of Intent' in Burma: Karen Ethno-Nationalism, Nationalism and Narrations of Nation," *The Pacific Review* 15, no. 4 (2002): 517–537.

14. *Population Distribution and Basic Demographic Characteristics*, Population and Housing Census of Malaysia 2010 (Putrajaya: Department of Statistic, Malaysia, 2011), 92.

15. In total, 96,422; Chinese are only 9.22 percent of Sabah's population. *Population Distribution and Basic Demographic Characteristics*, 92.

16. *Population Distribution and Basic Demographic Characteristics*, 93.

entity. As the following chapters explain, Sabah has experienced much intense Islamization and a drastic shift in demography. Since this study focuses on a Christian minority, Sarawak would be excluded. Only the contexts of Malay Peninsula (formerly Malaya, "Peninsular") and Sabah are studied.

CCS are also unique among the Chinese population in Malaysia. Animosity between Chinese and Muslims is much less in Sabah compared to the Peninsular. The struggle between the Malays and the "Communist Chinese" has never taken place in Sabah as in the Peninsular. The harmonious relationship with Muslims gives CCS an advantage in engaging with Muslims, although this advantage is fast disappearing in recent years due to reasons this study will address.

Meanwhile, CCS share a similar plight with the indigenous and predominantly Christian Kadazandusuns and Muruts (KDM) ethnic groups in various federal-state, cultural, and religious issues.[17] The KDM are the largest indigenous ethnic group in Sabah that has developed a relatively amicable relationship with the Chinese.[18] The KDM, especially non-Muslims, struggle to protect their indigenous rights and identity from being assimilated into the Malay ethnicity. The Chinese share with them this rejection of Malay nationalism.[19] Most of the CCS belong to Christian denominations with large indigenous congregations. As the KDM face the same aggression of Islamization, a practical and theological response to Malay hegemony by CCS will provide some insights on their common struggle. Similarly, the CCS might play a significant role among fellow Chinese. With nearly one-third (32.61 percent) of the Chinese in Sabah being Christians, CCS can assert a

---

17. Regina Lim, "Islamization and Ethnicity in Sabah, Malaysia," in *Encountering Islam: The Politics of Religious Identities in Southeast Asia*, ed. Yew-Foong Hui (Singapore: Institute of Southeast Asian Studies, 2012), 158–190; James Chin and Andrew Harding, eds., *50 Years of Malaysia: Federalism Revisited* (Singapore: Marshall Cavendish International, 2015).

18. Bernard Sta Maria, *Peter J. Mojuntin, the Golden Son of the Kadazan* (Melaka, Malaysia: Sta Maria, 1978), 25, https://koeln.ccc.de/media/pdf/TheGoldenSonOfTheKadazan(compact).pdf; K. G. Tregonning, *Under Chartered Company Rule – North Borneo 1881–1946* (University of Malaya Press, 1958), 32. Other records are: Danny Tze-Ken Wong, *Historical Sabah: The Chinese* (Kota Kinabalu, Malaysia: Natural History Publications, 2005), 51–55; Danny Wong, "A Hybrid Community in East Malaysia: The Sino-Kadazans of Sabah and Their Search for Identity," *Archipel* 84 (2012): 107–127.

19. The Kadazandusuns were at first hostile toward the Chinese who dominated the economy of Sabah, but later found Malay nationalism a greater threat. See the first person account of a prominent Kadazan politician in Herman J. Luping, *Sabah's Dilemma: The Political History of Sabah, 1960–1994* (Ann Arbor, MI: Magnus Books, 1994), 503–570.

significant influence toward fellow Chinese compared to their counterparts in the Peninsular.[20] The testimony of the CCS may play a prophetic role in showing a way for minorities in Malaysia to participate in nation-building.

The reasons discussed above show that CCS are in a unique position. Regrettably, CCS lack an overarching theological and ministry framework that enables them to respond to Malay hegemony, faithfully involve in nation-building, and missionally engage with the Malay Muslims. To rectify this, they need a practical theology.

The Need for Practical Theology

Practical theology is defined as a "critical, theological reflection on the practices of the church as they interact with the practices of the world with a view to ensuring faithful participation in the continuing mission of the triune God."[21] Practical theology employs ethnography to understand human experiences and discover underlying motives, worldviews, social dynamics, and meaning that motivate and animate church practices.[22] This is in contrast to systematic theology that interprets doctrine and tradition, and biblical studies that interpret the Bible.[23] Without neglecting Scripture and tradition, practical theology involves the context in the formulation of theological treaties and related solutions.[24]

---

20. *Population Distribution and Basic Demographic Characteristics*, 92. The Hakka Christians' influence can be seen clearly through the Basel Church and the Anglican Church, which started the majority of the schools in the state before the formation of Malaysia. See Delai Zhang, ed., *Sabah's Hakka Story* (Kota Kinabalu: Sabah Theological Seminary, 2015); Delai Zhang, *The Hakkas of Sabah: A Survey of Their Impact on the Modernization of the Bornean Malaysian State* (Kota Kinabalu, Malaysia: Sabah Theological Seminary, 2002).

21. John Swinton and Harriet Mowat, *Practical Theology and Qualitative Research* (London: SCM Press, 2011), Kindle, chap. 1.

22. Mary Clark Moschella, *Ethnography as a Pastoral Practice* (Cleveland, OH: Pilgrim Press, 2008), 38–40. In Swinton and Mowat, *Practical Theology*, "Introduction," chapters 1 and 2, Swinton argues that interpretation of the context is a "missing dimension" of the theological enterprise, which practical theology is rediscovering.

23. Swinton and Mowat, *Practical Theology*, chap. 1.

24. Swinton and Mowat, "Introduction," 1.

Methodology and Scope

The overarching methodological framework for this study is practical theology. It directs the methods used in the processes of studying the ministry context, identifying the ministry challenges, formulating theological reflection, and developing practical suggestion.[25] This study focuses on the two main denominations in Sabah. As the denomination with the largest number of Chinese members, the Basel Christian Church of Malaysia (BCCM/Basel Church) has a total of 19,147 members for their Chinese and English language congregations.[26] The Anglican Diocese of Sabah has about 7,000 average weekly worshippers in the Chinese and English language congregations. The total registered members of these Anglican congregations may well exceed 14,000. CCS can be more distinctly identified within these denominations, as their English-speakers are predominantly ethnic Chinese.[27] The Chinese in these two denominations also share the same historical root in the Hakka people (56.8 percent of all Chinese in Sabah).[28]

The number of Chinese believers and their cultural affiliation in the Roman Catholic Church in Sabah (RC) are less obvious.[29] The RC Kota Kinabalu Archdiocese's Sacred Heart Cathedral recorded about 2,000 average weekend worshippers who are Chinese-speaking.[30] This indicates the relatively smaller active number of Chinese RC members compared to the Anglican and Basel churches.[31] Considering its complexity, the RC is not

---

25. "Methods" are "specific techniques that are used for data collection and analysis," while methodology is "an overall approach to a particular field. It implies a family of methods that have in common particular philosophical and epistemological assumptions." Swinton and Mowat, *Practical Theology*, chap. 3.

26. The BCCM has a few name-changes in history; for convenience, it is referred to as the "Basel Church" in this study. Thomas Lip Tet Tsen, ed., *History of the Basel Christian Church of Malaysia (1882–2012)* (Kota Kinabalu: Basel Christian Church of Malaysia, 2015), 20–21, 620.

27. Among the churches of CCS, some consist of Chinese-speaking Chinese while others English-speaking Chinese. The English-speaking Chinese are racially Chinese, but culturally mixed, with a large proportion of them adopting certain Western cultures. The English-speaking Chinese are included in this study as a part of CCS.

28. Zhang, *Hakkas of Sabah*, 32.

29. Diocese of Kota Kinabalu, *Diocesan Organizational Pastoral Plan, 1998–2004* (Kota Kinabalu, Malaysia: DOPP Core Group, 1997), 1.

30. *Silver Jubilee of the Diocese of Kota Kinabalu 2002: Put Out into the Deep* (Kota Kinabalu, Malaysia: The Diocese of Kota Kinabalu, 2002), 75.

31. The Kota Kinabalu Archdiocese is one of the three dioceses in Sabah and the one with many Chinese believers, especially in the urban area where the cathedral is located. The other key Chinese congregations are in Sandakan, Tawau, and Kudat Diocese of Kota Kinabalu,

the primary focus in this study. The relatively smaller Methodist Chinese congregations, are also excluded.[32]

Instead of a survey, this study relies on documents and available publications from the abovementioned denominations and their contexts. The first two parts of this study are based on interpretations or narratives.[33] As this study follows narratives of the cultural groups concerned, data and information gathered are often "fragments and themes that emerge from particular situations and contexts."[34] The language used is often related to "themes and patterns, rather than systems and universal concepts."[35] In other words, this study aims to produce rich and thick descriptions rather than theory.[36]

Finally, this study intends to focus on the sociopolitical role of the CCS, with minimum discussion on their economic aspect. The economic prowess and influence of the Malaysian Chinese is well documented. In this work, attention will be on the sociopolitical aspects of Sino-Malay relation. For example, when discussing the overseas Chinese migration to Malaysia, their economic motive and later economic success are acknowledged, but the focus would be on their national and cultural identity. Such narrowing of focus is imperative for this religiocultural study.

Ministry Context

The first part of this study is comprised of two chapters. Chapter 1 explains the sociopolitical context of the CCS. It explains the root of Chinese Sabahans'

Diocesan Organizational Pastoral Plan, 1998-2004, 1. The Roman Catholics in Sabah are led by the Archdiocese of Kota Kinabalu which has two suffragan dioceses – the Diocese of Sandakan and Diocese of Keningau.

32. The Methodists recorded 2,185 in membership in 2017. "A Church after God's Own Heart: Leaflet Introducing the Methodist Church in Malaysia" (The Methodist Church in Malaysia, 2017).

33. "Ethnographic accounts and explanations are better understood as narratives rather than as scientific treatises." Moschella, *Ethnography*, 29.

34. Swinton and Mowat, *Practical Theology*, chap. 1.

35. Swinton and Mowat, chap. 1.

36. The three criteria of "falsifiable, replicable and generalizable" are not employed to create any theory. Swinton and Mowat, chap. 2. Interpretation of the situation produces knowledge that is required for future researches "to explore the possibility of transferability and to find models that describe a situation and that have transferable structures." Swinton and Mowat, chap. 2.

national identity.³⁷ It also describes the background of Chinese Sabahans' skepticism on the formation of Malaysia and how their reluctance toward the formation has since caused them to constantly negotiate for their nation-of-intent. Research on the Chinese in Sabah, particularly on CCS, is scarce. This work relies on Danny Wong's accounts of Sabahan Chinese, and Delai Zhang's works on the Hakkas, the earliest and pivotal clan within CCS.³⁸

Chapter 2 explains the origin and development of Malay nationalism and its evolvement to Malay hegemony, specifically, how Islamism emerged as the key tenet and driver for Malay hegemony today. Subsequently, this chapter describes the situation of functional dhimmitude in today's Malaysia. Rigorous academic works, subjective Malay writers, and some reputable surveys are used. The Malays' animosity toward the Chinese is also described. The main goal of this chapter is to explain the Malays' insistence on defining Malaysia according to their cultural nationalism.

Ministry Challenge

Part two of this study considers the two interrelated missional detachments of CCS. Chapter 3 describes how the clash of nationalisms hinders CCS from developing their Malaysian identity, distancing them from nation-building. Using the case of the Malaysian Chinese as a whole, this chapter explains the inclination of the CCS toward constitutionalism and multiculturalism.³⁹ The specific ways Malay hegemony invaded Sabah and alienated the CCS is discussed. With this, this chapter presents a gap between the disgruntled CCS and the Muslims, each with their own nation-of-intent and cultural distinction. Then, this chapter examines the various methods used by the Chinese in Malaysia and CCS to negotiate their nation-of-intent, and the limitations of these methods in the context of Malay hegemony. To this end, the mindset of the *dakwah* revivalists is analyzed and argued to be a hindrance to the civil

---

37. For this work, much effort is invested to understand the Malays from a Chinese perspective. A larger section is dedicated on Malay ethnogenesis compared to Chinese ethnogenesis. As a study, which aims to help the CCS to be missional, this is an obvious choice.

38. Danny Tze-Ken Wong, *The Transformation of an Immigrant Society: A Study of the Chinese of Sabah* (London: Asean Academic, 1998); Zhang, *Hakkas of Sabah*.

39. "Multiculturalism" is comprehensively defined in chapter 3 when the Chinese version of nation-of-intent is discussed.

negotiation of the CCS.[40] This chapter concludes that due to differences in nationalism and the pressure from Malay hegemony, the Chinese in Malaysia are indecisive about their Malaysian identity and commitment to the country.

Chapter 4 considers the absence of the missional engagement of the CCS with the Malays – the challenge of witnessing and evangelism. It describes how CCS retreated from their missional involvement in the society since the intensification of Malay nationalism. The withdrawal of the CCS from the public space and the privatization of their faith affect their witness to the Malay Muslims. With the emergence of Malay hegemony and additional restrictions, the evangelism work of the CCS to Malay Muslims faces serious setbacks. Meanwhile, the effectiveness and relevance of interfaith dialogue is also limited.

Theological Reflection

In chapter 5, the concept of incarnational mission is introduced. The concept of missional church is used to frame the meaning of incarnational mission within a missional ecclesiology. Incarnational mission is contended to be an expression of the mission of God. It continues the presence of Christ, represents the kingdom, and identifies with the people.

Chapter 6 explores the theological implications of applying incarnational mission in CCS's nation-building, social responsibility, and witnessing to the Malay Muslims. First, this chapter contends that incarnational mission should become the basis for national identity and nationalism. Then, through incarnational mission, the restoration of the gospel's social dimension is made possible. This provides CCS with the theological basis for their political theology and social engagement. Third, this chapter proposes an incarnational and comprehensive theology of witnessing which overcomes the deadlock of evangelism to the Malay Muslims.

---

40. *Dakwah* is understood as Islamic propagation in this book, as used in Mohamed Nawab, "Islamic Conservative Turn," 2; Azhar Ibrahim, *Contemporary Islamic Discourse in the Malay-Indonesian World: Critical Perspectives* (Petaling Jaya, Malaysia: Strategic Information and Research Development Centre, 2014), 36. See fuller definition of *dakwah* in Paul E. Walker, Reinhard Schulze, and Muhammad Khalid Masud, "Daʿwah," *The Oxford Encyclopedia of the Islamic World. Oxford Islamic Studies Online*, http://www.oxfordislamicstudies.com/opr/t236/e0182.

Proposed Application

Chapter 7 argues that social engagement is the preferred means to practically apply incarnational mission outlined in chapter 6. Social engagement is established as a proper theological expression for incarnational mission. Considering the context of Malay hegemony, social engagement is also sociopolitically suitable for CCS's incarnational mission. Furthermore, it is a fitting means for CCS to engage in nation-building and witness to the Malay Muslims. Finally, "dialogue of life and action" is proposed as the specific practice to implement social engagement.

Part I

Ministry Context

CHAPTER 1

Historical Context of Chinese Christians in Sabah

This chapter considers the historical context of the Chinese Christians of Sabah (CCS). Arriving in British North Borneo (later Sabah) as immigrants, CCS developed an affinity with the British crown colony. Consequently, they opposed the formation of Malaysia that signified the end of British rule in North Borneo. This historical background sets the foundation of CCS's nation-of-intent.

Chinese Christians as Immigrants in North Borneo

CCS were key members of early Chinese settlers in North Borneo. Their early settlement was characterized by their segregated social context and partnership with British and Western missionaries. Their homogenous nature had been largely maintained throughout British rule.

Chinese Immigrants in North Borneo

The early CCS were Chinese of the Hakka dialect group (Hakkas). The first group of Hakka Christians, believed to be fleeing from China after the failure of the Taiping Rebellion (1850–1864), arrived in Sandakan, and eventually became members of the Basel Church.[1] The other group of Christian Hakkas

---

1. Among them were the remnant of the Taiping rebels/revolutionists. Zhang, *Hakkas of Sabah*, 5–6, 11–13.

from China arrived in North Borneo under the initiative of the British North Borneo Chartered Company (Company) in 1882.[2] Learning from the mistake of its predecessor that failed to source sufficient workers, the Company took swift initiatives to ensure a supply of manpower to work the land,[3] and decided to bring in, among others, Hakka settlers and laborers from China.[4] Subsequent groups arrived through various schemes, which continued until after the Second World War (WWII).[5]

The agriculturally-oriented Hakka settlers had a higher tendency to stay in North Borneo than the other dialect groups, which were more business-oriented.[6] They also differed from other Chinese, as they were refugees seeking new beginnings.[7] They had determined to stay for the long-term.[8] Furthermore, the Hakka settlers, especially Christians recruited through the Basel Mission, were given land and incentives and they often came with family.[9] Favored by the British colonists, the Hakkas' initial migration to Kudat in the late nineteenth century was a great success.[10]

---

2. The concession of North Borneo was officially transferred to the British North Borneo Chartered Company by the American Trading Company in 1882. Wong, *Transformation of an Immigrant*, 10–11. For details, see K. G. Tregonning, "American Activity in North Borneo, 1865–1881," *Pacific Historical Review* 23, no. 4 (1954): 357–372; K. G. Tregonning, *A History of Modern Sabah, 1881–1963* (Kuala Lumpur: Published for the University of Singapore by the University of Malaya Press, 1965), 1–30; and Ranjit Singh, *The Making of Sabah, 1865–1941: The Dynamics of Indigenous Society* (Kota Kinabalu, Malaysia: Bahagian Kabinet dan Dasar, Jabatan Ketua Menteri, 2011), 113–130.

3. Wong, *Transformation of an Immigrant*, 10–11.

4. Wong, 13–14.

5. Wong, 19; Zhang, *Hakkas of Sabah*, 10. The arrival of more Chinese immigrants was also due to factors such as the Boxer Rebellion in China. Wong, 30, 55.

6. Tregonning, *History of Modern Sabah*, 131; Wong, *Transformation of an Immigrant*, 19, 37–38; Jessie G. Lutz and Rolland Ray Lutz, "The Invisible China Missionaries: The Basel Mission's Chinese Evangelists, 1847–1866," *Mission Studies* 12, no. 1 (1995): 204–227.

7. Wong, *Transformation of an Immigrant*, 27; Niew Hong Tong, "A Brief History of the Hakka Immigrates in East Malaysia," *Asian Culture*, no. 17 (June 1993): 191 (in Chinese), as cited by Wong, 18, 44.

8. Wong, 37–38.

9. H. Bienz, "Short History of The Borneo Basel Self-Established Church, Usually Called The Basel Mission, in North Borneo," *Journal of the Malaysian Branch of the Royal Asiatic Society* 39, no. 1 (209) (1966): 166–168; Danny Tze-Ken Wong, "Chinese Migration to Sabah Before the Second World War," *Archipel* 58, no. 3 (1999): 131–158; Wong, *Transformation of an Immigrant*, 19–20, 85–89. For in-depth case study, see Delai Zhang, ed., *The Hakka Experiment in Sabah* (Kota Kinabalu, Malaysia: Sabah Theological Seminary, 2007).

10. Anwar Sullivan and Patricia Regis, "Demography," in *Commemorative History of Sabah, 1881–1981*, ed. Anwar Sullivan and Cecilia Leong (Kota Kinabalu, Malaysia: Sabah

After Kudat, the Company worked with the Basel Mission and invited more Basel Christians to settle in Sabah, covering more areas along the West Coast.[11] The number of Christians in North Borneo increased rapidly. According to the census report of 1931, the Chinese were the second largest ethnic group in North Borneo, with the Hakkas comprising one-third of the total Chinese population.[12] By 1951, nearly 60 percent of all Chinese in Sabah were Hakkas; about 30 percent of the Hakkas were Christians.[13] The Chinese remained the second largest ethnic group in the 1960 and 1970 censuses.[14]

Chinese in a Segregated Social Context

The activities of the Chinese in North Borneo were mainly restricted to town and specific settler areas. As in other colonies, the British applied "divide-and-rule" tactics. According to the Company Charter, the Company "or its officers as such, shall not in any way interfere with the religion of any class or tribe of the people of Borneo, or of any of the inhabitants thereof."[15] The indigenes had little interaction outside of their habitat and their way of life was preserved. Only Chinese were recruited by the Company.[16] As a result, the Chinese in urban and sub-urban areas had little contact with the indigenous people in the rural areas.[17]

Apart from the Chinese-indigene segregation, most Christian Hakkas remained detached from other non-Christians. The social circle of the CCS has had a relatively self-sufficient, enclosed, mono-cultural, and mono-religious beginning. The Basel Church, for example, began as a homogenous Hakka

---

State Government, Centenary Publications Committee, 1981), 553–554; Owen Rutter, *British North Borneo: An Account of Its History, Resources and Native Tribes* (Kota Kinabalu: Opus Publications, 2008), 131–132; Wong, *Transformation of an Immigrant*, 19–20, 29–33.

11. Wong, *Transformation of an Immigrant*, 55–58.
12. Anwar Sullivan and Regis, "Demography," 562.
13. In 1951, there were 44,505 Hakkas among a total of 74,374 Chinese in Sabah, while the total population was 334,141. In 1921, Hakkas were 18,153 among 39,256 Chinese, Appendix 4. L. W. Jones, *North Borneo Report on the Census of Population 1960* (Kuchen: Government Printing Office, 1962) in Wong, *Transformation of an Immigrant*; Zhang, *Hakkas of Sabah*, 32.
14. Anwar Sullivan and Regis, "Demography," 567–571.
15. British North Borneo Chartered Company, *British North Borneo Company Charter* (Ithaca, NY, 1878), 9, http://archive.org/details/cu31924078409665.
16. Wong, *Transformation of an Immigrant*, 85.
17. Rutter, *British North Borneo*, 33–34.

church and remained so until the 1970s.[18] The Basel Christians normally settled within an area as landowners, with the school and church establishment as their focal point, making their environment homogenous and their identity distinct.[19]

In short, ethnogenesis in these early Chinese immigrants happened in a relatively independent and isolated environment.[20] The parochial attitude of the Chinese in general and CCS in particular has been prevalent from the very beginning of Chinese immigration. Interactions with other ethnicities were exceptions or simply a means to business.

Chinese as Partners to the British Colonists

Referring to the Chinese in 1922, Rutter, a British historian, commented, "North Borneo could never have gone a mile along the road of progress had not her doors been opened to the adventurous inhabitants of the Celestial Empire."[21] According to Rutter, the Chinese were honest, intelligent, and industrious; and they contributed to the development of North Borneo as the partners of the British.[22] Chinese participation in the North Borneo government began in the early days of the Company. From 1931, the Chinese had representatives in various advisory, legislative, and governing organizations.[23] Participation in these organizations was vital to the well-being of the Chinese. It ensured healthy cooperation between the Chinese and the Company for their common interests.

After WWII, the British needed the Chinese to help reconstruct North Borneo, so they took steps to prevent the Chinese from returning to China. They became involved in Chinese education for the first time to "mold the

---

18. Zhang, *Hakkas of Sabah*, 45.

19. Danny Tze-Ken Wong, "The Basel Christian Church and 130 Years of the History of Sabah: A Survey," in *Sabah's Hakka Story*, ed. Delai Zhang (Kota Kinabalu, Malaysia: Sabah Theological Seminary, 2015), 90.

20. Chee-Beng Tan, "Ethnic Groups, Ethnogenesis and Ethnic Identities: Some Examples from Malaysia," *Identities* 6, no. 4 (1997): 441–480. Interference of Chinese schools was bordering on absence during colonial period. Tregonning, *History of Modern Sabah*, 183.

21. Rutter, *British North Borneo*, 81.

22. Rutter, 81.

23. The organizations were Clan Associations, Chinese Chamber of Commerce, Kapitan Cina, Legislative Council, Chinese Advisory Board and Chinese Consul. The Kapitans, representatives in the Legislative Council and the Chinese Advisory Board were appointed by the government, while the rest were Chinese-initiated. Wong, *Transformation of an Immigrant*, 98.

Chinese into permanent residents of the state."[24] This was part of the efforts to encourage the Chinese to regard themselves as citizens of North Borneo, with all the advantages of citizenship accorded to them.[25]

The Chinese also filled the leadership gap in government.[26] Immediately after the war, the Advisory Council was established to assist the Governor in administering the colony. The Chinese were present since its inauguration and they remained a key component in the years to come, with four to five Chinese representatives included in the Council from 1947 to 1950.[27] These leaders played a vital role in protecting the interests of the Chinese and were pivotal in rebuilding North Borneo after the war.[28] From 1950 to 1963, The Legislative Council and the Executive Councils replaced the Advisory Council. Again, Chinese presence was strong.[29] To a large extent, the transformation of the Chinese from immigrants to citizens was complete.

The Formation of Malaysia

The formation of Malaysia interrupted CCS's process of localization as citizens of North Borneo. The Malaysia proposal was not expected by the CCS. Reluctantly, CCS were forced to adapt to their new country.

The Malaysia Proposal

In 1961, Malaya Prime Minister Tunku Abdul Raman (Tunku) proposed that Malaya, Singapore, and the Bornean states (Brunei, Sarawak, and North Borneo) would join to form the Federation of Malaysia.[30] In order to incorporate Singapore into Malaya, the Borneo states were invited so that their indigenous population (especially Muslims) would balance up the number of Chinese in Singapore.[31]

---

24. Wong, 173.
25. Wong, 177.
26. Wong, 175–176.
27. Government Gazette, 15 July, 1947, and North Borneo News, 1 September, 1949, quoted in Zhang, *Hakkas of Sabah*, 37.
28. Zhang, 241.
29. Tregonning, *History of Modern Sabah*, 239.
30. Zhang, *Hakkas of Sabah*, 242.
31. Edwin Lee, *The Towkays of Sabah: Chinese Leadership and Indigenous Challenge in the Last Phase of British Rule* (Singapore University Press, 1976), 62–63, in Zhang, *Hakkas of*

Initially skeptical, Bornean leaders were eventually persuaded by the British and the Malayan leaders to change their minds.³² The Muslim-indigenous group in North Borneo, led by Mustapha Harun, welcomed the idea of Malaysia as they "supported a strong central government under Federation, Islam as the national religion, and Malay as the national language."³³ In contrast, North Borneo Chinese did not expect such a move and remained adamant that Malaysia was a poor option to them.

Chinese Opposing the Formation of Malaysia as North Borneans

By the 1960s, the Chinese had made North Borneo their home having politically, socially, and economically attached to the land. With 77 percent of them local-born, North Bornean Chinese dominated the non-European economy.³⁴ Many of them had seceded their ties with China due to political differences.³⁵ They were also a part of the ruling class. As the ethnic group that received better education, they occupied key positions in the government. The Chinese political strength prior to Sabah's independence was shown during the first local election in 1962. The Chinese were well represented in all of the town boards and assumed chairmanship in all major towns.³⁶ The Chinese were concerned that their interests would be affected by Malays with the formation of Malaysia. Their "position . . . in business and society would be undermined, in contrast with the benefits they had derived from maintaining close relations with the colonial regime."³⁷ Bornean Chinese

---

Sabah, 244–245, 242; C. Paul Bradley, "Communal Politics in Malaysian Borneo," *The Western Political Quarterly* 21, no. 1 (1968): 130.

32. Zhang, *Hakkas of Sabah*, 244.
33. Bradley, "Communal Politics," 130.
34. Bradley, 130.
35. The Chinese in North Borneo maintained a closer tie with the Kuomintang (Nationalist Party of China) of Taiwan instead of the Communist China.
36. Town boards – (Kota Kinabalu, Sandakan, Tawau, Kudat, Beaufort, Tenom) Chairmanship – Kota Kinabalu, Sandakan, Tawau and Tenom. Zhang, *Hakkas of Sabah*, 257–258.
37. Danny Tze-Ken Wong and Hui Ling Ho, "The Chinese in Sabah and Sarawak Politics: Ensuring a Role in Government," in *Malaysian Chinese and Nation-Building: Before Merdeka and Fifty Years After*, Vol. 2, ed. Phin Keong Voon (Kuala Lumpur: Centre for Malaysian Chinese Studies, 2008), 528.

were decidedly cool to the Malaysian proposal. . . . Their principal fear was that the Alliance's Malay political leaders in Kuala Lumpur would dominate [and] subordinate Borneo and discriminate against the Chinese . . . they opposed Islam as a state religion and wanted English retained as an official language. While they were willing that indigenes be given special educational opportunities due to their backward position, the Chinese opposed constitutional status for such privileges.[38]

The Chinese also opposed the proposal because their business elite, commonly referred as *towkays*, preferred British rule which benefited them.[39] They considered the idea of Malaysia uncertain, risky, and unequal.[40] This is made plain in item 106 of the Cobbold Commission Report, written in 1962:

> In North Borneo . . . a major strand in the opposition to Malaysia among the Chinese lies in genuine fear of discrimination . . . affecting their education, language and culture generally, and reducing them to the status of what is popularly known as "second-class citizens" . . . there is fear among the Chinese business community that Malaysia would involve a new and heavier tax structure. At present also, as a racial group, the Chinese enjoy educational, economic and commercial superiority over the indigenous population. They are wary of the prospect that, with Malaysia, they might suffer from competition with Singapore or from discriminatory arrangements made in the process of correcting the present imbalance of economic status between themselves and the indigenous people.[41]

The lack of support from CCS for the formation of Malaysia can be deduced from their loyalty to the British. Such loyalty was not unprecedented among Christian minority living in a context dominated by another religio-cultural force. At the brink of Indian independence, the Indian Christians

---

38. Bradley, "Communal Politics," 130.
39. Zhang, *Hakkas of Sabah*, 243.
40. Zhang, 243–244.
41. Cameron Cobbold, "Report of the Commission of Enquiry, North Borneo and Sarawak, 1962," in *The Birth of Malaysia: A Reprint of the Cobbold Report, the I.G.C. Report and Malaysia Agreement*, ed. James Kim Min Wong (Kuching, Malaysia, 1962), 43.

"saw everywhere the benefits of missionary enterprise, the founding of churches, the spread of education, the uplift of the depressed classes . . . and believed that if the British left, all these projects and achievements would be under threat, if not actually undermined by an unsympathetic Hindu majority."[42] The CCS shared similar sentiment toward British rule, and similar concerns on the threats of others.[43]

The Chinese Conceded Defeat

Chinese rejection of the Malaysia idea was expressed through their consistent objections to various attempts by the proponents of the proposals in the Malaysia Solidarity Consultative Committee.[44] However, the Chinese were constantly frustrated by the Malayan and British through the Cobbold Commission, which was to them, merely "a partisan body in favor of the Malaysia Proposal."[45]

It was at this juncture that communal politics gained pace in North Borneo. Eventually, the Chinese were becoming isolated as the only racial group opposing the Malaysia Proposal.[46] The largest indigenous group, the KDM, eventually accepted the Malaysia Proposal:

> For the Kadazan there can be no other guarantee for their future than for North Borneo to obtain independence by joining Malaysia. Self-Government first would mean that the heirs, when the British leave would be the Chinese, owing to their educational and economic superiority. . . . Only through Malaysia,

---

42. Geoffrey A. Oddie, "Indian Christians and National Identity, 1870–1947," *Journal of Religious History* 25, no. 3 (2002): 364, referring to *The Guardian*, 30 June 1932; also the experience of Bishop Azariah in Susan Billington Harper, *In the Shadow of the Mahatma: Bishop Azariah and the Travails of Christianity in British India*, 1st ed. (Grand Rapids, MI: Routledge, 2000), 345. Unlike Indian Christians though, CCS have no record referring to the British colonization as divine providence.

43. For general records on CCS' positive impression on the British rule and Western missionaries, see Gordon Boughton, *Sabah Anglican Diocese Golden Jubilee History 2012* (Kuala Lumpur: The Anglican Diocese of Sabah, 2012); Tsen, *History of the Basel Christian Church*.

44. Zhang, *Hakkas of Sabah*, 249–251.

45. Citing James Angil, James P. Ongkili, *The Borneo Response to Malaysia, 1961–1963* (Singapore: Donald Moore Press, 1967). The Cobbold Commission devised clever techniques to blur the line between those who agreed and those who opposed by splitting the opposing group into many factions. See Lee, *Towkays of Sabah*, 119, in Zhang, *Hakkas of Sabah*, 251–252.

46. Zhang, *Hakkas of Sabah*, 252.

with a happy multi-racial country like Malaysia, . . . can the racial problems of the Borneo territories also be solved. The extension of special privileges to the native peoples will give them a chance to catch up with their more advanced Chinese brothers.[47]

Such communalism further distanced the Chinese from the indigenous groups and left the Chinese with few political options. As the Chinese failed to thwart the Malaysia Proposal, they changed their aim to safeguarding Chinese interests, which were mainly on cultural issues such as religious freedom and English as the official language. Unfortunately, both were later overwritten after the formation of Malaysia.

Summary: The Cultural Isolation of the CCS and Their Fondness for the British

This chapter describes the origin of CCS. Having fled from China for a better life in Sabah, CCS clearly enjoyed favor from the British. They settled as the citizens of British North Borneo. As they were forced to accept the formation of Malaysia, they began to struggle to protect their version of nationalism, which has its foundation in their historical roots. Their acceptance of British education, detachment from the indigenes, and resentment toward the Malays and Muslims would eventually form the basis of their very own nation-of-intent.

---

47. Bernard Sta Maria, *Peter J. Mojuntin*, 48.

CHAPTER 2

The Rise of Malay Hegemony

This chapter describes the evolution of Malay nationalism to Malay hegemony. It traces the emergence of Islam as the main driver for the above. The resulting reality of functional dhimmitude in Malaysia is then described.

Malay Ethnogenesis, Immigrants' Threat, and Colonial Struggle

Ethnogenesis is the process where a group of people form their ethnic awareness.[1] A commonly held "Malay" consciousness in Southeast Asia emerged in the sixteenth century.[2] It was shared among subjects of various sultanates. Their common civilizational style was perceived by outsiders as the marker of an ethnicity.[3] Malays' consciousness as a united people was a reaction to the threats of colonialism and arrival of new immigrants in the eighteenth century.[4] This reaction was the result of economic competition and religious differences.[5] It evolved into a sense of insecurity that has persisted as a constant theme in Malay ethnogenesis. Future Malays would repeatedly remind themselves to be diligent because otherwise the "name 'Malay' might

---

1. Tan, "Ethnic Groups, Ethnogenesis," 3.
2. Anthony Milner, *The Malays* (Chichester, UK: Wiley-Blackwell, 2008), 93–94.
3. Milner, *The Malays*, 93–94. For further discussion on "Malayness," see Milner, 242.
4. Howard M. Federspiel, "Modernist Islam in Southeast Asia: A New Examination," *The Muslim World* 92, no. 3–4 (2002): 373–374; Milner, *The Malays*, 8–9, 128.
5. Milner, *The Malays*, 110, 121, 131, referring to Kassim Ahmad, *Kisah Pelayaran Abdullah* (Kuala Lumpur: Dewan Bahasa dan Pustaka, 1964), 29, and R. A. Datoek Besar and R. Roolvink (eds.), *Hikajat Abdullah* (Jakarta/Amsterdam: Djambatan, 1953), 304.

disappear from this world."⁶ Malays have since ridden on a certain "race-based reactionary nationalism" in their pursuit of control and "survival."⁷ The colonial segregation policy and vernacular education system contributed further to a future pluralist Malaysia devoid of any concept and motivation for racial integration.⁸

The People (*Bangsa*) Movement

The Malays gradually organized themselves into a *bangsa* (people or nation) movement in the nineteenth century. This movement began by consolidating and actualizing a race-based nation of people with the shared Malay consciousness among subjects from various sultanates.⁹ By the dawn of the twentieth century, key Malay intellectuals began to formulate and articulate the concept of *bangsa*. Much effort was directed "in making the Malays a community and identity independent of . . . the sultanate."¹⁰ Attempts were made to transfer the loyalty and ownership of the custom from the rulers to the *bangsa*.¹¹ Rulers were to be relegated to mere "symbols" which serve to unite the *bangsa*.¹² A trans-sultanate *bangsa Melayu* (Malay nationality) became an alternative identity to "subjecthood." The concept of *bangsa* received wide acceptance as a formidable force against the oppressions of the colonists and immigrants, at the expense of the rulers.

The Islamic Influence

Islam has been a key influence in Malay ethnogenesis. Though it had been in the region for hundreds of years, Islam rose to prominence through its

---

6. Milner, *The Malays*, 131, 110.

7. Bridget Welsh, "Umno's Reactionary GE13 'Victory,'" 2013, http://bridgetwelsh.com/2013/05/umnos-reactionary-ge13-victory/.

8. A. B. Shamsul, "Identity Construction, Nation Formation, and Islamic Revivalism in Malaysia," in *Islam in an Era of Nation-States: Politics and Religious Renewal in Muslim Southeast Asia*, ed. Robert W. Hefner and Patricia Horvatich (Honolulu, HI: University of Hawaii Press, 1997), 209; Milner, *The Malays*, 120.

9. Among them are the determined reformer Munshi Abdullah and the newspaper editor Mohd. Eunos Abdullah. Milner, *The Malays*, 231.

10. Milner, *The Malays*, 132, 233.

11. Milner, *The Malays*, 130, 132, 153. On the dynamics regarding the transfer of loyalty from the patrimony of a ruler to a sense of community or national identity, see Gill, *Nature and Development*, 159–160.

12. Milner, *The Malays*, 130, 153, 233.

endorsement by the Malay rulers in the sixteenth century.[13] By the nineteenth century, the Syariah-minded Islamists gained greater influence in the presence of colonial power, often due to weak monarchy.[14] By the early twentieth century, Malays were urged to put their confidence in their identity as members of the global Muslim community.[15] They were taught to become great like the Arabs through the knowledge of Syariah and obedience to Allah's laws.[16] The Islamists reminded Muslims of their primary obligation toward the *ummah* (the Islamic community), instead of the monarchy or *bangsa*.[17] They condemned un-Islamic cultural beliefs and practices, including the "rituals and beliefs of the royal courts."[18] The Islamists' value system became the alternative for the feudal value system.[19]

From late nineteenth to early twentieth century, the emphasis on Islam as "the primary bond for community" gained traction amid challenges from those who insisted on *bangsa*.[20] The similarities between the Syariah-minded and the *bangsa*-minded were proven to be greater than their differences as they both considered the monarchy, the colonists, and the foreigners their common enemies. Both groups rejected the irrational, uncritical acceptance of traditional values and myths.[21] Yet, the Islamists distinguished themselves by using local expressions and the Arabic language, which were more familiar to the Muslims and "convey to 'Malay' readers a convincing tone of piety."[22] Contrarily, the Western appearances of the *bangsa*-minded distanced them from the masses.[23]

---

13. Milner, 40–42.
14. Milner, 139, "Shari'ah" – Syariah.
15. Milner, 138, 142–143.
16. Milner, 142–143.
17. Milner, *The Malays*, 138. Ummah is "umat" in Malay. Anthony Milner, *The Invention of Politics in Colonial Malaya: Contesting Nationalism and the Expansion of the Public Sphere* (Cambridge: Cambridge University Press, 2002), chaps. 6 and 7.
18. Milner, *The Malays*, 216.
19. Shaharuddin Maaruf, *Malay Ideas on Development: From Feudal Lord to Capitalist*, 2nd ed. (Singapore: Strategic Information and Research Development Centre, 2014), 1–50, 170.
20. Milner, *The Malays*, 138–143.
21. Milner, 142–143.
22. Milner, 142–143.
23. Munshi Abdullah, a key figure in the "bangsa" movement was criticized precisely for being perceived as pro-colonist. Shaharuddin, *Malay Ideas*, 29–30.

The Islamists also sought to initiate social reform based on Islamic principles.[24] The religious scholars were claimed to be legitimate "heads of religion" that should rule the *ummah*.[25] The Islamists advocated "Muslim nationalism," which denotes "the conscious effort on the part of Muslims to organize themselves politically with the stated intention of gaining control of the state apparatus and with the long-term view of building a nation-state that reflects the aims and aspirations of the Muslims of that community."[26]

Thereon, Malays were referred to as "the Muslims in Malaya" instead of subjects of a certain sultanate.[27] Not only did Islamists succeed in lifting the Malay morale by relating them to the global *ummah*, but Islam, together with the emergence of the *bangsa* movement, also created a "Malay self-consciousness" that relies on "Islam as the unifying factor and philosophical system which gels different Malay sub-groups together."[28] As the masses were increasingly convinced by the Islamic interpretation of their identity, the old world of sultanate was being replaced by "new (though competing) concepts of community based on both religion and race."[29] Today, modern Malays identify themselves first as Muslim, and second Malays.[30] This is confirmed in lengthy discourse by different Malay authors and credible surveys.[31] Islam has

---

24. Milner, *The Malays*, 138.

25. Milner, 144.

26. Muslim nationalism "…not necessarily intended to create an Islamic state, which would be a nationstate that is modeled on Islamic understandings of law and power." Farish A. Noor, "Muslim Nationalism in Southeast Asia," *Oxford Islamic Studies Online*, http://www.oxfordislamicstudies.com/article/opr/t343/e0042. A Malay-Muslim nationalism would fulfill the definition of "nation" mentioned earlier – emotion, identity, culture, myth, and memories, and an intention to implement Islamic laws and customs. Liow calls it "religious nationalism" – "a condition where religious identity and nationalism are blended together, resulting in a situation where religious groups are bent on asserting their presence toward the ends of establishing or defending their own conception of nationhood in religious terms." See Liow, *Religion and Nationalism*, 44–45. The concept of "state"/nationalism in Islam is contentious, but the focus here is on describing the situation, rather than making a judgment, similar to the empirical approach adopted by Ahmad Suaedy in "Islam and Minorities: Managing Identity in Malaysia," *Al-Jami'ah: Journal of Islamic Studies* 48, no. 1 (2010): 4.

27. Milner, *Invention of Politics*, 230; Milner, *The Malays*, 142–143.

28. Federspiel, "Modernist Islam in Southeast Asia," 373–374; Timothy P. Barnard, ed., *Contesting Malayness: Malay Identity Across Boundaries* (Singapore: NUS Press, 2004), 12–18; Milner, *The Malays*, 5.

29. Milner, *The Malays*, 144.

30. Asrul Zamani, *The Malay Ideals* (Kuala Lumpur: Golden Books Centre, 2002), 13.

31. Cheng Wee Teo, "More Malays Say They Are Muslim First: Malaysian Poll," *The Straits Times* (Kuala Lumpur, 12 August 2015), http://www.straitstimes.com/asia/se-asia/more-

become "a sufficient portal to Malayness, in the form of '*masuk Melayu*' (becoming Malay)."[32] The Malay identity has become synonymous with Islam.[33]

Independence and the Formation of the "Malay Nation-State"

The *bangsa* and Islamic movements eventually succeeded in pushing for Malayan independence in 1957. The struggle toward independence was however, led by a Western trained aristocrat, a Malay prince, Tunku Abdul Rahman (Tunku).[34] He led the main Malay party, the United Malay National Organization (UMNO). UMNO's raison d'être was

> to protect and promote Malay political, sociocultural, religious, and economic interests. Its early goals as a secular political party led by westernized aristocrats were directed to unifying and channeling Malay nationalism and to gaining independence from the British, and later to maintaining political dominance while making compromises necessary in a multiethnic coalition.[35]

---

malays-say-they-are-muslim-first-malaysian-poll; Sheith Khidhir Abu Bakar, "Study Finds More Malay Youths Say They Are Muslims First," *FMT News*, 21 September 2017, https://www.freemalaysiatoday.com/category/nation/2017/09/21/study-finds-more-malay-youths-say-they-are-muslims-first/.

32. Judith Nagata, "Boundaries of Malayness: 'We Have Made Malaysia: Now It Is Time to (Re)Make the Malays but Who Interprets the History?,'" in *Melayu: The Politics, Poetics and Paradoxes of Malayness*, ed. Maznah Mohamad and Syed Muhd Khairudin Aljunied (Singapore: NUS Press, 2013), Kindle, 397–400; Shamsul, "Identity Construction," 209.

33. Adrian Vickers, "'Malay Identity': Modernity, Invented Tradition and Forms of Knowledge," in *Contesting Malayness: Malay Identity across Boundaries*, ed. Timothy P. Barnard (Singapore: NUS Press, 2004), 27, citing Clive Kessler, "Archaism and Modernity: Contemporary Malay Political Culture" in *Fragmented Vision: Culture and Politics in Contemporary Malaysia*, ed. Joel S. Kahn and F. Loh Kok Wah, Asian Studies Association of Australia Southeast Asia Publications 22 (Sydney: Allen and Unwin, 1992), 133–157.

34. "It was the colonial encounter that provided this new generation of Southeast Asian Muslim activist-intellectuals with the vocabulary and ideas that served as the framework for their Muslim nationalist aspirations: They . . . adopted modern concepts like the nation-state, citizenship . . . but with the aim of fighting for independence from colonial rule instead." Farish, "Muslim Nationalism."

35. Diane K. Mauzy, "United Malays National Organization," *The Oxford Encyclopedia of the Islamic World*. Oxford Islamic Studies Online, http://www.oxfordislamicstudies.com/article/opr/t236/e0824.

For the bangsa-minded, UMNO leading other communal parties was the hopeful replacement for the monarchy. Tunku and UMNO succeeded in gaining the support of the masses, while Islam remained the main cultural-religious system. The Western idea of a nation-state was forced to accommodate Malay nationalism as a new constitution was drafted. Two definitions in the new constitution became the main points of contention in the future – namely, the status and definition of the "state" and "Malay."

To the non-Malays, the constitution guarantees a "bargain" Malays made with them for Malaysia to retain "important symbols of Malay identity, but … to be democratic, secular, and extended equal rights to all through a common citizenship."[36] Malaya, to the non-Malays, was for "Malayans" – Malayan Nationalism (later Malaysian-Malaysia or "Malaysia for *bangsa* Malaysia").[37] The Malays have otherwise claimed that it was a "social contract" that gave "expanded citizenship rights in return for unquestioned Malay political dominance."[38] As a result, two nationalisms emerged from different interpretations of the constitution. Malays tend to cling on to a cultural nationalism – an understanding of nationalism based not on legal terms but on cultural preference.[39] To them, the new country was the "Malay Nation-State" (later, "Malay-Malaysia") and the immigrants were fortunate to be given the right to stay.[40] According to a poll in 2006, only 35 percent of Malays consider

---

36. Colonial Office, "Constitutional Proposal for the Federation of Malaya," and "Federation of Malaya, Constitutional Proposals." John Funston, "UMNO – From Hidup Melayu to Ketuanan Melayu," in *The End of UMNO?: Essays on Malaysia's Dominant Party*, ed. Bridget Welsh (Petaling Jaya, Malaysia: Strategic Information and Research Development Centre, 2016), 22.

37. Ahmad Fauzi Abdul Hamid, "All-Inclusive Civic Territorial Nation," in *Islamisme Dan Bahananya: Cabaran Besar Politik Malaysia Abad Ke-21* (Islamism and Its Discontents: A Major Challenge to Twenty-First Century Malaysian Politics), Siri Syarahan Umum Pelantikan Profesor (Penang, Malaysia: Universiti Sains Malaysia, 2018), 23; Milner, *The Malays*, 166. This was already a compromise from the version of "Malayan nationalism" which was initially planned by the British through the Malayan Union. Boon Kheng Cheah, *Malaysia: The Making of a Nation* (Singapore: Institute of Southeast Asian Studies, 2002), 1–47.

38. Funston, "UMNO," 22.

39. Ahmad Fauzi Abdul Hamid, "Exclusive Ethnic-Malay Genealogical Nation," in *Islamisme Dan Bahananya*, 23.

40. "The Malay Nation-State" was coined by Cheah, who accurately detects and describes the elements of Malay dominance in the process of independence. Cheah, *Malaysia*, 3.

themselves Malaysians first, while 52 percent of them identify themselves as Malays first.[41]

Meanwhile, "Malayness was distilled into constitutional and legal formulae, and . . . 'remade' by the Malaysian constitution."[42] According to the constitution, "Malay" means "a person who professes the religion of Islam, habitually speaks the Malay language, conforms to Malay custom."[43] This definition effectively sealed the primacy of Islam in Malay ethnogenesis. Tunku's UMNO intended to establish a secular state, but the position of Islam as the religion of the federation was ambiguous.[44] Constitutionally, there was no explicit commitment to secularism and this was left to be exploited in the future.[45] The non-Muslims in Malaya, and later the non-Muslim Borneans reluctantly accepted the conditions of Islam as the official religion and special Malay rights, as they believed Malaya (and later, Malaysia) was a state based on the Western concept of nation where constitutionalism and multiculturalism were honored and maintained.[46]

The conflict of two nation-of-intents, "Malaysian-Malaysia" and "Malay-Malaysia," came into direct confrontation after the formation of Malaysia. When Singapore's leader, Lee's nation-of-intent, the "Malaysian-Malaysia" was seen as a threat to the opposing "Malay-Malaysia" nation-of-intent, Singapore was expelled from the federation in 1965, two years after the formation of Malaysia. Non-Malays in Malaysia continued with their Malaysian-Malaysia nation-of-intent, albeit with much more compromise due to the loss of a large proportion of Chinese population to Singapore.

---

41. Merdeka Center for Opinion Research, *Public Opinion Poll on Ethnic Relations: Experience, Perception & Expectations* (Bangi, Selangor, Malaysia: Merdeka Center for Opinion Research, 21 March 2006), 8, https://merdeka.org/v2/download/public-opinion-poll-on-ethnic-relations-experience-perception-expectations-march-2006/.

42. Nagata, "Boundaries of Malayness," 384–390.

43. Article 160(2) of the Malaysian Constitution.

44. Funston, "UMNO," 20.

45. Liow, *Religion and Nationalism*, 138.

46. For competing nation-of-intent of the various non-Malay groups, see Shamsul and Sity, "Nation, Ethnicity."

The Rise of Malay Supremacy

A form of feudalism took the helm of the country from independence to 1971, with Tunku as the key figure.[47] Tunku was feudalistic. He kept ordinary Malay "subjects" from governance.[48] He did not intend to create a capitalist class among the Malay.[49] Furthermore, Tunku was perceived as promoting pluralism and "his concessions to the non-Malays seemed to be a betrayal to Malay interest."[50] The Syariah-minded have also been suspicious of Tunku's Western outlook.[51] Meanwhile, the Chinese continued to dominate the economy, enjoying the "non-Malay capitalism" just as they did prior to independence.[52] Feudalism and "colonialism" which have been the cause of poverty during the colonial time continued to haunt the daily lives of the Malays.

The racial riot on 13 May 13 1969 was the consequence of Malays' dissatisfaction with their economic and political status. In the aftermath of the riot, Tunku was forced to resign and capitalistic nationalism took over as the dominant discourse of the Malay race.[53] It was represented by Mahathir Mohamed (Mahathir), who championed Malay economic empowerment through affirmative action through the New Economic Policy (NEP, 1970).[54] Purportedly, by narrowing the income gap between the Chinese and the Malays, interethnic conflict would be avoided.[55] The NEP also provided state-sponsored education opportunities to Malay-Muslims that exposed them

---

47. "Traditionalistic nationalism," according to Shaharuddin Maaruf. Shaharuddin, *Malay Ideas*, 129–156.

48. Milner, *The Malays*, 72–73; Shaharuddin, *Malay Ideas*, 51–73.

49. Malay rulers in the past actually developed "colonial capitalism" and "non-Malay capitalism" with the colonists and the Chinese but kept their subjects poor to secure their power. Shaharuddin, *Malay Ideas*, 62–67, 105–128; Milner, *The Malays*, 72.

50. Cheah, *Malaysia*, 79.

51. Tunku's interest in horseracing and gambling, and his elitist, aloof appearance further distanced him from the masses, who by this time had subscribed to an Islamic nationalism.

52. Shaharuddin, *Malay Ideas*, 70–73, 105–128.

53. Shaharuddin, 170–176.

54. Suaedy, "Islam and Minorities," 24–25; Mahathir Mohamad, *The Malay Dilemma* (Singapore: Marshall Cavendish, 2008).

55. *Malaysia Human Development Report 2013*, ed. Jeffrey Hardy Quah (United Nations Development Programme, Malaysia, January 2014), 233, http://www.mhdr.my/page/161/Download-MHDR-2013/.

to Islamism.⁵⁶ The National Culture Policy (NCP, 1971) was introduced.⁵⁷ It was drafted with Islamic values at heart, believing that these values would unite all citizens.⁵⁸ A new focus on Islamic propagation was initiated, with the National Fatwa Committee established in 1970.⁵⁹ Retrospectively, these developments can be considered as violence against the non-Malays initiated by the domineering Malays to strengthen their hegemony.⁶⁰

The UMNO-dominated government utilized the policies to actualize Malay nationalism. NEP was a means to assert the "reactionary race-based nationalism," and "'Race' became the structural basis. . . . Political, economic and social arrangements were organized in terms of 'race,' and all types of competition for resources and influence were conceptualized in this way."⁶¹ With an agenda to revert fully to Malay-Malaysia, and under the pretext of capitalistic nationalism, the ideology of Malay Supremacy was ,introduced in 1986.⁶² Monash defines Malay Supremacy ("Ketuanan Melayu") as

> The ideological, socio-structural and historical stratification process by which the population of Malay descent has gained and intentionally sustain, to its own best advantage, the dynamic mechanics of upward or downward socially mobility over the non-Malay population, on a national scale, using Malay ethnicity and Islam as the main criteria for allocating resources and making political decisions.⁶³

---

56. Ahmad Fauzi Abdul Hamid and Che Hamdan Che Mohd Razali, *Middle Eastern Influences on Islamist Organizations in Malaysia: The Cases of ISMA, IRF and HTM* (Singapore: ISEAS Publishing, 2016), 2.

57. The National Department for Culture and Arts, "National Culture Policy JKKN," *Official Website of The National Department for Culture and Arts*, http://www.jkkn.gov.my/en/national-culture-policy.

58. Funston, "UMNO," 141.

59. Funston, 141. Fatwa – "Authoritative legal opinion given by a mufti (legal scholar) in response to a question posed by an individual or a court of law." John L. Esposito, ed., "Fatwa," in *The Oxford Dictionary of Islam* (New York, NY: Oxford University Press, 2003), http://www.oxfordislamicstudies.com/article/opr/t125/e646.

60. Suaedy, "Islam and Minorities," 23; Ilan Peleg, *Democratizing the Hegemonic State: Political Transformation in the Age of Identity* (Cambridge, UK: Cambridge University Press, 2007).

61. Milner, *The Malays*, 231.

62. Funston, "UMNO," 50.

63. Paul Monash, *Malay Supremacy: A Historical Overview of Malay Political Culture and an Assessment of Its Implication for the Non-Malays in Malaysia* (Auckland: Maygen Press,

Malay Supremacy enjoyed general acceptance from the Malays. The subsequent years saw even the political-and-economic driven Malay Supremacy losing its initial characteristics as it evolved into a certain Malay hegemony, which was driven by Islam. Instead of merely a "criterion" in Malay Supremacy, Islam experienced further revival in the years after NEP, which the following section now turns to.

Islamization as a Political Necessity

Islamization has become a necessity for the post-independence Malayan (and later Malaysian) government to gain support from the Malays. This is the consequence of the sustained Islamic revivalism. It is also due to political rivalry and the government's intention of becoming the new champion of the Muslims in the country.

The Emergence of Islamic Revivalism (*Dakwah*)

As described earlier, the Islamists succeeded in consolidating their position in the process of Malay ethnogenesis, making Islam the main unifying and cultural identity of the Malays.[64] Thereon, Malays repeatedly found Islam as their refuge in crisis.[65] Time and again, Islamic revivalism emerged and flourished when secular mechanisms failed to resolve their social and economic grievances.[66] During 1975 and 1979, the revivalist group, Malaysian Muslim Youth (Angkatan Belia Islam Malaysia, ABIM) became a credible political opposition against the allegedly corrupted UMNO.[67] ABIM was dominated by university students from the liberal arts. The more radical, less tolerant and conservative Islamic Representative Council (IRC) eventually emerged to popularity during this period, operating in campuses and attracting mostly science students informed by "sectarian Islamic groups in the Middle East

---

2003), ix.

64. Shamsul, "Identity Construction," 210.

65. Shamsul, 212, 222.

66. Shamsul, 222; Julian C. H. Lee, *Islamization and Activism in Malaysia* (Singapore: Institute of Southeast Asian Studies, 2010), 20.

67. Shamsul, "Identity Construction," 215.

and South Asia."⁶⁸ Eventually, the more moderate *dakwah* lost ground to this radical version of *dakwah*.⁶⁹ Islam's position in Malay ethnogenesis was further strengthened through these *dakwah* movements.⁷⁰ As the champion of Malay ethnogenesis, UMNO was impelled to increase its attention to Islam and it subsequently adopted its own Islamization strategy.⁷¹

UMNO and PAS

UMNO was also forced to enhance its Islamic outlook due to the provocation from the Pan-Malaysian Islamic Party (PAS).⁷² PAS projects itself as the true Malay-Muslim party. Inspired by the 1979 Iranian revolution, PAS adopted a new form of leadership headed by the *ulamas*.⁷³ It also maintained a close relationship with the Muslim Brotherhood.⁷⁴ PAS "jettisoned its Malay nationalist orientation in favor of a more universalistic Islamic focus, similar to the one adopted by the IRC group of the student *dakwah*."⁷⁵ Meanwhile, instigated by the Iranian Shi'ism revival, Saudi Arabia began to financially support Sunni movements throughout the world, including ABIM.⁷⁶ Thus, "In the government's estimation, the combination of the student-based *dakwah* movement and [PAS] was politically explosive."⁷⁷ In view of this, Mahathir launched a systematic process of Islamization through the federal government

---

68. Conservative – "the rejection of a progressive re-interpretation of Islamic teachings and it refers to an adherence to established doctrines and a social order." Mohamed Nawab, "Islamic Conservative Turn," 3, referring to Martin van Bruinessen, *Contemporary Developments in Indonesian Islam: Explaining the "Conservative Turn"* (Singapore: Institute of Southeast Asian Studies, 2013). Shamsul, "Identity Construction," 215. ABIM was more open to various Islamic thoughts compared to IRC's focus on Salafism. Maszlee Malik, "Salafism in Malaysia: Historical Account on Its Emergence and Motivations," *Sociology of Islam* 5, no. 4 (2017): 16–17.

69. Shamsul, "Identity Construction," 223.

70. Shamsul, 210.

71. Shamsul, 210, referring to D. K. Mauzy and R. S. Milne, "The Mahathir Administration in Malaysia: Discipline through Islam," *Pacific Affairs* 56, no. 4 (1983–1984): 617–648.

72. Milner, *The Malays*, 219.

73. Mohamed Nawab, "Islamic Conservative Turn," 4–5.

74. Mohamed Nawab, 5–6. It must be noted that the Iranian Revolution did not result in much doctrinal influence in Malaysia due to its Shi'ism, and there are significant differences between the Wahabism of Saudi Arabia and the teaching of the Muslim Brotherhood. Yet, Malaysian Muslims seemed to have gathered fractions of these teachings for their own benefit.

75. Shamsul, "Identity Construction, 217.

76. Mohamed Nawab, "Islamic Conservative Turn," 5.

77. Shamsul, "Identity Construction," 217.

and UMNO-controlled states.[78] He even co-opted the key leader of ABIM, Anwar Ibrahim, into UMNO, further garnering and intensifying systematic Islamization through the government machinery.

Complying with the populist *dakwah* movement was necessary because the Islamists and Syariah-minded are more concerned with piety rather than economic development that Mahathir's capitalist nationalism championed. UMNO and the government were distancing themselves from the grassroots who were often left out in development and held a revivalist view of Islam.[79] For this group, affirmative actions and improvement of the Malay economic status were secondary to the agenda of Muslim nationalism. Meanwhile, the success of NEP in penetrating every sector of the economy also rationalized the need to similarly expand the Syariah Court to cover every aspect of this "modern Malay polity."[80]

The revivalists, as they became increasingly shaped by Islamism, have also been arguing that economic equality is not a solution for inter-ethnic relations in Malaysia.[81] They dismiss "integration with non-Muslims" as a way forward for unity among different races in Malaysia.[82] To them, there is no possibility of unity in a country with different faiths.[83] Instead, they turn to Islam as the only means for true integration and inter-ethnic unity. Asrul Zamani, for example, believes that the racial tension in Indonesia that led to violence against the Chinese, could have been avoided had the Chinese embraced Islam.[84]

To gain political currency, UMNO has to compete with PAS as to which of them is the more "Islamic" party.[85] Meanwhile, PAS has always intended

---

78. Fred R. von der Mehden, "Islamic Movements in Malaysia," in *The Oxford Handbook of Islam and Politics*, ed. John L. Esposito and Emad El-Din Shahin (Oxford: Oxford University Press, 2013), 587–599, http://www.oxfordislamicstudies.com/article/opr/t9001/e005.

79. Muhammed Abdul Khalid, *The Colour of Inequality: Ethnicity, Class, Income and Wealth in Malaysia* (Petaling Jaya, Malaysia: MPH Group Publishing, 2014).

80. Raymond L. M. Lee and Susan E. Ackerman, *Sacred Tensions: Modernity and Religious Transformation in Malaysia* (Columbia, SC: University of South Carolina Press, 1997), 53–54.

81. Asrul, *Malay Ideals*, 8. On the relation between *dakwah* revivalists and Islamism, see Azhar, *Contemporary Islamic Discourse*, 41.

82. Asrul, *Malay Ideals*, 9–11. For the rejection of "Pluralism", see Azhar, *Contemporary Islamic Discourse*, 174–184.

83. Asrul, *Malay Ideals*, 9.

84. Asrul, 12.

85. Funston, "UMNO," 110–119.

to make UMNO its ideological captive and political hostage by instigating UMNO to implement more conservative Islamic policies.[86] In an attempt to "out-Islam" PAS, Mahathir even declared Malaysia as an Islamic state on 29 September 2001, although the country was not governed based on Syariah.[87] The competition between UMNO and PAS has not only intensified the process of Islamization, but has also resulted in increased conservativism.[88] Increasingly, Muslims in Malaysia are offered a "purer" or more "authentic" form of Islam, and Muslim nationalism, which rejects multiculturalism, has become a well-accepted ideology among the Malays. Electoral politics has been adopted by Islamist groups and political parties to eliminate multiculturalism and pursue the full implementation of Islamic law.[89]

Eventually, the government under the leadership of UMNO initiated "the mainstreaming of Islam into all domains of Malaysian social life."[90] Islam has been positioned to dominate the public domain by being a "civil religion."[91] Islam, instead of Malay traditional values, has been favored as the "vehicle for moral reform" in Malaysia by the government.[92]

From Islamization to the Emergence of Malay Hegemony

Islamization in Malaysia is a result of ethnogenesis, but Islamic revivalism has since had a life of its own. After intentional Islamization by the government, the revivalist version of Islam further expanded and eventually became the

---

86. Clive Kessler, "UMNO, Then, Now and Always?," in *The End of UMNO?: Essays on Malaysia's Dominant Party*, ed. Bridget Welsh (Petaling Jaya, Malaysia: Strategic Information and Research Development Centre, 2016), 150–151; Azhar, *Contemporary Islamic Discourse*, 47.

87. Kevin Tan, "Malaysia a Fundamentalist Islamic Country, Says PM," *Malaysiakini*, 17 June 2002, https://www.malaysiakini.com/news/11804.

88. Fred R. von der Mehden, "Islamic Movements in Malaysia"; Kessler, "UMNO?," 152–153.

89. This is best illustrated via the struggle of ISMA. Ahmad Fauzi and Che Hamdan, *Middle Eastern Influences*, 9–10. A more radical position is held by Hizbut Tahrir Malaysia that rejects electoral democracy. Ahmad Fauzi and Che Hamdan, 14–15.

90. Shamsul, "Identity Construction," 210.

91. Virginia Matheson Hooker, "Reconfiguring Malay and Islam in Contemporary Malaysia," in *Contesting Malayness: Malay Identity across Boundaries*, ed. Timothy P. Barnard (Singapore: NUS Press, 2004), 159.

92. Hooker, "Reconfiguring Malay," 160.

prime mover of the national narrative. Islam has now become a "chief symbol and *guiding spirit* of a new form of Malay distinctiveness."[93] The process of Islamization and *dakwah* has "redefined Malay ethnicity," further galvanizing the role of Islam as "a pillar" in the sociopolitical life of the Malays.[94] Indeed, in today's Malay ethnogenesis the *bangsa* and Syariah-minded have merged.[95] The earlier Bangsa-minded nationalists that advocated Malaya-Raya (a joint Malay Nation with Indonesia) or those who advocated Malaysian-Malaysia such as UMNO founder Onn Jaafar (and to a certain extent, Tunku) have all lost their influence. Today, Muslim nationalism is a given, with different groups advocating different degrees of ethnocentrism. PAS, for example, is less racially exclusive, while other organizations, such as ISMA, are more Malay-centric.[96] Islam has evolved from being an identity marker to the force that directs every aspect of Malay life and Malaysian sociopolitical life.

The Islamized Public Space

The outcome of the revivalist movement is most significantly demonstrated by the domineering attitude of the state and its Islamic authority.[97] Yapp succinctly describes,

> The dominant Muslim party . . . by using State apparatus, assert a form of cultural superiority by providing the fundamental outlook in the form of the sovereignty of Islam (Ketuanan Islam) in the whole of Malaysia society. This ideology – the values and beliefs of the dominant Muslim party – has resulted in the Muslim majority beginning to make claims on and exert control

---

93. Milner, *The Malays*, 220, referring to Judith A. Nagata, *1984: The Reflowering of Malaysian Islam* (Vancouver: University of British Columbia Press), 72 (my emphasis).

94. Milner, 220; Shamsul, "Identity Construction," 207.

95. The more liberal Bangsa-minded nationalists that advocated Malaya-Raya (a joint Malay Nation with Indonesia) or those who advocated Malaysian-Malaysia such as UMNO founder Onn Jaafar (and to a certain extent, Tunku) have all lost their influence.

96. Ahmad Fauzi and Che Hamdan, *Middle Eastern Influences*, 7.

97. Shamsul, "Identity Construction," 218. Some have questioned the impact of the Syariah-minded *dakwah* in Malay society, arguing that although Malays do identify themselves first as Muslims, they are ambivalent toward the *dakwah* movement and doctrine. However, judging from the result of election and the support which PAS receives, the majority Malays seem to desire a Syariah-oriented society, similar to the version which the *dakwah* movement aims for. Milner, *The Malays*, 218.

over the other social-religious communities and exert its rulership over social institutions and processes.[98]

Muslim nationalism has been asserting itself in the public domain. The federal Department of Islamic Development (JAKIM), has since the 1970s, played an important role in radicalizing Muslims and Islamization. To JAKIM, "non-Muslims must bend to Islamic laws and regulations as they are living in Muslim-majority Malaysia."[99] The English legal system should be replaced with Syariah law that applies to all Malaysians.[100] This is in line with the revivalists' inclination toward Islamism, where only Syariah is accepted as the authorized legal system.[101] The concept of *tawhid* (God's oneness) is extended to legitimize Muslim rule, and Syariah as the only basis for governance.[102] Subsequently, state authorities, acting as champions of Islam, have enacted laws and regulations which assume the superiority of Syariah over the Malaysian constitution and in the process, trespassed federal jurisdiction.[103] The Malays in general, agree with this position because granting more freedom of expression to the Syariah law is a crucial way to express their religious commitment.[104] In fact, since the status of the Syariah Court was elevated, the Civil Court has lost its jurisdiction in many cases.[105] In recent years, this is expressed through the bipartisan support enjoyed by the ongoing attempts to amend Syariah Court Act 1965 (Bill 355), generally referred to as RUU355 (Rang Undang-undang/Bill 355).[106] Both UMNO and PAS are

---

98. Eugene Yapp, "The 'Copyright' Controversy of 'Allah': Issues and Challenges of the Malaysian Church," in *The Church in a Changing World: An Asian Response*, ed. Bruce J. Nicholls, Theresa R. Lua, and Julie Belding (Quezon City: Asia Theological Association, 2010), 147–156.

99. James Chin, "From Ketuanan Melayu to Ketuanan Islam: UMNO and the Malaysian Chinese," in *The End of UMNO?: Essays on Malaysia's Dominant Party*, ed. Bridget Welsh (Petaling Jaya, Malaysia: Strategic Information and Research Development Centre, 2016), 195.

100. Asrul, *Malay Ideals*, 113.

101. Ahmad Fauzi, *Islamisme Dan Bahananya*, 16.

102. Azhar, *Contemporary Islamic Discourse*, 41; "Tawhid-Oxford Islamic Studies Online," http://www.oxfordislamicstudies.com.fuller.idm.oclc.org/article/opr/t243/e340?_hi=1&_pos=2.

103. Shad Saleem Faruqi, "The Bedrock of Our Nation," *The Malaysian Bar*, 30 March 2007, http://www.malaysianbar.org.my/general_opinions/ comments/bedrock_of_our_nation.html, in Ahmad Fauzi, *Islamisme Dan Bahananya*, 17.

104. Asrul, *Malay Ideals*, 101; Ahmad Fauzi, *Islamisme Dan Bahananya*, 16–17.

105. Funston, "UMNO," 113–116.

106. To increase Syariah court's power on criminal cases and open the way for Hudud to be implemented, see "'Say No to RUU355 for Malaysia's Sake' | The Star," *The Star Online*

united in supporting the bill.[107] Islamization of public space is felt at the level of ordinary daily lives of the non-Malays. Consequently,

> Relations between Muslims and non-Muslims (read: Malay and non-Malay) have become tense and awkward at times because of the influence of strict Islamic codes of behavior promoted by the dakwah movement.... One example that demonstrates how the dakwah ethos has permeated every layer of society and affected everyday forms of social interaction at the grassroots level can be seen in Malay Muslim dietary rules or food taboos. Many Muslims now will not eat food brought by non-Muslim colleagues to social gatherings, be they at the workplace or at the homes of non-Muslim colleagues.[108]

As Islamism took over the public space, having already taken over the government and sociopolitical agencies, and assumed an authoritative position in Malay ethnogenesis, it attempted to further materialize Muslim nationalism. Having now merged with the concept of Malay-Malaysia, this religious force has become an integral part that directs Malay nationalism. Malay Supremacy has transformed into "Islam hegemony" or "Malay hegemony."[109] Today, young Malays see them as two sides of a coin.[110] Even moderate Muslims concede to its superiority.[111]

(Kuala Lumpur, Malaysia, 7 May 2017), https://www.thestar.com.my/news/nation/2017/05/07/say-no-to-ruu355-for-malaysias-sake; Ahmad Fauzi, *Islamisme Dan Bahananya*, 19.

107. Ahmad Fauzi, 17. This is a far cry from Amanat Haji Hadi that denounced UMNO members as infidels on the grounds that they were obliged to a colonial system of governance; the same Haji Hadi Awang is the one who tabled the private Bill of 355. Ahmad Fauzi and Che Hamdan, *Middle Eastern Influences*, 4.

108. Shamsul, "Identity Construction," 219.

109. Chin, "From Ketuanan Melayu," 204–205. "Ketuanan Melayu" is Malay supremacy; "ketuanan Islam" is Islam hegemony.

110. Chin, 205.

111. Ahmad Fauzi, for example, laments the loss of Malaysia's multiculturalism and pluralistic nature to Islamism. Ahmad Fauzi, *Islamisme Dan Bahananya*, 40. Islamization, which is seen as a noble move by the moderates, has been hijacked by "Salafization." Ahmad Fauzi, 42.

The Irrepressible Malay Hegemony

Malay hegemony is the result of Islamization taking "on a life of its own, beyond the control of political institutions and actors."[112] Liow argues that

> In this respect, the Government's hesitance to formally and publicly address issues that have emerged out of the policing of religious practice by state religious departments, its disinclination towards Muslim intellectuals and civil-society groups seeking a "third way" of Islam beyond the UMNO-PAS paradigm . . . is telling of the extent to which the stakes have been raised since the process of Islamization was set in motion three decades ago.[113]

Islamization, according to Julian Lee, has the potential of undermining the "very structures of authority on which it rests."[114] Islamization became out-of-control in the post-Mahathir era. Mahathir's Vision 2020 Malaysian society that depicted a Malaysian-Malaysia (*bangsa* Malaysia) is but today a rejected idea in the face of Malay hegemony.[115] Badawi as the successor of Mahathir failed in his attempt to introduce the moderate Islam Hadhari.[116] The government under Badawi's successor Najib leadership has since succumbed to pressures from conservatives. To remain in power, UMNO has been working closely with "a range of extreme ethnonationalist groups, most notably Perkasa, Pekida and ISMA."[117] ISMA (Muslim Student Solidarity Front or Ikatan Siswazah Muslim Malaysia) in particular, with its motto of "Malay Consensus, Islam Sovereign," detests Islamists who are perceived to have any association with multiculturalism.[118] It epitomizes Malay hegemony with its ethnocentrism and radical Islamism. The emergence of groups such as ISMA

---

112. Joseph Chinyong Liow, "Political Islam in Malaysia: Legitimacy, Hegemony and Resistance," in *Islamic Legitimacy in a Plural Asia*, ed. Anthony Reid and Michael Gilsenan (New York: Routledge, 2008), 187.

113. Liow, "Political Islam," 187.

114. Lee, *Islamization and Activism*, 135.

115. Shakila Yacob, "Political Culture and Nation Building: Whither Bangsa Malaysia?," *Malaysian Journal of Social Policy and Society* 3 (2006): 42.

116. Suaedy, "Islam and Minorities," 11; Funston, "UMNO," 144; Ahmad Fauzi, *Islamisme Dan Bahananya*, 15.

117. Funston, "UMNO," 145.

118. Ahmad Fauzi and Che Hamdan, *Middle Eastern Influences*, 7.

makes the older, more localized *dakwah* groups like ABIM look moderate in comparison while gradually replacing them as the champions of Islamism.[119]

The fact that a series of incidents in which extremist remarks and actions have gone unpunished in Malaysia certainly point to the possibility that the Muslim majority in the country has quietly but surely accepted Muslim nationalism and a conservative Islam. Malays have directed their "feudalistic" loyalty toward Islamism, as they seek Islamic approval on every aspect of their lives.[120] Their concern is how to be a "good Muslim" – according to the conservative *dakwah* version of Islam. From 2009, many acts and threats of violence against non-Muslims have gone unpunished or ignored by authorities. The non-Muslims protested, but few voices from the Muslims were heard. Muslim extremists dragged a cow's head through a street to protest against Indians, fire-bombed churches, impounded Bibles using the term Allah, and threatened to burn all Bibles with the word Allah.[121] Though officially opposing the Islamic State (IS), the Prime Minister Najib has expressed his admiration of IS.[122] In a 2015 survey, the IS received favorable view from 11 percent of Malaysian Muslims surveyed. Malaysia scored the second highest percentage among eleven countries with significant Muslim populations. Only 4 percent of Muslims surveyed in neighboring Indonesia supported the IS.[123] This indicates Malaysian Muslims' sympathy and identification toward "Salafi-jihadisme" – a version of Islamism much influenced by, among others, Sayyid Qutb.[124]

Between General Elections (GE)12 and GE13, losing support from non-Muslims, and PAS becoming less threatening, UMNO became radicalized

---

119. "Manhaj Malazi" or "Malaysian method" of Islamic struggle is distinctive of ABIM. Ahmad Fauzi and Che Hamdan, 3. On ISMA, see Ahmad Fauzi and Che Hamdan, 6–10.

120. Lee, *Islamization and Activism*, 132–133.

121. Funston, "UMNO," 110–111; Liow, *Religion and Nationalism*, 153–173.

122. Melissa Chi, "Be Brave like ISIL Fighters, Najib Tells Umno," *Malay Mail* (Kuala Lumpur, Malaysia, 24 June 2014), https://www.malaymail.com/s/693209/be-brave-like-isil-fighters-najib-tells-umno.

123. Funston, "UMNO," 117; Jacob Poushter, "In Nations with Significant Muslim Populations, Much Disdain for ISIS," *Pew Research Center*, 17 November 2015, http://www.pewresearch.org/fact-tank/2015/11/17/in-nations-with-significant-muslim-populations-much-disdain-for-isis/.

124. Ahmad Fauzi, *Islamisme Dan Bahananya*, 38. Some Malaysians have been involved in terrorist groups. This brand of Salafism, however, is considered by moderates as different from pure Salafism, such as that contained in the Amman Message. Ahmad Fauzi, *Islamisme Dan Bahananya*, 41.

by taking up fully the ideology of Malay hegemony.¹²⁵ The society was divided by Malays differentiating themselves against non-Muslims.¹²⁶ With religious tones, the rhetoric of calling for arms against the "infidels" legitimized. Extremists such as Ibrahim Ali could threaten a holy war against Christians without being prosecuted.¹²⁷ The UMNO mouthpiece newspaper, *Utusan*, even "claimed an opposition conspiracy to establish Christianity as the official religion."¹²⁸ Such allegiance has been repeatedly used to gain popularity. These are only possible when the matters raised would gain political currency from the masses. This shows the popular view and stance of the Muslim majority in the country. Pressure groups that have no political burden, notably Perkasa, Pekida, and ISMA, relentlessly and insatiably demand the government's response to their Islamic agenda.¹²⁹ Associating with these groups, UMNO projects itself as the protector of one race and religion instead of a multiracial and pluralistic nation.¹³⁰ UMNO has "capitulated to and made itself a captive of a kind of Islamist radicalism."¹³¹ In fact, it is hard to see any government of Malaysia surviving without taking this stance, effectively making Malaysia a hegemonic state where "one ethnopolitical group dominates society's political process by controlling state institutions and policies so as to promote its interests more or less exclusively."¹³² In Malaysia, the promoted interest is a mixed Malay-ethnocentric Islamism, or in short, Malay hegemony.

The Defeat of the Moderates

The emergence of a Malay hegemony is a significant setback suffered by moderate Islam in Malaysia. The rejection of Islam Hadhari, for example, signifies the rejection of key moderate Islamic ideas which would be welcomed by both the moderate Muslims and non-Muslims today. The moderate Muslims in Malaysia tolerate traditionalist Sufism. They oppose Salafism, accept electoral democracy, and reject ethnocentrism, as demonstrated by the National Trust

---

125. Kessler, "UMNO?," 155–156, 162.
126. Kessler, 156.
127. Funston, "UMNO," 97; Liow, *Religion and Nationalism*, 163.
128. Funston, "UMNO," 97.
129. Kessler, "UMNO?," 161.
130. Kessler, 154–155.
131. Kessler, 162.
132. Peleg, *Democratizing the Hegemonic State*, 1.

Party (Parti Amanah Negara, or Amanah).[133] Amanah's key themes in its political struggle are *maqasid Syariah (Sharia), Islam Rahmatan lil-Alamin* (inclusive and compassionate Islam), and *fiqh Malaysia* ("interpretation of Islamic jurisprudence within a Malaysian context").[134] The concept of *maqasid Syariah*, for instance, is accepted by the main political party that champions Malaysian Malaysia, the Democratic Action Party (DAP).[135] *Maqasid Syariah* rejects the literal understanding and application of Syariah, which is seen as "legalistic Islam."[136] The same idea is also shared by today's moderate Islamist NGOs like ABIM, IKRAM (Pertubuhan IKRAM Malaysia, or IKRAM Malaysia), and IRF.[137] They are still Islamists who are only considered moderate because they are willing to "delay" the full implementation of Islamic law in the multicultural context of Malaysia.[138] The moderates' stance as Islamists and their fight for Muslim nationalism remain,[139] but they are willing to use the electorate and accept the modern context of nation state, and wish to be called "democrat Muslims" instead of "political Islamist."[140] They are also more inclusive – willing to work with non-Muslims. In fact, Amanah accepts non-Muslims as members.[141]

---

133. Maszlee Malik, "Rethinking the Role of Islam in Malaysian Politics: A Case Study of Parti Amanah Negara (AMANAH)," *Islam and Civilization Renewal Journal* 8, no. 4 (2017): 457–472.

134. Wai Weng Hew, "The Battle of Bangi: The Struggle for Political Islam in Urban Malaysia," in *Towards a New Malaysia?: The 2018 Election and Its Aftermath*, ed. Meredith L. Weiss and Faizal S. Hazis, 1st ed. (Singapore: National University of Singapore Press, 2020), 198; Felicitas Opwis, "Maqāṣid Al-Sharīʿah," in *The [Oxford] Encyclopedia of Islam and Law*, Oxford Islamic Studies Online, n.d., http://www.oxfordislamicstudies.com/opr/t349/e0113.

135. "Maqasid Syariah" or "the aims of the Shariah" focuses on the purpose of Syariah rather than literal implementation. See Opwis, "Maqāṣid Al-Sharīʿah."

136. Maszlee, "Rethinking the Role of Islam," 462.

137. Ahmad Fauzi, *Islamisme Dan Bahananya*, 29–32.

138. For instance, members of Amanah are still keen to implement *hudud*. Maszlee, "Rethinking the Role of Islam," 463.

139. They are bound by the Islamic worldview, where *tawhid* requires *dakwah*, and the distinction between Muslims and non-Muslims within any Islamic jurisprudence remains. While they may say that the non-Muslims are protected when Islam prospers in Malaysia, this statement itself already distinguishes the status between the Muslims and the non-Muslims. In other words, moderate Islam in Malaysia is still Islamism (though less ethnocentric). Hew, "Battle of Bangi," 208.

140. Maszlee, "Rethinking the Role of Islam," 463.

141. Maszlee, 464.

Sadly, moderate Islam in Malaysia is surpassed. G25, a group of twenty-five prominent senior Malay leaders and scholars, attempted to project a moderate voice of Islam. Their voices were suppressed, and their book banned by the government.[142] The shrinking space for civil society in Malaysia due to Malay hegemony has also limited the voice of moderate Islam.[143] Moderates' support among the electorates is also limited to the minority urban middle class.

The moderates' tolerance toward a multicultural society is shunned. Efforts to dialogue with non-Muslims on the grounds of liberalism and multiculturalism are attacked and quickly put under siege by the forces of Malay hegemony through public denouncements, use of media, and even rallies. From the 1990s, moderate Islam has been marginalized as the national narrative in Malaysia is dominated by a simplistic discourse depicting the struggle between two opposing forces of Islamism and secularism.[144] Any association with liberalism or multiculturalism is considered complicit with the West and secularism. The Muslim community is expected to choose between these two polarities. Consequently, moderate Islam is repudiated by the Malay hegemony narrative, where the polarization between two antagonistic and extreme ideologies is fictionized, exaggerated, and pronounced to be mutually exclusive and irreconcilable.

Functional Dhimmitude as the Expression of Malay Hegemony

With Malay hegemony, non-Muslims in Malaysia today have come under functional dhimmitude. Under Malay hegemony, the status of non-Muslims is interpreted by the Islamic perspective instead of a secular and constitutional perspective. This leads to non-Muslims in Malaysia today being regarded as *dhimmi*.

---

142. The Malaysian Insight, "G25's Book on Role of Islam in Malaysia Banned," 2017, https://www.themalaysianinsight.com/s/8837/. For G25, see "About Us | G25 Malaysia," *G25 Malaysia*, https://www.g25malaysia.org/about-us-1. The G25 is associated with the moderate Islamic Renaissance Front (IRF). Ahmad Fauzi, *Islamisme Dan Bahananya*, 32.

143. According to Freedman, a "moderate Islam" country is one that has effective NGOs or a functioning civil society. Amy L. Freedman, "Civil Society, Moderate Islam, and Politics in Indonesia and Malaysia," *Journal of Civil Society* 5, no. 2 (2009): 107–127.

144. Such polarization into two camps also happens across political parties. Ahmad Fauzi, *Islamisme Dan Bahananya*, 22.

Dhimmitude Explained

Dhimmitude is a neologism popularized by Bat Yeʾor, delineating the condition of "*dhimmi*."[145] Bat Yeʾor traces the concept of dhimmi to *jihad* and Muhammad's treaty with non-Muslims in his early conquest.[146] The concept of *jihad* divides the world into *dar al-Harb* (territory of war, illegally controlled by infidels) and the *dar al-Islam*, the territory of Islam. *Jihad* is the constant state of war that only ends with the dominion of Islam over all unbelievers.[147] Restoring the possessions in *dar al-Harb* to the Muslims is a rightful duty.[148] The prisoners of war resulting from *jihad* are called *dhimmis*.[149] They are non-Muslims granted a treaty of protection that suspends the conquerors' right to execute them due to their unwillingness to convert to Islam.[150] It is merely a suspension of the conqueror's right where non-Muslims are tolerated in the conquered land.[151] The *dhimmi* are to be exempted from battle (*jihad*) as they are not a part of the *ummah*.

This gives weight to Bat Yeʾor's argument that the ideological framework of dhimmitude is *jihad*. In other words, dhimmitude is the ideological consequence of a world defined by the realms of Muslims and non-Muslims.

---

145. Sidney H. Griffith, *The Church in the Shadow of the Mosque: Christians and Muslims in the World of Islam* (Princeton, NJ: Princeton University Press, 2008), 16.

146. The works of Bat Yeʾor are included as they relate well with the situation and experiences of non-Muslims in Malaysia. They are valuable sources that do not succumb to romanticization of Islam. Theodore Pulcini, "Review of Islam and Dhimmitude: Where Civilizations Collide," by Bat Yeʾor, *Middle East Journal* 56, no. 4 (2002): 736–738. Her works are obviously lacking in historical method (see Sidney H. Griffith, "Review of The Decline of Eastern Christianity under Islam: From Jihad to Dhimmitude, Seventh-Twentieth Century," by Bat Yeor, Miriam Kochan, and David Littman, *International Journal of Middle East Studies* 30, no. 4 (1998): 619–621), polemic, and at times lack of academic rigor, but they address the potentiality of the ideology of "dhimmitude" nested within Islamic doctrine which can be invoked by rulers or jurists, based on their doctrinal or sociopolitical preferences.

147. Bat Yeʾor and Jacques Ellul, *The Dhimmi: Jews & Christians under Islam*, trans. David Maisel, rev. enl. ed. (Vancouver, Canada: Fairleigh Dickinson University Press, 1985), 45; Yeʾor, *Decline of Eastern Christianity*, 40. Dhimmis include both people of the Book (Christians and Jews), and others. See Suaedy, "Islam and Minorities," 14.

148. Yeʾor, *Decline of Eastern Christianity*, 40.

149. *Dhimmi* is an adjective form designating the persons of *adh-dhimmah*, or "covenant of protection" that has the verbal root in Arabic that denotes "to affix blame" or "to find fault." Griffith, *Church in the Shadow*, 16.

150. Yeʾor, *Decline of Eastern Christianity Under Islam*, 40–41. Though, initially, these non-Muslims referred only to "People of the Book" (the Jews, Christians, and Sabians), followers of other faiths are eventually included as well. Suaedy, "Islam and Minorities," 14; Uriah Furman, "Minorities in Contemporary Islamist Discourse," *Middle Eastern Studies* 36, no. 4 (2000): 2.

151. Yeʾor and Ellul, *The Dhimmi*, 46.

According to this worldview, Muslims are expected to be involved in *jihad* as an ongoing struggle. Hence, the legitimacy of dhimmitude is assumed as it is an inevitable outcome of *jihad*.

Muhammad's treaty with the non-Muslim tribe at Khaybar is said to be an early form of dhimmitude. Non-Muslims that surrendered were spared and allowed to retain their own religion in the land if they paid a tribute named *jizya*.[152] The *dhimmi*'s status as tributary is a sign of submission to Islam. The *jizya* serves as a sign of submission, as well as the substitute for direct participation in *jihad*.[153]

These concepts that govern dhimmitude are in the Qur'an, where the Muslims are commanded to fight and subjugate the non-Muslims to Islamic rule and the paying of *jizya*.[154] Some have attempted to explain away the negative connotation of *jiyza*, but the subjugation of *dhimmi* cannot be denied.[155] Non-Muslims could only choose between converting to Islam, becoming a *dhimmi*, or be put to death.[156]

An early form of dhimmitude existed from the early stage of Islamic development, but its establishment is best demonstrated through the introduction of the "Pact of Umar."[157] By the ninth century, the concept of dhimmitude was consolidated and defined comprehensively by law.[158] The Pact of Umar stipulated the dhimmitude as an isolated and discrete group within the Islamic political arrangement whose existence is at the mercy of Muslim's tolerance.[159]

---

152. Ye'or and Ellul, 44; Furman, "Minorities in Contemporary Islamist," 13.

153. Ye'or and Ellul, 44; Furman, 5–6.

154. Griffith, *Church in the Shadow*, 10, referring to Q Tawbah 9:29.

155. M. A. S. Abdel Haleem, "The Jizya Verse (Q.9:29): Tax Enforcement on Non-Muslims in the First Muslim State," *Journal of Qur'anic Studies* 14, no. 2 (2012): 72–89. While this work attempts to explain away the negative connotation of dhimmitude, it confirms the relation between *jiyza* and *dhimmi*.

156. "People of the Book" is commonly used to refer to Christians and Jews, but in the context of dhimmitude, Zoroastrians and others are sometimes included. Samuel Hugh Moffett, *A History of Christianity in Asia, vol 1: Beginnings to 1500*, 2nd ed. (Maryknoll, NY: Orbis Books, 1998), vol. 1, chap. 16.

157. Griffith, *Church in the Shadow*, 15–16.

158. Griffith, 15–16.

159. Muslim jurists based the stipulations regarding *dhimmi* on the case of Khaybar, effectively implying dhimmitude as the consequence of *jihad*.

It is similar to the concept of "second class citizen" in a modern state.[160] In Griffith's words,

> The legal disabilities that governed their lives required subservience, often accompanied by prescriptions to wear distinctive clothing and to cease from the public display of their religion, and, of course, to refrain from inviting converts from among the Muslims. Christian wealth, buildings, institutions, and properties were often subject to seizure.[161]

The *dhimmi* must be "considerate of the sensibilities of their Muslim neighbors in public."[162] Yet, "Whilst the Islamists require that 'protected-people' do not offend Muslims' sensitivities, they do not offer a reciprocal undertaking."[163] Non-Muslims were not allowed to "serve in key decision-making positions, as rulers of the state, as army commanders, or as judge."[164] "In later Ottoman times, this arrangement came to be called the millet system."[165]

The *dhimmis* are always the "minority." In the context of a region ruled by Muslims, "the criteria for distinguishing between 'minority' and 'majority' are not quantitative, but rather cultural and political, that is, determined by religion and control of the government."[166] The minorities under Islamic rule could be numerically majority, and yet considered as "minorities." "Muslims may be a numerical minority of the population, but they are always the 'majority' because of their religious and cultural superiority and the Divine law which determines that Islam and Muslims must rule."[167] As a consequence of this, "Islamists determine the status of different groups by their religion."[168] So in this context, "minority" always refer to the non-Muslims ruled by Muslims. From their early conquest to the time of the Crusaders, Muslims were not a

---

160. Griffith, *Church in the Shadow*, 16.
161. Griffith, 16.
162. Furman, "Minorities in Contemporary Islamist" 4.
163. Furman, 4.
164. Furman, 5.
165. Griffith, *Church in the Shadow*, 16; M. O. H. Ursinus, "Millet," *The Encyclopaedia of Islam* 7, 61–64.
166. Furman, "Minorities in Contemporary Islamist" 2.
167. Furman, 3.
168. Furman, 3.

numerical majority in the countries they ruled.[169] Yet, they gradually dominated not just the demography of population, but the social and cultural condition of these lands.[170]

Some have attempted to downplay the plights of *dhimmis*,[171] claiming that "humanity has never known such an exemplary model of relations between the majority – or the ruling class – and the minority that is under its protection."[172] Dhimmitude is seen an expression of grace and mercy on the part of the Muslims.[173] However, this is based on the rationale that the *dhimmi* is the alternative to death or conversion to Islam. Levy-Rubin argues that the Pact of Umar is in fact a sign that Muslims' attitude toward the non-Muslims had grown "harsher and less tolerant with time."[174] She draws such a conclusion after comparing earlier treaties and the Pact of Umar. Apparently, over time, the concept of dhimmitude has grown beyond its relationship with *jizya*, becoming more an ideological apparatus, implemented not based on its original jurisprudence or doctrinal technicalities. Referring to dhimmitude, Furman explains, "here and there, one finds awareness of the need to escape the frozen doctrinaire framework and to try to refresh it without contradicting it."[175]

Even in the setting of a modern state, the concept of *dhimmi* remains the primary reference for managing non-Muslims by Muslim-dominated governments.[176] It is believed that "contemporary Islamists continue to regard the classic *dhimmi* regime as the basis for relations between Muslims and non-Muslims in the Islamic state."[177] Consequent to the adoption of the Western

---

169. Griffith, *Church in the Shadow*, 11.

170. Griffith, 14.

171. Maher Y. Abu-Munshar, *Islamic Jerusalem and Its Christians: A History of Tolerance and Tensions* (London: Tauris Academic Studies, 2007).

172. Furman, "Minorities in Contemporary Islamist," 3.

173. Abdul Haleem, "The Jizya Verse."

174. Milka Levy-Rubin, "Shurut Umar and Its Alternatives: The Legal Debate throughout the Eighth and Ninth Centuries over the Status of the Dhimmis," *Jerusalem Studies in Arabic and Islam* 30 (2005): 204.

175. Furman, "Minorities in Contemporary Islamist," 19.

176. Suaedy, "Islam and Minorities," 4; Richard C. Martin, "From Dhimmis to Minorities: Shifting Constructions of the Non-Muslim Other from Early to Modern Islam," in *Nationalism and Minority Identities in Islamic Societies*, ed. Maya Shatzmiller, 1st ed. (Montreal: McGill-Queen's University Press, 2005), 3–21.

177. Furman, "Minorities in Contemporary Islamist," 19.

political system, dhimmitude is not stipulated explicitly anymore, even in Muslim dominated countries. Yet, there is abundant scriptural, doctrinal, and traditional rationale to legitimize dhimmitude. Though it may not be in an actual legal form, it is at least ideologically in force. This is pertinent in countries which experience Islamist revivalism, such as Malaysia.

In Malaysia, discussions on the concept of *dhimmi* emerged in the 70s within PAS but it was not discussed in the public due to its sensitivity.[178] In recent years, due to the development described in this chapter, it has resurfaced.[179] In general, Malaysian Muslims consider dhimmitude a legitimate concept for the coexistence of non-Muslims in the context of a Muslim-governed Malaysia.[180] Echoing its development, dhimmitude is understood as a theological and ideological concept rather than a mere jurisprudence or governance method. The main concern today is for the non-Muslims to submit to the Islamic rule rather than paying the *jizya*.[181]

Functional Dhimmitude in Malaysia Today

In 2013, the government under the dominance of UMNO unreservedly declared that the Arabic word for God, Allah is only to be used by Muslims, notwithstanding the ruling of the High Court which ruled otherwise.[182] In September, "JAKIM's weekly sermon called for action in defense of Islam by Muslims over the use of the word '*Allah*' for God by the 'enemies of Islam.'"[183] The "position of Islam was being 'threatened from every corner' and such

---

178. Suaedy, "Islam and Minorities," 19.

179. Kit Siang Lim, "Non-Muslim Malaysians as 'Kafir Zimmi'/ "Kafir Harbi" – New Faultline in Nation-Building," *DAP*, 2003, https://dapmalaysia.org/all-archive/English/2003/oct03/lks/lks2716.htm; Nur Hasliza Mohd Salleh, "Mujahid: Jangan Ada Lagi Gelaran Kafir Harbi, Zimmi," *Free Malaysia Today*, 24 July 2018, https://www.freemalaysiatoday.com/category/bahasa/2018/07/24/mujahid-jangan-ada-lagi-gelaran-kafir-harbi-zimmi/; Yayasan Dakwah Islamiah Malaysia, "Tiada Lagi Gelaran Kafir Harbi, Zimmi Dalam Sistem Kewarganegaraan (No More Kafir Harbi, Dhimmi Titles in System of Citizenship)," *Yayasan Dakwah Islamiah Malaysia*, 3 October 2019, http://www.yadim.com.my/v2/tiada-lagi-gelaran-kafir-harbi-zimmi-dalam-sistem-kewarganegaraan/; Muhammad Firdaus Zalani, "Kafir Harbi-Zimmi Perlu Difahami Dalam Kerangka Menyeluruh," *Majlis Ulama ISMA*, https://muis.org.my/2019/10/kafir-harbi-zimmi-perlu-difahami-dalam-kerangka-menyeluruh/.

180. Hussin Mutalib, *Islam in Malaysia: From Revivalism to Islamic State?* (Singapore: NUS Press, 1993), 66–70.

181. Muhammad Firdaus, "Kafir Harbi-Zimmi Perlu."

182. Funston, "UMNO," 112. The Allah issue is just one dispute among others. See Liow, *Religion and Nationalism*, 135–173.

183. Funston, "UMNO," 112–113.

defense was a 'holy struggle.'"[184] According to one of the state muftis, non-Muslims who objected to this defense committed treason as JAKIM's sermons were endorsed by the rulers.[185]

The Court of Appeal eventually overturned the High Court's ruling in October, effectively barring the use of Allah by non-Muslims. The basis for the ruling is twofold. First, it was argued that freedom of religion is based on Article 3(1) that stipulates, "Islam is the religion of the Federation; but other religions may be practiced in peace and harmony in any part of the Federation." Use of Allah by non-Muslims will result in conflict and disharmony, and thus violates the Article.[186] Second, it was ruled that Allah is "not integral to Christian faith."[187] This ruling has long lasting repercussions. It reinterpreted the meaning and motive of Article 3(1). The Article was meant to guarantee the freedom to practice other religions. However, the "decision made non-Muslim religious practice subject to not offending Muslims, regardless of the nature of this offence."[188]

Ultimately, in this case, the authority, under the pressure of the Muslim groups, asserts that Allah belongs to Muslims exclusively.[189] Regardless of the complexity of the legal technicalities of the case, the prevalent sentiment was most revealing. Evidently, political leaders and the majority Malay today consider minorities in Malaysia as *dhimmis*. The Christians, according to the Malays, should be grateful, as they were given a privilege to dwell in Malay land.[190] Kessler argues that the interpretation of the constitution and law today is largely based on this mindset when it comes to issues in relation to race and religion. This attitude can be seen through the rhetoric of the minister whose stern warning to the Christians is, "don't create trouble, '*Allah*' exclusive to Muslims."[191] Kessler considers such warning "a diagnostically telling

---

184. Funston, 113.
185. Funston, 107–108, 113.
186. Funston, 113.
187. Funston, 113.
188. Funston, 113. Although technically the ruling applied only to the Catholics' publication, *Herald*, a "precedent has been set for a much broader application."
189. Yapp, "'Copyright' Controversy," 147–156.
190. Clive Kessler, "The Dhimmi and an Old New 'Rationale,'" *New Mandala*, http://asiapacific.anu.edu.au/newmandala/2014/07/24/the-dhimmi-and-an-old-new-rationale/.
191. Kessler, "Dhimmi and an Old New," referring to "Don't Create Trouble, 'Allah' Exclusive to Muslims, Former Home Minister Tells Churches," *Malaysia Today*, 10 July

locution. That is how the *dhimmi*, the so-called protected religious minorities, of medieval Islamic society were addressed. That is how they were spoken to and reminded of their place, a subordinated one, and their rights, which were limited and conditional."[192]

Indeed, "Dhimma literally means 'pledge and guarantee' . . . the contract for protection that was made with Christians . . . when they agreed to live within the Muslim state."[193] The basis for peaceful co-existence between Muslim and non-Muslim, according to the Qur'an, is based on four tenets: human brotherhood, religious tolerance, justice and fair treatment, and loyalty and alliance. Yet, non-Muslims must not be perceived as threatening to fulfill the third tenet, justice and fair treatment.[194] Amicable attitude toward non-Muslims "can change if they become the aggressor, threaten to break a truce, or present an obstacle to the delivery of the message of Islam."[195]

In the case of the use of Allah, Christians insist on their right to use the term to refer to God. The authority considers this to be a threat to Islam in Malaysia. Christians were deemed by Muslims to have breached the constitution. They are thought to be not practicing religion "in peace in harmony" as stated in the constitution.[196] Based on the definition of *dhimmi* above, they have become "threatening," as it was perceived that the use of Allah would confuse Muslims in the country. Kessler argues that it is "that same logic and mind-set that also seem to inform the Court of Appeal's judgment in this name of Allah matter." If so, indeed "the Common Law tradition, 'the discourse of constitutional legality,' is in a beleaguered and precarious situation."[197]

Such rhetoric and attitude toward minorities in Malaysia is by no means enough to technically constitute a full dhimmitude. Even though in the Islamic worldview the Muslims are always the ruling "majority," with only slightly more than 60 percent of the population being Muslims, dhimmitude

---

2014, http://www.malaysia-today.net/2014/07/10/dont-create-trouble-allah-exclusive-to-muslims-former-home-minister-tells-churches/.

192. Kessler, "Dhimmi and an Old New."

193. Maher Y. Abu-Munshar, "In the Shadow of the 'Arab Spring': The Fate of Non-Muslims under Islamist Rule," *Islam and Christian-Muslim Relations* 23, no. 4 (2012): 496.

194. Abu-Munshar, "In the Shadow of the 'Arab Spring,'" 489–494.

195. Abu-Munshar, 492.

196. Article 3, The Federal Constitution of Malaysia.

197. Kessler, "Dhimmi and an Old New."

in Malaysia is demographically implausible.[198] Still, as Kam Weng Ng pointed out, with the rationale of Malay hegemony, "Perhaps, non-Muslims are already 'functional *dhimmis*' in Malaysia. Non-Muslims are already subject to Islamic *dhimmi* policies without bearing the official status of *dhimmi*."[199]

Many other evidences point to the emergence of functional dhimmitude in Malaysia. In 2013, non-Muslims of a school were instructed to have their meals in the toilet during the fasting month.[200] Again, it was the sensitivity of the Muslims that needed to be protected. The headmaster was not even sanctioned. Instead, parents were intimidated by police and their children had to be transferred to another school. One of the state *muftis* in Malaysia openly referred to non-Muslims in Malaysia as *dhimmi* – supposedly to "defend" non-Muslims from being labeled as "*kafir harbi*" (belligerent infidels).[201] The change of road names to Islamic names, the Islamization of school syllabus, and the insistence on Muslim superiority in all areas of society are reminiscent of historic dhimmitude.[202] Notwithstanding one's perception of dhimmitude, this concept is undeniably foreign to the non-Muslims and a natural consequence of Malay hegemony.

Summary: From Malay Nationalism to Malay Hegemony

The evolution of Malay ethnogenesis into Malay hegemony is a demonstration of how Islamism might empower a nation or people in their pursuit of self-determination. The Islamists have since the early stage of Malay ethnogenesis, played an important role. Their influence during colonial time was significant. The Islamists thrived together and eventually intertwined with the *bangsa* movement in their joint cause of Malaya independence. Thereon, Islamism has been playing an increasingly important role, supporting and

---

198. For further explanation, see Abu-Munshar, "In the Shadow," 499–500.

199. Kam Weng Ng, "The Dhimmi Syndrome: The Psychological Degradation of the Oppressed," *Krisis & Praxis* (blog), http://www.krisispraxis.com/archives/2006/11/the-dhimmi-syndrome-the-psychological-degradation-of-the-oppressed/.

200. Chin, "From Ketuanan Melayu," 203.

201. "Asri: You Can't Simply Label Non-Muslim Citizens 'Kafir Harbi,'" *Free Malaysia Today*, 24 June 2016, http://www.freemalaysiatoday.com/category/nation/2016/06/24/asri-you-cant-simply-label-non-muslim-citizens-kafir-harbi/.

202. Ye'or, *Decline of Eastern Christianity*, 239–240.

shaping Malay ethnogenesis and nationalism in every crisis the Malays faced. Ultimately, Islamism became the object and beneficiary of political competition. It gave birth to Malay hegemony – a version of Malay nationalism that is primarily directed by conservative Islam.

The Islamic turn to conservativism in Malaysia described in this chapter can be demonstrated through the five indicators outlined by Mohamed Nawab Mohamed Osman.[203] First, the number of Malaysian Muslims who subscribe to conservative Salafism has increased significantly. The *dakwah* movement has certainly contributed to this phenomenon. Under Salafism, reasoning and theologizing suffered a further setback and gave way to fundamentalism that interpreted Islam merely as a way of life predetermined by its sacred texts.[204] Second, Islam has become the dominant influence in government policy making. The dominance of JAKIM is a clear example. Third, there has been sustained support and pressure for a thorough implementation of Islamic law and the promulgation of an Islamic state in Malaysia. Fourth, the rise of Islamist NGOs and pressure groups and their influence have helped to steer the government and the public toward a more conservative stance. Finally, the rights of religious minorities have been undermined. Furthering Mohamed Nawab's last point, this study argues that minorities such as CCS who argue for equal rights and Malaysian Malaysia are ignored because they are considered as *dhimmi*.

---

203. Mohamed Nawab, "Islamic Conservative Turn," 3–4.

204. Islamism, however, influences all Islamic schools of thought, not just Salafism. Ahmad Fauzi, *Islamisme Dan Bahananya*, 41.

Part II

Ministry Challenge

CHAPTER 3

The Clash of Nationalisms and Social Withdrawal of the Sabah Chinese Christians

This chapter describes the clash between CCS's nationalism and Malay hegemony, and CCS's subsequent social withdrawal. The various ways in which CCS negotiate their version of nationalism in the public space are discussed. The limitations and ineffectiveness of these negotiations are also explored. This chapter surveys the above problems by first considering the larger context of Malaysian Chinese and Malaysian Christians as a whole, before focusing on the context of CCS.

The Clash of National Discourses

The clash of nationalisms in Malaysia is inevitable as both the Malays and the non-Malays have competing nation-of-intent. Malay nationalism has been extensively described in chapter 2. The following sections describe the nation-of-intent and nationalism of the Malaysian Chinese, which are shared by the CCS.

The Cultural Nationalism of Malaysian Chinese

For overseas Chinese, embracing the nation-state identification of their new home outside of China takes time and requires various conditions.[1]

---

1. Gungwu Wang, "Chinese Ethnicity in New Southeast Asia Nations," in *Ethnic Relations and Nation-Building in Southeast Asia: The Case of the Ethnic Chinese*, ed. Leo Suryadinata,

For centuries, the Chinese in Malaysia have retained much of their cultural heritage. They see themselves as both Chinese and Malaysian, and these identities are neither mixed nor mutually exclusive.[2] The Chinese in Malaysia are often called "Malaysian Chinese," an expression that indicates, "being Malaysian is expressed through being Chinese in the Malaysian context."[3]

The Malaysian Malaysia, Multiculturalism, and Constitutionalism

To preserve their cultural identity, the Malaysian Chinese, including the CCS, have resorted to multiculturalism.[4] Multiculturalism holds a multiculturalist position in a pluralist society. It rejects the monoculturalist position where the dominant group dismisses diversity and attempts to assimilate minorities.[5] As described in chapter 2, the Malaysian Chinese prefer Malaysian-Malaysia to Malay-Malaysia because the former is multiculturalist and the latter, monoculturalist.[6] Thus, a nation-of-intent based on multiculturalism is the best option for them to safeguard their cultural identity and prevents assimilation. For the Malaysian Chinese, the means to champion their nation-of-intent is constitutionalism. They insist that Malays have misinterpreted the constitution. They maintain that the constitution guarantees a Malaysian-Malaysia.[7]

Politics/Social Issues: Southeast Asia (Singapore: Institute of Southeast Asian Studies, 2004), 7.

2. Chee-Beng Tan, "Chinese Identities in Malaysia," in *Chinese Overseas*, Comparative Cultural Issues (Hong Kong: Hong Kong University Press, 2004), 109, http://www.jstor.org/stable/j.ctt2jbzp1.9.

3. Tan, "Chinese Identities in Malaysia," 109.

4. While the use of multiculturalism only became prominent much later, non-Malays in Malaysia, including Lee Kuan Yew who led Singapore, had been subscribing to its principles and concepts in their political struggles.

5. Bhikhu Parekh, *Rethinking Multiculturalism: Cultural Diversity and Political Theory* (Basingstoke, UK: Macmillan, 2000), 6.

6. The term "multiculturalism" was first used in the Malaysian context by Goh. Daniel P. S. Goh et al., eds., *Race and Multiculturalism in Malaysia and Singapore* (London: Routledge, 2009), 1–16. Thock refers to this "nation-of-intent" as "civic nationalism." Ker Pong Thock, "Discoursing Nation-Building and Civil Society Formation," in *Malaysian Chinese and Nation-Building: Before Merdeka and Fifty Years After, Vol. 2*, ed. Phin Keong Voon (Kuala Lumpur: Centre for Malaysian Chinese Studies, 2008), 586.

7. Thock, "Discoursing Nation-Building and Civil Society Formation," 590, quoting Liok Ee Tan, *The Politics of Chinese Education in Malaya, 1945–1961* (Oxford University Press, 1997), 310. "'Malayan social contract' was no explicit or recognized part of the discussions leading to Merdeka in 1957; that it is merely a retrospective 'construct,' an idea that was later fashioned, with a partisan political purpose, and then imputed, or 'read back,' by its inventors into the Federal Constitution – or their revisionist ideas of its provisions and meaning." Clive Kessler,

Malaysian Christians also share a similar nation-of-intent. Judging from their support of the liberal ideas of democracy, human rights, and freedom based on constitutionalism, it is safe to conclude that they too, like the other non-Muslims, advocate Malaysian-Malaysia, with multiculturalism as their core social model.

Political Identity and Multiculturalism in Malaysia

The foundation for multiculturalism within a political domain is a shared political identity by all citizens. Yet, political identity is contested by the different nationalisms in Malaysia.[8] Political identity is a legal identity of all citizens in a state. It vitally provides criteria to adjoin all citizens in their commitment to the state.[9] In the case of Malaysia, the definition of political identity has been dominated by the Malays.[10] Since the introduction of NCP, other ethnicities are coerced into accepting the newly reformulated political identity based on Malay and Islamic values.[11] Understandably, such a move is due to the fact that fundamentally,

> Islam rejects the idea of "melting" the members of the various communities together to form a single civil and national society, or the possibility of establishing relations of cooperation and full equality between the members of the various communities on the basis of an overarching federal law, with each community preserving its cultural and religious identity.[12]

So far, non-Malays have resisted such attempts of assimilation. Specifically, they reject Islam as an integral component in the formulation of national identity.[13] In other words, non-Malays in Malaysia reject Islamism, regardless

---

"Foreword: Where Malaysia Stands Today: A Personal Introduction to a Timely Collection of Essays," in *Misplaced Democracy: Malaysian Politics and People*, ed. Sophie Lemiere (Petaling Jaya, Malaysia: Strategic Information and Research Development Centre, 2014), viii.

    8. As this study relates "national identity" and nationalism to ethno-nationalism, the term "political identity" is used to refer to the state-related, legal identity often associated with citizenship.

    9. Parekh, *Rethinking Multiculturalism*, 230–231.

    10. Parekh, 232.

    11. Parekh, 232.

    12. Furman, "Minorities in Contemporary Islamist Discourse," 17–18.

    13. Parekh, *Rethinking Multiculturalism*, 234.

of its level of moderateness. They reacted defensively, distancing themselves further from the Malays.[14] They seek a nation-of-intent that is based on a political identity that recognizes the legitimacy of their culture, protects them, and accepts them. Otherwise, holding onto their Malaysian political identity becomes a challenge. This creates an identity crisis, which has caused many CCS to detach from nation-building.

Malay Hegemony Alienated the Chinese Christians in Sabah

For centuries, the Chinese have been suspicious of Islam.[15] As a complete "way of life," Islam is a direct challenge to Chinese culture. In fact, "Responding to the reality that they live within a Malay hegemonic state, the Chinese have absorbed cultural elements previously considered as the exclusive preserve of Malays."[16] Yet, they have remained extremely unaccommodating toward Islam.[17] They rarely convert to Islam and use Islam as an ethnic boundary marker to differentiate themselves from the Malays.[18] They would also "reject the establishment of an Islamic state in Malaysia."[19]

The Malaysian Chinese have a long history of resisting Malay nationalism and Islam.[20] They opposed NCP in the 1970s and state-sponsored Islamization

---

14. Parekh, 234–235.

15. Evidently, the Chinese assimilate easily in Buddhist countries such as Thailand. Yet, in both Muslim majority countries, Indonesia and Malaysia, the Chinese have rejected Islam. See Jean DeBernardi, "Chinese in Southeast Asia," *Encyclopedia of World Cultures, Vol. 5, East and Southeast Asia*, 74–75.

16. "Of the three attributes of Malayness . . . Malay rulers, the Malay language, and Islam – only Islam has remained clearly outside the experience of most Chinese." Pek Koon Heng, "Chinese Responses to Malay Hegemony in Peninsular Malaysia 1957–96," *Southeast Asian Studies* 34, no. 3 (December 1996): 521.

17. Heng, "Chinese Responses to Malay Hegemony in Peninsular Malaysia 1957–96," 521. The negative impression of Islam in the eyes of Malaysian Chinese is well documented, even by Muslim scholars. Chuah, for example, lists thirteen reasons why Malaysian Chinese reject Islam. See Osman Abdullah @ Hock Leng Chuah, "Methodology of Da'wah to the Non-Muslim Chinese in Malaysia: A Preliminary Observation," *Ulum Islamiyyah, The Malaysian Journal of Islamic Sciences* 5, no. 1 (2006): 73–76.

18. Yeok Meng Ngeow, "Islamization and Ethnic Identity of the Chinese Minority in Malaysia" (University of Malaya, 2011), 23, 25, http://eprints.um.edu.my/582/1/ICAS_of_NGEOW_YEOK_MENG%5B1%5D.pdf; Chuah, "Methodology of Da'wah," 68.

19. Heng, "Chinese Responses to Malay Hegemony," 521.

20. Thock, "Discoursing Nation-Building," 585–586.

in the 1980s and 1990s, as they were perceived as cultural threats.[21] The uncompromising stance of the Chinese against Islam is "equilibrium to the imposition of Islamic values into the public sphere."[22] To the Malays, Islam is a means to unite all ethnicities in Malaysia. Yet, the Chinese perceive Islam as a threat to their ethnic identity.[23] They react against Malay hegemony by preserving their culture tenaciously, especially through education.[24] This is true throughout Malaysia, including Sabah.

Malaysian Chinese also consider Malay hegemony a threat to constitutionalism and nation-building.[25] The Chinese felt that "their political, economic and social power had been gradually eroded because of the government policy of Islamization."[26] UMNO and the government, in their efforts to counter PAS, put little emphasis on engaging the Chinese.[27] The Chinese were shocked and felt betrayed by Mahathir's declaration in 2001 that Malaysia was an Islamic state.[28] Lim Kit Siang, quoted by Lee, described Mahathir's declaration as "a tectonic shift in Malaysian politics where the undisputed constitutional and nation-building principle for forty-four years of Malaysia as a democratic, secular, and multi-religious nation has been abandoned."[29] Most Malaysian Chinese, like Lim, consider Malaysia a secular state hijacked by Islamism.

---

21. A. B. Shamsul, "Text and Collective Memories: The Construction of Chinese and Chineseness from the Perspective of a Malay," in *Ethnic Relations and Nation-Building in Southeast Asia: The Case of the Ethnic Chinese*, ed. Leo Suryadinata, Politics/Social Issues: Southeast Asia (Singapore: Institute of Southeast Asian Studies, 2004), 128–129.

22. As in the case of the Kelantanese society. Ngeow, "Islamization and Ethnic Identity," 24. "Policies that have profound impacts on the livelihood and lifestyle of the Chinese minority are rejected for fear of loss of such identity."

23. Chuah, "Methodology of Da'wah," 68.

24. Ngeow, "Islamization and Ethnic Identity," 24; Thock, "Discoursing Nation-Building," 590.

25. P. G. Lim, "Towards National Integration: Of the Constitution, Governance and Ethnicity," *INSAF* 32, no. 1 (2003): 18; Phin Keong Voon, "Whither the Malaysian Nation-State?," in *Malaysian Chinese and Nation-Building: Before Merdeka and Fifty Years After. Vol. 2*, ed. Phin Keong Voon (Kuala Lumpur: Centre for Malaysian Chinese Studies, 2008), 739.

26. Chuah, "Methodology of Da'wah," 68; Amini Amir Abdullah, "Islamic Revivalism, Religious Freedom and the Non-Muslims in Malaysia: A Preliminary Discussion," *Pertanika* 11, no. 2 (2003): 133.

27. Chin, "From Ketuanan Melayu," 172.

28. Chin, 187.

29. Kam Hing Lee, "Differing Perspectives on Integration and Nation-Building in Malaysia," in *Ethnic Relations and Nation-Building in Southeast Asia: The Case of the Ethnic Chinese*, ed. Leo Suryadinata, Politics/Social Issues: Southeast Asia (Singapore: Institute of Southeast Asian Studies, 2004), 102.

Malay Nationalism and Islamization in Sabah

Malay nationalism has always been considered a foreign invasion by the non-Muslims in Sabah. It was formally introduced in Sabah during Mustapha's term as chief minister from 1967.[30] Eager to show the Peninsular his commitment to Malay nationalism, he "wanted Sabah to be Muslim and Sabah's language to be Malay, in order to bring the state closer to the situation in the Peninsula."[31] Mustapha's intention to unify Sabah with "one language, one religion and one culture" was consistent with the NCP.[32] Mustapha's successor Harris Salleh continued with the Malay nationalism programs.[33]

Islamization in Sabah follows the patterns in the Peninsular. Islam was integrated into Malay nationalism. The concept of "*masuk Melayu*" or "becoming Malay" through embracing Islam was popularized in Sabah in the 1960s and 1970s as a way for people to be recognized as "Sabahan" and "Malaysian." Evidently, Islamization in Sabah was an attempt by the federal and the state governments to unite Sabah under the NCP. In the 1960s and the 1970s, Islamization was intense and systematic. It was executed with coercion, intimidation, deception, and enticement in the name of "nationalism." The United Sabah Islamic Association (USIA) was established in 1969 for this purpose. It was given "funds to advance Islamic influence and co-ordinate a push towards converting the people to Islam in a series of mass proselytization."[34]

Islamization in Sabah was threefold.[35] First, it began by weakening the churches through the expulsion of Christian missionaries.[36] Second, Islamization in Sabah was carried out by enticing, threatening, and persecuting

---

30. Zhang, *Hakkas of Sabah*, 142. Brunei Muslims have for many years observed Malay customs and used the Malay language. Singh, *Making of Sabah, 1865–1941*, 63. Yet, Brunei Malays in Sabah were dispersed and lack a shared ethnic consciousness in Sabah. Only after the Second World War, was the promotion of the Malay bangsa movement recorded. Milner, *The Malays*, 134.

31. Bruce Clifford Ross-Larson, *The Politics of Federalism: Syed Kechik in East Malaysia* (Singapore: Ross-Larson, 1976), 107, as cited in Zhang, *Hakkas of Sabah*, 142.

32. Luping, *Sabah's Dilemma*, 534. The Declaration of National Culture Policy in 1971 has upheld Islam and Malay culture. See Luping, *Sabah's Dilemma*, 515; Chuen Hoe Yow, "The Chinese in Sabah and Sarawak Politics: Ensuring a Role in Government," in *Malaysian Chinese and Nation-Building: Before Merdeka and Fifty Years After. Vol. 2*, ed. Phin Keong Voon (Kuala Lumpur: Centre for Malaysian Chinese Studies, 2008), 564.

33. Lim, "Islamization and Ethnicity in Sabah," 169–170.

34. Zhang, *Hakkas of Sabah*, 144.

35. Luping, *Sabah's Dilemma*, 535.

36. Luping, 541–560.

non-Muslim community leaders into embracing Islam.[37] By co-opting the support of non-Muslim leaders, Mustapha managed to make Islam the official religion of Sabah in 1971. The third step was converting the masses. Threats of "denying job opportunities and economic access were normal."[38] Those who converted to Islam were given benefits in the forms of "money, promotions and timber areas."[39] Some Christian activities were also banned in 1974.[40] By 1975, USIA claimed 93,000 conversions.[41]

In 1976, Harris initiated the Sabah Islamic Council (Majlis Ugama Islam Sabah /MUIS).[42] While Mustapha was actively involved in the effort of mass proselytization and took credit for its operation under USIA, Harris and MUIS worked without similar publicity.[43] However, aggressive Islamization continued through proselytization and various government policies.[44] Muslim population increased and Sabah experienced a "transformation of the demography."[45] From 1976 to 1985, "the total Muslim population increased from 40 percent to 50 percent within ten years through mass village conversion and large-scale foreign immigration into Sabah."[46] The increase of population of Sabah between 1970 and 2000 saw a shocking 285 percent growth from 0.64 million to 2.4 million, an impossibility in natural circumstances.[47] Consequently, there have been strong but unproven suspicions that

---

37. Zhang, *Hakkas of Sabah*, 145.
38. Luping, *Sabah's Dilemma*, 562–564.
39. Zhang, *Hakkas of Sabah*, 145, referring to Ross-Larson, *Politics of Federalism*, 108.
40. Zhang, 145.
41. Zhang, 146. For comparison, Sabah population in 1980 was 929,299. Malaysian Information Department website, http://pmr.penerangan.gov.my/index.php/profil-malaysia/7962-demografi-penduduk.html.
42. Zhang, 146.
43. Luping, *Sabah's Dilemma*, 567.
44. Luping, 567.
45. Lim, "Islamization and Ethnicity in Sabah, Malaysia," 169–170.
46. Lim, 169–170.
47. Chin, "Forced to the Periphery: Recent Chinese Politics in East Malaysia," 117; while overall, Malaysia population grew from 10.4 to 22.2 million, or at 113 percent in the period. Sarawak's growth was 106 percent, from 0.98 million to 2 million. According to *Sabah Statistics Yearbook 2015* (Putrajaya, Malaysia: Department of Statistics, Malaysia, 2016), there is an increase of 490.62 percent from 653,604 to 3,206,742 in Sabah's population between 1970 and 2010.

the phenomenon is due to a "deliberate policy of 'importing' Muslim voters from Indonesia and the Southern Philippines."[48]

Malay Hegemony a Betrayal to the Sabah Chinese

Under Malay hegemony, the fate of the Chinese and CCS are interwoven, as they were both betrayed. The CCS, having been co-governing with the British and lacking an anti-colonial nationalism, naturally favor a secular, multicultural state based on Western liberal democracy where laws and human rights are the foundations.[49] Thus, they found difficulty in adapting to the Malay-Muslim nationalism of the federal government that put ethno-nationalism, Islamic values, and anti-West sentiment before fair governance and meritocracy.

Sabah Chinese were appalled to find that Malaysian nationalism, which they accepted with great compromises, was hijacked and turned into Malay nationalism after the 1969 riot. They were not directly involved in the 1969 racial riot in the Peninsular and were reluctant to bear the consequences of Malay Supremacy that resulted from the riot.[50] While the more Westernized Chinese were concerned about their rights and justice, the cultural Chinese majority rejected the Malay-Islam nationalism as it infringed upon their basic aspirations of economic wellbeing and cultural integrity.

Islamization left a lasting effect on CCS. It produced only a negligible number of Chinese converts. Yet, it changed the demography of Sabah and further impeded indigenization of the Chinese as Malaysian.[51] Through the transformation of the demography, the Muslims "have managed to become an absolute majority in terms of electoral politics."[52] Subsequently and unsurprisingly, the Chinese in Sabah suffered a decline in their political weight.

Due to Malay hegemony, the Sabah Chinese today suffer similar difficulties faced by the Malaysian Chinese in general. The failure of a former chief minister of Sabah to build a statue of a sea goddess at a key Chinese town

---

48. Chin, "Forced to the Periphery," 116; Kamal Sadiq, "When States Prefer Non-Citizens over Citizens: Conflict over Illegal Immigration into Malaysia," *International Studies Quarterly* 49, no. 1 (2005): 101–122.

49. Wang, "Chinese Ethnicity," 9.

50. *Malaysia Human Development Report 2013*, 233.

51. Chin, "Forced to the Periphery," 117.

52. Chin, 117.

due to the objection from the state government is an example of Malay hegemony. It was alleged that "the statue could not be built as it was too close to a mosque and that there was a fatwa against the statue."[53]

Civil Negotiations by the Chinese Christians

Civil negotiation is a form of negotiation, which is non-violent and operates within the framework of democracy and civil society.[54] It is a mediation that aims to mitigate conflicts; hence it is a limited form of social engagement, as social engagement goes beyond conflict resolution. Civil negotiation may be carried out within the government through the political parties' internal negotiation, meetings of representatives between concerned groups, or mass civil movements. As a form of negotiation, its premise is essentially the interpretation and protection of the legal rights of the parties involved. Engagement with the masses and building of relationship are secondary.

Chinese Civil Negotiation

The Malaysian Chinese have initiated various civil negotiations with the ruling regime to fight for Malaysian-Malaysia. The civil negotiation of the Malaysian Chinese is best illustrated through the appeals made by their guilds and associations. The Chinese Guilds and Associations (CGA) are often the preferred choice of representatives compared to the Chinese political parties.[55] In 1985, the CGA launched the "Joint Declaration by Chinese Guilds and Associations of Malaysia" through their Civil Rights Committee.[56] Instead of only focusing on the Chinese community, the declaration appealed for equal rights for all Malaysian citizens. The declaration shows the multicultural

---

53. Chin, 120. Chin alleges that personal conflict might have played a part in the matter, but the reasons given by the government were based on a sentiment according to Malay hegemony.

54. Civil society is "that set of diverse non-governmental institutions which is strong enough to counterbalance the state and, while not preventing the state from fulfilling its role of keeper of the peace and arbitrator between major interests, can nevertheless prevent it from dominating and atomizing the rest of society." Ernest Gellner, *Conditions of Liberty: Civil Society and Its Rivals* (London: Penguin Books, 1994), 5.

55. Thock, "Discoursing Nation-Building," 575–577. Most CGAs are educationist associations, as Malaysian Chinese consider Chinese education as their means to preserve their cultural distinctiveness.

56. Thock, "Discoursing Nation-Building," 593.

nature of the Malaysian Chinese's nation-of-intent.[57] It was a response to NCP, increased influence from the *dakwah* groups, and Islamization. CGA's civil negotiation is also reflected in the 1999 *suqiu* (Petitions and Appeals), which was endorsed by 2,905 CGA.[58] Again they appealed for multiculturalism via constitutionalism, seeking equality.[59] The affirmative policies of the government prioritizing Malays in education and economic development were contested. All CGA's civil negotiations failed miserably. The Chinese were accused of ingratitude and were met with hostility from the Malays.

Christians' Civil Negotiation as a Response to Islamization

Malaysian Christians' civil and political negotiation is triggered by their needs to respond to Islamization.[60] Specifically, they reacted against government actions

> such as legal amendments that allowed state intervention into non-Muslim religions, reduced allocation ratios for non-Muslim places of worship (as compared to the building of mosques), the conversion of non-Muslim minors, the legal prohibition of preaching to Muslims, the introduction of hudud laws and many others . . . restrictions on numerous activities like sharing the gospel, registering as a denomination, meeting as a group, buying land, conducting kindergartens, and recruiting church workers.[61]

Malaysian Christianity is "a prime example of a minority faith spurred towards political response by pressures from a secular state gradually taking on a non-secular bias in favor of a majority faith."[62] In 2005, Peter G. Riddell lists

---

57. Thock, 593–594.
58. Thock, 577.
59. Lee, "Differing Perspectives on Integration," 94–95.
60. Liow, *Religion and Nationalism*, 156.
61. Alwyn Lau, "Intimating the Unconscious: Politics, Psychoanalysis and Theology in Malaysia" (PhD diss., Monash University, 2016), 9. See also Eu Choong Chong, "The Christian Response to State-Led Islamization in Malaysia," in *Religious Diversity in Muslim-Majority States in Southeast Asia: Areas of Toleration and Conflict*, ed. Bernhard Platzdasch and Johan Saravanamuttu (Singapore: Institute of Southeast Asian Studies, 2014), 290–320.
62. Lau, "Intimating the Unconscious," 9.

five responses from the non-Muslims in Malaysia as they face Islamization.[63] They are: lobbying the government, participating in the political process, engaging with Muslims through dialogue, contextualizing the faith to rid its foreign image, and undertaking advocacy and apologetics. Much of the above remain true today. Mostly, the above are performed and represented by Christian umbrella bodies, among them, the Christian Federation of Malaysia (CFM), Council of Churches of Malaysia (CCM), and National Evangelical Christian Fellowship (NECF). Their primary role is to "pressure" the ruling regime through constitutionalism.[64] Their points of contention are the interpretation of two articles in the constitutions that concern the freedom of religion, and Islam as the official religion in Malaysia.[65] Their motive for negotiation is to safeguard the "rights" of Christians in the country. Their methods include press statements, representation, educating Christians, and attempting the five methods mentioned by Riddell.

However, the acts of lobbying the government and initiating dialogue have largely been ignored.[66] Malaysian Christians have been "systematically excluded from discussion and debate on Islamization and its implications."[67] Such purposeful exclusion further proves that non-Muslims are being treated as *dhimmi*. Any criticism or comment on Islamization has been regarded by Muslims as highly offensive, even though policies involved concern the whole Malaysian society.[68] Meanwhile, Christians' Western image has been consolidated through their active participation in various political processes and civil actions. Christians have in recent years taken legal actions against the government, notably, in the cases of Lina Joy's apostasy and the Allah

---

63. Peter G. Riddell, "Islamization, Civil Society, and Religious Minority in Malaysia," in *Islam in Southeast Asia: Political, Social and Strategic Challenges for the 21st Century*, ed. K. S. Nathan and Mohammad Hashim Kamali (Singapore: Institute of Southeast Asian Studies, 2005), 173–184.

64. Chong, "Christian Response," 295–300; Riddell, "Islamization, Civil Society," 181–184.

65. These articles in the constitution have been interpreted differently by the advocates of the two nationalisms, as shown in the Allah case described in chapter 2.

66. Riddell, "Islamization, Civil Society," 173.

67. Robert Hunt, "Christian Theological Reflection and Education in the Muslim Societies of Malaysia and Indonesia," *Studies in World Christianity* 3, no. 2 (1997): 215, quoted in Riddell, 173.

68. Hunt, "Christian Theological Reflection," 215, quoted in Riddell, 173.

controversy.⁶⁹ Yet, though such advocacy is necessary, detachment from Muslims has been perpetuated and worsened.

Civil Negotiations of the Chinese Christians in Sabah

The Chinese were largely silent throughout the process of Islamization in Sabah. In the 1970s, CCS did send a letter to oppose the expulsion of missionaries, but they considered the persecution under the Malay nationalism and Islamization a blessing in disguise because it drove away nominalism in the church.⁷⁰ There seemed to be very little concern about the restriction of evangelism to the Muslims or the difficulties a Muslim apostate might have faced. These concerns only surfaced in recent years. Then, CCS regarded the restraints which they practiced a great virtue, as they sacrificed for "the larger goal of nation building," believing that a multi-religious society would emerge in a relatively short time.⁷¹ Zhang also opines that such diplomatic stances of the church prevented conflicts like those in Northern Ireland, Sri Lanka, and southern Philippines.⁷² So, CCS "advocated consultations and dialogues and sought compromises to defuse tension."⁷³ Yet, such passive and reactionary acts reveal the shortsightedness of the church at the time. Islamization was allowed to gain many converts and tilted the political balance between the non-Muslims and Muslims in Sabah. As the CCS retreated from engaging with their sociopolitical context, Islamization could continue to indoctrinate Malaysian and Sabahan Malays with a sense of Malay superiority and increasingly legitimize Muslim nationalism as the main national discourse.

The CCS may be passive in their reaction as a religious body, but they remain steadfast to Malaysian nationalism. In recent years, they have resisted Malay hegemony through the Sabah Council of Churches (SCC), which stands in solidarity with CFM, CCM, and NECF. Indeed, "the collective Christian responses are more or less coordinated and thus similar" when

---

69. Liow, *Religion and Nationalism*, 135–173. "Malaysia's best-known Christian convert, Lina Joy, lost a six-year battle on Wednesday to have the word 'Islam' removed from her identity card, after the country's highest court rejected the change." "Malaysia's Lina Joy Loses Islam Conversion Case," *Reuters*, 30 May 2007, https://www.reuters.com/article/us-malaysia-religion-ruling-idUSSP20856820070530.

70. Boughton, *Sabah Anglican Diocese*, 120.

71. Zhang, *Hakkas of Sabah*, 147.

72. Zhang, 147.

73. Zhang, 148.

it comes to their understanding of Christian political activism.[74] The recent SCC's involvement with various political and civil engagements attests to the stance of CCS, which is based on multiculturalism and constitutionalism.[75]

The Limitations of Civil Negotiations

Civil negotiation is a common means to contend one's nation-of-intent through the electoral or legal means.[76] Ng, seeing that a functional *dhimmi* is emerging in Malaysia, believes this prevents an "implicit submission to dhimmitude . . . to explicit submission to dhimmitude."[77] However, Lee opines that with the discourses fought out in public, support will determine the outcome.[78] Support of a discourse may not mean that the conflicting discourses are given adequate space to be debated. Likewise, election is also risky, as election "may confirm the legitimacy of a bad or corrupt electoral structure."[79] Undertaking a legal challenge "likewise affirms the courts' legitimacy and risks creating an unwanted legal precedent which will worsen real prospects for future legal challenges."[80] The outcome of the Lina Joy and Allah cases are examples. The problem, contends Lee, is the absence of a mechanism that allows discourses to be properly competed. The media that is going in different directions, with mainstream and social media not converging, is making logical discussion of differing opinions difficult. The conflicting discourses have no space to even converge and "have a good fight." Azeem Fazwan Ahmad Farouk points out that the lack of ethnic integration and cooperation among the civil society organizations and the lack of space for democratization in Malaysia's political environment have weakened the role of civil negotiation.[81] Lim similarly

---

74. Lau, "Intimating the Unconscious," 7.
75. For example, see Sabah Council of Churches, "Press Statement by Sabah Council of Churches on Kelantan's Hudud Enactment," Press Release, 30 March 2015, http://www.majodi.org/v4/index.php/news/675-press-statement-by-sabah-council-of-churches-on-kelantan-s-hudud-enactment.
76. Lee, *Islamization and Activism*, 135–136.
77. Ng, "Dhimmi Syndrome."
78. Lee, *Islamization and Activism*, 135–136.
79. Lee, 136.
80. Lee, 136.
81. Azeem Fazwan Ahmad Farouk, "The Limits of Civil Society in Democratising the State: The Malaysian Case," *Kajian Malaysia, USM* 29, no. 1 (2011): 91–109. Civil society is pluralist in nature. See Mohammed Arkoun, "Locating Civil Society in Islamic Context," in

bemoans the inability of the state to negotiate secular space for dialogues due to the prominence of the Malay hegemony agenda.[82] Ramasamy criticizes the Malaysian state for utilizing a "combination of coercive and non-coercive measures" to curtail the effectiveness of the civil society.[83] These result in the disappearing of reasoning, inclusiveness, and the efficacy of civil society. Unfortunately, this harmonizes well with a patrimonial society like Malaysia where the government treats the state apparatus like its "private inherited property."[84]

As Islamism is now interwoven with Malay self-determination, Malaysia has lost its original foundation of nation-building that saw different races with different religious backgrounds coming together to pursue independence and in agreement of mutual respect.[85] A selective amnesia today by political figures and Malay extremists on the existence of such an agreement gives them an excuse to dismiss the need for dialogues; though most of the time, they do so to gain political currency.[86] Furthermore, the subversive changes in the attitude of the majority Malays, which increasingly see the minority as *dhimmi*, not only sync with the ongoing Malay hegemony policies, but also diminish the openness and willingness to discuss and dialogue. Civil negotiations also fail because of the inherent *dakwah* movement's rigid spirituality and fundamentalist doctrine, the overly Western outlook of the Chinese and Christians in their sociopolitical activism, and cultural differences.

The *Dakwah* Revivalists' Sentiment toward Civil Negotiation

Muslims in Malaysia are greatly influenced by the *dakwah* revivalists, so understanding the sentiments and mindset of the *dakwah* revivalists helps to explain the ineffectiveness of CCS's civil negotiations. *Dakwah* means proselytizing of non-Muslims and ensuring faithful adherence to Islamic teaching

---

Civil Society in the Muslim World: Contemporary Perspectives, ed. Amyn B. Sajoo (London: I. B. Tauris in Association with The Institute Of Ismaili Studies, 2004), 48–49.

82. Lim, "Islamization and Ethnicity," 178–179.

83. P. Ramasamy, "Civil Society in Malaysia: An Arena of Contestation?," in *Civil Society in Southeast Asia*, ed. Hock Guan Lee (Singapore: Institute of Southeast Asian Studies, 2004), 214.

84. For the relationships between patrimonial culture, civil society, and Islam, see Arkoun, "Locating Civil Society," 53–54.

85. Lim, "Islamization and Ethnicity in Sabah," 178–179; Lee, *Islamization and Activism*, 40.

86. Ng, "Dhimmi Syndrome."

by the *ummah*. The *dakwah* revivalists strive to "revive" Islam as a way of life for all Muslims through activism.[87] They see a need to reinvent the image of the Malay-Muslim community to attract the non-Muslims to Islam.[88] The revivalists' activism was carried out through the *ulamas'* teaching that aims to promote and safeguard the right Islamic practices.[89]

Like the early Islamists in Malaysia, the revivalists advocate an overarching Islamic paradigm for every area of human life. Influenced by the ideologies of Islamist thinkers such as Abul A'la Maududi and Sayyid Qutb,[90] they reject nationalism and secularism per se.[91] The modern understanding of nationalism is seen as a Western product that deceives Muslims with human-made concepts, a betrayal to Muslim's idealistic pan-Islamic "golden era of the caliphate."[92] The revivalists aim to establish Islamic blueprints based on the Syariah, which would sustain the *ummah* through the challenge of competing ideologies from the West.[93] They condemn the current Common Law legal system of its Western values.[94] They believe that the independent, modern state of Malaysia is still colonized by the West unless the "man-made law" from the West is replaced by Syariah.[95] They demonize Western modern and secular lifestyles and consider the full implementation of the Syariah law necessary to restore the glorious past of Malay history.[96] In short, they reject "Westernization," and aim to assert Islamic values in every aspect of human life and to replace all Western elements or institutions.[97] Ultimately, the establishment of an Islamic state or "an Islamic socio-political order in

---

87. However, Azhar Ibrahim opines that their "concerns with addressing larger societal issues remains largely peripheral in comparison to their efforts to ensure fellow Muslims observe religious duties and subscribe to correct thinking based on the 'Islamic paradigm.'" Azhar, *Contemporary Islamic Discourse*, 36–37.

88. Asrul, *Malay Ideals*, 33.

89. Azhar, *Contemporary Islamic Discourse*, 37.

90. Ahmad Fauzi, *Islamisme Dan Bahananya*, 25–26.

91. Abdullah Saeed, "Trends in Contemporary Islam: A Preliminary Attempt at a Classification," *The Muslim World* 97, no. 3 (2007): 399. Though actually, their struggle belongs to a type of "cultural nationalism," as explained earlier.

92. Azhar, *Contemporary Islamic Discourse*, 74.

93. Milner, *The Malays*, 216.

94. Milner, 216.

95. Saeed, "Trends in Contemporary Islam," 399–400.

96. Azhar, *Contemporary Islamic Discourse*, 36.

97. Saeed, "Trends in Contemporary Islam," 399.

Muslim societies" is preferred.⁹⁸ Muslim groups which have any connection with the West are shunned and deemed as deviant.

Today, the revivalists antagonize liberalism and its ideological offspring, secularism and constitutionalism.⁹⁹ Multiculturalism too is claimed to be a subversive ideology, which aims to overthrow Islam in Malaysia.¹⁰⁰ Allegedly, multiculturalism has its root in the "liberal separation of religion from social order," which is "in direct conflict with the very nature of the worldview of Islam."¹⁰¹ It is only through a "common religious worldview" of Islam, they claim, that Malaysia can foster national unity.

A Critical Assessment on Christian Civil Negotiation

Generally, Christians' civil negotiation, much like the Chinese, is ineffective in Malaysia. Both the Malaysian Chinese and Christians negotiate based on the premise of multiculturalism and constitutionalism, but the Malay Muslims do so on the premise of Malay hegemony. The failure of negotiation is due to the deeply-rooted negative image of Chinese Christians in the eyes of Malay Muslims and the approaches that Christians have adopted. Civil negotiations by Christians in Malaysia have been blindly based on rationalism and liberalism. In responding to the Allah issue, Ng proposes that, "certain non-negotiable criteria must apply and be accepted by all parties without which dialogue becomes virtually impossible. These axioms include: the freedom of religion, the separation of religion and state, and the belief that dialogue in the interests of democratic pluralism is the best solution."¹⁰² Ng even suggests the inclusion of "international political pressure groups" as a

---

98. Saeed, 399.

99. Liberalism is one of the most loathed ideologies for the Malaysian Muslims. Khairil Ashraf, "20 NGO Islam Ikrar Sokong Parti Lawan Sekularisme Pada PRU14," *Free Malaysia Today*, 3 March 2018, http://www.freemalaysiatoday.com/category/bahasa/2018/03/03/20-ngo-islam-ikrar-sokong-parti-lawan-sekularisme-pada-pru14/; Khalif Muammar, "Islam dan Liberalisme" (Institut Kajian Strategik Islam Malaysia (IKSIM)), http://iksim.my/iksim/uploads/files/Makalah/Islam%20dan%20Liberalisme%20(Bahagian%20I).pdf.

100. Md. Asham Ahmad, "Debunking Multiculturalism," *The Star Online*, 22 August 2006, https://www.thestar.com.my/opinion/letters/2006/08/22/debunking-multiculturalism/; for IKIM, see http://www.ikim.gov.my/new-wp/.

101. Md. Asham, "Debunking Multiculturalism."

102. Lau, "Intimating the Unconscious," 24–25. Multiculturalism is also one of the ideologies which Ng regards as essential. See Kam Weng Ng, "Multiculturalism – How Can It Be Wrong?," *The Star Online*, 25 August 2006, https://www.thestar.com.my/news/nation/2006/08/25/multiculturalism--how-can-it-be-wrong/.

means of support for Christians in Malaysia under the threat of Islamization.[103] However, from the *dakwah* revivalists' perspective these are the very Western liberal elements that they intend to banish from Malaysia. These are wrong approaches of attempting to impose the Western version of civil society to a sociopolitical context that is historically and culturally different.[104] Such demands would certainly result in heightened antagonism from Muslims. In fact, the Muslims have made it clear that their main responsibility is to protect the use of Allah against the Christians who in the name of human rights and freedom of religion threaten the peace of the country by encouraging Muslim apostates.[105] Hence, the liberal ideas of rights and freedom are liabilities in these negotiations because they produce no convergence of interests and conceptual agreement between the two parties, and rather, only the provocation of negative perceptions and emotions.

When supporters of different nation-of-intent presuppose different sets of conditions for discussion, intellectual dialogue collapses. Only the learned that are in the minority, are the exception. Christians' attempts to rationally discuss issues have fallen onto deaf ears, or worse, created a confrontational image for themselves. Unfortunately, most Christians seemed to have persisted on this route. CFM, for example, while it has rightfully upheld the need for civil negotiation, has limited its efforts to rational approaches.[106] Christians are encouraged to join a political party or civil organization, participating in community work, and civil protest.[107] Yet, their method of advocacy projects a liberalistic outlook. Christians' championing of freedom and rights is legitimate, but as they portray themselves as advocates of Western ideologies, they have worsened instead of resolving the disputes at hand.

In sum, public or civil negotiations of Malaysian Christians, including those of CCS, are problematic. They are incidental and reactionary, serving

---

103. Kam Weng Ng, "Creating Social Space for Mission: Paradigm Shift in Mission in Malaysia," *Transformation* 20, no. 4 (2003): 224.

104. Arkoun, "Locating Civil Society," 55.

105. Majlis Agama Islam Selangor (Selangor Islamic Religious Council), *Pendedahan Agenda Kristian (Exposing the Christian Agenda)* (Shah Alam, Malaysia: Majlis Agama Islam Selangor, 2014), 120, http://www.mais.gov.my/en/.

106. "About Us – Christian Federation of Malaysia (CFM)," 2018, https://cfmsia.org/about-cfm/.

107. Kam Weng Ng, "A Christian Social Vision for Nation Building," *Berita NEFC*, February 2008, 6.

only to counter issues which infringe their rights. Otherwise CCS would remain private, lack a public presence, and remain segregated. Socially, Malaysian Christians including CCS remain detached from the Muslims. Their engagements are also limited to the five methods outlined by Riddell, which do not include strategy and method to socially engage with the Muslim masses. As CCS are reactionary, their present engagements lack in-depth theologizing, especially in relation to nationalism and ethnogenesis.

Summary: Unsettled "Malaysian" Identity, Detachment from Nation-Building

The clash of nationalisms has resulted in identity crisis and social withdrawal of CCS. CCS's nation-of intent, based on multiculturalism, is in conflict with Malay hegemony. Consequently, CCS do not find it compelling to commit to nation-building, nor to concede their national identity to the political identity defined by Malay hegemony. Malay hegemony has also alienated CCS, forcing them to retreat from the public domain. The civil negotiations of the CCS remain occasional and produce poor results.

The clash of nationalisms is best demonstrated through the social polarization in the Malaysian society today. In 2006, 97 percent of Chinese in Malaysia surveyed expected all cultures and religions to be given equal rights in the future, while only 38 percent of Malays surveyed thought the same, too.[108] Similarly, a more recent survey reveals "Malays associated 'Malaysian-ness' with being Malay."[109] They reject an integrated Malaysian national identity comprising characteristics of other ethnicities. The non-Malays aspire otherwise.[110] Meanwhile, not a single Chinese aspires that Malaysia becomes a more Islamic country in the future, but 43 percent of Malays surveyed hope so.[111] Generally, Malaysians expect each ethnic group to maintain their

---

108. Merdeka Center for Opinion Research, *Public Opinion Poll*, 38.

109. Ananthi Al Ramiah, Miles Hewstone, and Ralf Wölfer, *Attitudes and Ethnoreligious Integration: Meeting the Challenge and Maximizing the Promise of Multicultural Malaysia* (Kuala Lumpur: CIMB Foundation, 12 January 2017), 74.

110. Ananthi, Hewstone, and Wölfer, *Attitudes and Ethnoreligious Integration*, 74.

111. Merdeka Center for Opinion Research, *Public Opinion Poll*, 38.

own cultural identity in the future.¹¹² A clear sign of polarity is the use of cultural markers to differentiate one from the "other." On this, the Chinese schools are considered "critical to the maintenance of Chinese community and Chineseness," while "Islam is perceived in the context of the Malay community as the definer of Malayness."¹¹³ The researchers opine, "Over time, this asymmetry may push groups further apart and create an anxiety within non-Malays in particular, that calls for Malaysian-ness by the majority-led government are an attempt to assimilate, rather than meaningfully and respectfully integrate all Malaysians."¹¹⁴

Weakened Commitment of the Malaysian Chinese in Nation-Building

The clash of nationalisms erodes the commitment of the Chinese and CCS to nation-building. The political identity of the Chinese that gives them legal right as citizens in the state, has not been able to provide them with a sense of belonging and inspire them with patriotism. The discrimination that the Malaysian Chinese suffer has distanced them from the main national discourse, and Malay hegemony has now motivated them to migrate.¹¹⁵ Had the Chinese been included in the main national discourse, the transfer of their loyalty from their culture to the state might have been smoother.¹¹⁶

The Detachment of the CCS from Nation-Building

Like the other Chinese, the clash of nationalisms also disoriented CCS's Malaysian identity and distanced them from nation-building. There is "an absence of a vision of a shared future for all Malaysians" among the Christians in Malaysia.¹¹⁷ Christians' tendency to migrate has tarnished the reputation of Christians in Malaysia, causing others to question their loyalty.¹¹⁸ Still,

---

112. Merdeka Center for Opinion Research, 39. The Malays scored 69 percent and the Chinese 66 percent.

113. Shamsul, "Text and Collective Memories," 127.

114. Ananthi, Hewstone, and Wölfer, *Attitudes and Ethnoreligious Integration*, 74.

115. "Nearly half of Chinese surveyed have a strong desire to emigrate from Malaysia." Ananthi, Hewstone, and Wölfer, *Attitudes and Ethnoreligious Integration*, 4.

116. Wang, "Chinese Ethnicity," 10.

117. Peter Rowan, *Proclaiming the Peacemaker: The Malaysian Church as an Agent of Reconciliation in a Multicultural Society* (Oxford: Regnum Books International, 2012), 140.

118. Keat Peng Goh, "Church and State in Malaysia," *Transformation* 6, no. 3 (1989): 20.

in a recent survey among Christians, 52 percent of respondents consider themselves as uncommitted citizens, and only 16 percent rate themselves as very committed citizens.[119] In the same survey, only 38 percent said "no" to emigrating to another country given a chance, with 30 percent saying "yes" and 32 percent unsure.[120] The number of Christians emigrating remains higher in proportion compared to others.[121]

For Christians who have awakened from political indifference, their approach of engagement has been reactionary, ineffective, and uncritically based on Western liberalism. Their engagement approaches are also limited, aiming only to protect their rights. There is no constructive change in their theology and attitude toward nation-building. They are still detached from nation-building. They lack a clear Malaysian identity, hence their minority mindset, ghettoism, and dhimmitude status are perpetuated.[122] They need a serious theological reflection on their political identity and their role in nation-building, which is considered in part three of this work.

---

119. Rowan, *Proclaiming the Peacemaker*, 135–136.

120. Rowan, 137.

121. Though the reasons for migration may not be a direct indication of national commitment, their relation is highly probable. See Rowan, 175–177; Merdeka Center for Opinion Research, *Public Opinion Poll*.

122. Ghettoism is "a form of escape within the borders of one's country that entails a gradual disengagement with wider society and the adoption of a survival mode of existence." Rowan, *Proclaiming the Peacemaker*, 176–177.

CHAPTER 4

Absence of Chinese Christians in Sabah's Mission Engagement with the Malay Muslims

The mission engagement of CCS with Muslims has deteriorated since the rise of Malay nationalism. Under Malay hegemony, they lost their means to directly engage with Sabah society through education. They withdrew from mission engagement with the Muslims as evangelism to Muslims became restricted. CCS's mission engagement with Muslims was also hindered by the absence of interfaith dialogue.

Early Mission Engagement in the Immigrant Church

CCS's lack of mission engagement with Muslims is not a present-day scenario. The early settlement of CCS had no mission to the non-Chinese. They focused on pastoral covering. Their ministry model was centripetal. It was homogenous, monolingual, and had very little contact with other ethnic groups.

Pastoral Covering

CCS's mission engagement began with pastoral covering.[1] Early Hakka Christians in Kudat consisted of believers of various denominations. They

---

1. For earliest evidence pointing to Chinese presence in the Anglican churches in Sabah, see Boughton, *Sabah Anglican Diocese*, 19, 27, 30.

had converted to Christianity in China through the Basel Mission, the Church Missionary Society (CMS, known as "The Churchmen"), the Berlin Mission, and the Methodist Mission.[2] In 1888, William Henry Elton of the Society of Propagation of the Gospel (SPG) visited Kudat and was requested by Chinese Christians to send a minister.[3] Elton concluded his pastoral visit by promising to send a pastor with the condition that the Chinese from different denominations would congregate as one group.[4] Eventually, Elton built a school and a church during 1889 and 1890 and sent a minister named Richard Richards to provide pastoral covering. As a result, the various Chinese Christian groups worshiped together in the new St. James' Anglican Church.[5]

In contrast, although the Basel Church recorded home worship as early as 1882, their pastoral covering was not clergy-oriented.[6] Even when the first Basel Church gathering was recorded in 1886, there was no minister. Thus, when St. James' Anglican Church began in 1890, about half of its membership was Basel members.[7] It was only in 1905 that the Basel Mission sent a priest to Kudat.[8] By then, many Basel Christians had converted to Anglicanism under the leadership of Fong Hau Kong.

The Centripetal Mission Churches

CCS's early missions followed a centripetal model much like the case of St. James' Church. Throughout North Borneo, Anglican Chinese congregations were started in response to Chinese believers seeking pastoral covering. When they found an Anglican minister, the minister would gather them, appoint a lay reader, and arrange services. The minister followed up with regular visits if a residential priest was not available.[9] The Basel Church was family

---

2. Simon Chin, "St. James' Church – 97 Years in Kudat," in *Diocese of Sabah*, ed. Kay Keng Khoo (Kota Kinabalu, Malaysia: Anglican Diocese of Sabah, 1987), 70.

3. Brian Taylor, "SPG and North Borneo," in *Diocese of Sabah*, ed. Kay Keng Khoo (Kota Kinabalu, Malaysia: Anglican Diocese of Sabah, 1987), 17.

4. Boughton, *Sabah Anglican Diocese*, 27. The catechist, missionary, and teacher were often the same person in those days, who is referred to as "minister" or "pastor" here.

5. Boughton, 28.

6. Zhang, *Hakkas of Sabah*, 9–10.

7. Wong, *Transformation of an Immigrant*, 36, referring to British North Borneo Herald, 1 April 1889, and Baptism Record of St. James 1892–1941; Boughton, *Sabah Anglican Diocese*, 28.

8. Wong, *Transformation of an Immigrant*, 36.

9. Boughton, *Sabah Anglican Diocese*, 30–37.

and home-based. Chinese-speaking Basel congregations were established at places where the believers resided. The Basel Church was less clergy-oriented. They relied heavily on lay preachers as they transplanted their lay-led family worship from China to North Borneo.[10] The Basel Church grew by following the development spearheaded by the Company, populating new areas and starting new congregations through lay preachers.[11] The Anglicans, following the parish model, built English churches (chaplaincy) in major towns with Chinese language services.[12] Their church buildings and mission schools attracted many Chinese believers.

The early Chinese Christians in North Borneo had no record of specific evangelistic missions to non-Christians. Their social engagement was education through the mission school.[13] Outreach remained restricted by the segregated social context. There was no purposeful missionary engagement to other Chinese dialect groups or the indigenes. For the Anglican Chinese, the mode of church was colonial, Western, and Anglo-Catholic. Like many mission churches in the age of colonialism, their church life was based on a parish-centered Christendom mindset. Their emphases were on "church" (fellowship), "quality," and "Asian ministry" (indigenization of leadership).[14]

The Basel Church mission to other people groups was absent before the 1950s.[15] The Basel Church operated within a self-sufficient homogenous community. It has been a predominantly Chinese-speaking church, with its Malay-speaking and English-speaking general councils formed only in 2003 and 2009.[16] Clearly, the mission engagement of CCS in different denominations was limited by their homogenous and centripetal natures.

---

10. Zhang, *Hakkas of Sabah*, 46–47.

11. Zhang, 51–53.

12. Boughton, *Sabah Anglican Diocese*, 30–41; Ping Chung Yong, "Message from Bishop of Sabah," in *Diocese of Sabah 35th Anniversary, 1962–1997*, ed. Tuk Su Koo (Kota Kinabalu, Malaysia: Anglican Diocese of Sabah, 1997), 5; Brian Taylor, *Elton Hill Diary: Story of the Founding of St. Michael's Church, Sandakan, Sabah, Malaysia* (Hong Kong: Lai Hing & Company, 1976).

13. Tregonning, *History of Modern Sabah*, 174–175.

14. Taylor, "SPG and North Borneo," 20.

15. Tsen, *History of the Basel Christian Church*, 147–151.

16. Tsen, 24–25.

Mission Schools

Historically, the Roman Catholics, Anglicans, and the Basel Church were the only education providers in North Borneo until the emergence of a Chinese private school in 1913 and the first government school in 1915.[17] The mission schools were CCS's key social enterprises and mission outreach in North Borneo.[18] By 1963, there were 121 mission schools, compared to 146 government schools and 116 Chinese schools.[19] A mission school was almost certain to accompany every establishment of a local church.[20] The majority of students were Chinese as they were attracted by the greater opportunities presented by the mission school education.[21] Although the Chinese had never grown past more than 25 percent of Sabah's population, they became more influential than other ethnic groups because of better education provided by the mission schools, which was recognized by the British colonial government.[22]

Chinese Christians in Sabah Losing Mission Engagement

With the formation of Malaysia, North Borneans eventually lost their mission engagement. They lost control of the mission schools because of Malay nationalism. Their ministry context was also changed by the invasion of Malay nationalism and the formation of Malaysia.

Losing the Mission Schools

Mission schools under the CCS were practically lost due to the 1970 directive that required the schools to surrender curriculum and administration

---

17. K. M. George, "Historical Development of Education," in *Commemorative History of Sabah, 1881–1981*, ed. Anwar Sullivan and Cecilia Leong (Kota Kinabalu, Malaysia: Sabah State Government, Centenary Publications Committee, 1981), 472–475.
18. Boughton, *Sabah Anglican Diocese*, 32.
19. George, "Historical Development of Education," 491.
20. Boughton, *Sabah Anglican Diocese*, 36–38.
21. Wong, *Transformation of an Immigrant*, 74. Deducing from the report by the Inspector of Schools, the majority of school pupils in 1922 were Chinese. George, "Historical Development of Education," 494.
22. Wong, *Transformation of an Immigrant*, 105, 185.

fully to the control of the federal government.[23] Under NCP, mission schools were required to help forge a Malaysian culture based on Malay nationalism. Christian symbols were not allowed to be openly displayed in many places. The curriculum was also redesigned, and the Bible as a subject was moved out of regular class time. Worship places for Muslims forced their way into mission schools' compounds.[24] Foreign Christian teachers had their working permits revoked and their departure weakened the Christian ethos in the schools.[25] Christians bemoaned these changes and tried to preserve the Christian ethos in mission schools.[26] Through the Malaynization of the educational system and with Malay hegemony, more Malay Muslim teachers were sent to teach in Sabah, including in the mission schools. Subsequently, CCS lost their main missional contact with the people. Evangelism opportunities in the mission schools have since been limited.

A Different Mission Field

After independence, Chinese Christians discovered that there were less "sheep looking for a shepherd." Meanwhile, the church could not afford to stay within the comfort zone of the segregated social space created by colonists anymore. A Christendom mindset and the centripetal model had become unsustainable for the new era.

Anglicans and the Roman Catholics started Malay-speaking missions in the 1950s among the indigenes. Yet, mission to Muslims had never been on the agenda of the CCS. As Malay nationalism entered Sabah, evangelism to Malay Muslims was restricted. The CCS's potential harvest field for conversion was immediately limited to only non-Muslims.

---

23. George, "Historical Development of Education," 500; K. M. George, "The Contributions of Mission Schools to the Development of the Church and the State of Sabah," in *Diocese of Sabah Silver Jubilee, 1962-1987*, ed. Kay Keng Khoo (Kota Kinabalu, Malaysia: Anglican Diocese of Sabah, 1987), 29-30; Choon Neo Tay, "The Role of Mission Schools in Nation Building: A Report for the Conference of Christian Mission Schools in Malaysia," *Pelita Methodist* 34 (August 2009): 1-2.

24. Boughton, *Sabah Anglican Diocese*, 17.

25. Geok Oon Chan and Boon Hock Lim, "The Mission to Reclaim Mission Schools," *Berita NECF* (November-December, 2008): 10-11.

26. Boughton, *Sabah Anglican Diocese*, 125-126.

Breakthrough in Evangelism, Absence of Social Engagement

Despite the changes in their sociopolitical context, CCS experienced breakthrough in evangelism. This was achieved in the absence of sustained and deliberate social engagement. Since losing their influence in mission schools, social engagement of the CCS in the 1980s was through their involvement in charities and welfare organizations.[27] Often, these were event-based. Others included involvement in Prison Fellowship Malaysia,[28] medical camps, and welfare and disaster relief.[29] However, these were responses to special needs rather than purposeful social engagement for the public good. CCS such as the Anglicans were engaging society to "save souls" without any consideration to challenge the sociopolitical structure or engage with long-term social issues. There was no formal effort to engage Muslims due to legal restrictions.

Anglican urban churches began to reach out to non-Christian Chinese in the 1970s and 1980s. Local churches such as the Cathedral embarked on various evangelistic programs. Church planting, a service center for healthcare, and new social gatherings were initiated for evangelism opportunities.[30] The Chinese Anglicans were also involved in various mass evangelistic gatherings.[31] Unfortunately, they adopted an understanding of evangelism that dichotomizes word and work.[32] Following the theological climate of the day, evangelism was separated from social action.[33] As a result, the "salvation of souls" became the focus. There was no exploration of mission through social engagement. Even the two lines' mention of "social missionary work" in the Diocesan Synod Declaration in 1993 was focused on activities, while multiple-page documents were dedicated to strategy for "evangelistic" outreach in the same period.[34] Similar situations are common among Malaysian evangelical Christians. Hwa Yung alleges that the negligence of social engagement by

---

27. Boughton, 191.
28. Boughton, 213.
29. Boughton, 263.
30. Boughton, 163–166.
31. Boughton, 191–192.
32. A problem described by Scott W. Sunquist, *Understanding Christian Mission: Participation in Suffering and Glory* (Grand Rapids, MI: Baker Academic, 2013), 320.
33. Sunquist, *Understanding Christian Mission*, 320.
34. Tuk Su Koo, ed., *Diocese of Sabah 35th Anniversary, 1962–1997* (Kota Kinabalu, Malaysia: Anglican Diocese of Sabah, 1997), 39–45.

Malaysian evangelicals in general is the result of modernist-fundamentalist debates in the US.[35] The evangelicals distanced themselves from social responsibility, which they associated with the modernist-liberal camp. They focused on proclamation as the means for witnessing the gospel, reducing evangelism to verbal transmission of propositional truth. While some have reaffirmed sociopolitical responsibility after the Lausanne Covenant in 1974, most Malaysian Christians remain ignorant of the holistic nature of the gospel. Being labeled as practicing a "social gospel" is a real fear among the churches.[36]

Further, evangelicals in Malaysia "tend to conform to the secularization thesis where religion is placed in the private realm without much public relevance."[37] A survey report by NECF in 2001 indicates that a large majority of evangelicals invest in evangelism programs and "feel at ease talking about their faith to others."[38] Yet, evangelicals "tend to shy away from societal issues such as poverty and religious freedom."[39] Only slightly more than a quarter of evangelical pastors and only about one-tenth of church members "were personally involved in community care, social justice or nongovernmental organizations."[40] Evangelicals tend to live in a ghetto, gravitating their lives around their church.[41] The same survey reveals that, "36 percent of churches did not organize any activities that involved interaction with non-Christians in their neighborhoods. On the average, churches surveyed spent only 8 percent of budgets on social concern and community involvement."[42]

---

35. Hwa Yung, *Beyond AD 2000: A Call to Evangelical Faithfulness* (Kuala Lumpur: Kairos Research Centre, 1999), 35, referring to George M. Marsden, *Fundamentalism and American Culture*, 2nd ed. (New York: Oxford University Press, 2006).

36. Rowan, *Proclaiming the Peacemaker*, 147.

37. Eu Choong Chong, "Modernity, State-Led Islamisation and the Non-Muslim Response: A Case Study of Christians in Peninsular Malaysia" (School of Social Sciences, University Sains Malaysia, 2010), 243–244, https://www.academia.edu/6751048/Modernity_State-led_Islamisation_and_the_non-Muslim_Response_A_case_study_of_Christians_in_Peninsular_Malaysia.

38. Chong, "Modernity, State-Led Islamisation," 243–244.

39. Chong, 243–244.

40. Chong, 243–244.

41. Chong, 243–244.

42. Riddell, "Islamization, Civil Society," 177, referring to Edmund Ng, "A Post-Survey Analysis: Towards Greater Community Involvement," *Berita NECF*, 2002, http://www.necf.org.my/newsmaster.cfm?&menuid=2&action=view&retriveid=77.

In short, evangelical Christians in Malaysia have privatized their faith. Unlike the Roman Catholics, they withdraw from the public space as they lean toward "a church-government divide where its emphasis is on the spiritual welfare of its members, eschewing political involvement."[43] Significantly, the survey discovers that "48 percent of evangelicals rarely interact with Muslims," indicating the social distance between Christians and Muslims.[44]

Evangelicals in Malaysia have also succumbed to developmentalism, which is "a discourse that emphasizes individual freedom in the pursuit of economic goods and activities without emphasizing the corresponding pursuit of individual liberty and civil rights."[45] With developmentalism, private economic gains are disjointed from the common good.[46] Those who subscribe to developmentalism see no reason to be involved in political activism. They operate with a middle-class mindset and to them, "wealth accumulation eclipsed social transformation."[47] They strive for affluence and political stability, which in turn, is necessary for economic growth, even if "authoritarian policies are employed."[48] Thus, developmentalism explains "the shortage of reformist zeal in the Malaysian middle class, an essentially materialist and self-centered community."[49] Lau contends, "With the rise of middle-class Christians, developmentalism reduced Christian involvement in social activism while personal evangelism is given the main focus."[50] This scenario is common across the whole of Malaysia, and is prevalent among the CCS.

Meanwhile, some Malaysian Christians, especially evangelicals, are influenced by the charismatic movement, and because of their privatization of faith and shunning of social action, concentrate on prayer. This result is a privatized and pietistic spirituality that choose to separate the "sacred" from the "secular." Chong relates this "spiritual" way to engage civil society to the

---

43. Chong, "Modernity, State-Led Islamisation," 242.
44. Chong, 244.
45. Chong, 249.
46. Chong, 249.
47. Lau, "Intimating the Unconscious," 10–11.
48. Lau, 10–11.
49. Lau, 10–11, referring to Francis Kok-Wah Loh, "Developmentalism and the Limits of Democratic Discourse," in *Democracy in Malaysia: Discourses and Practices*, ed. Francis Kok-Wah Loh and Boo Teik Khoo (Surrey, UK: Curzon Press, 2002), 19–50. Lau notes the lack of direct evidence in Loh's thesis.
50. Lau, 10–11.

Malaysia National Prayer Network (MNPN). Launched in 2008, this network aims at "mobilizing all believers . . . to engage in prayer that 'call upon God for revival of the Church and transformation of our nation.'"[51] Often, prayer is mistaken as an easy shortcut to social transformation.

Christians' social engagement has also received much criticism and skepticism from the church. According to some, "The focus of the church . . . should be the realm of the sacred, and politics has no right to intrude into the sacred realm."[52] Some adopt escapism, seeing the world as a "sinking ship" to be abandoned and the church as the "life-boat."[53] As a result, the "on-going divide between private spirituality and public justice" becomes the main reason Malaysian Christians suffer social withdrawal.[54] The privatization of the gospel and social withdrawal of Malaysian Christians are phenomena confirmed by Rowan's research and Ng's observations.[55] There is a prevalent separation of the sacred and the secular, and of the temporal and the spiritual among the Malaysian Christians.[56]

The Limitations of Evangelism and Interfaith Dialogue

The mission engagement of the CCS with Muslims has also sufferred much setback because of Malay hegemony. The *dakwah* movement and its sentiment toward Christians are key obstacles that Malaysian Christians face in their missions to the Malays. Malay hegemony has also contributed to the ineffectiveness of interfaith dialogues.

The *Dakwah* Revivalists' Sentiment toward Christians

The limitations of evangelism and interfaith dialogue in CCS's efforts to engage Muslims are the result of a conservative *dakwah* revivalist sentiment. The

---

51. Chong, "Modernity, State-Led Islamisation," 262–263.
52. Chong, 267.
53. Hwa, *Beyond AD 2000*, 36, referring to Moody's "life-boat" analogy.
54. Lau, "Intimating the Unconscious," 20.
55. Rowan, *Proclaiming the Peacemaker*, 148–149, referring to Kam Weng Ng, "Spirit and Kingdom: Power and Manifestation in Mission," Poimen (Kuala Lumpur: Malaysia Bible Seminary, January-March, 1994), 20–21.
56. Chong, "Modernity, State-Led Islamisation," 267–269.

Malaysian conservative Islam is a product of its own context and is interwoven with Malay ethnogenesis. According to Asrul Zamani who wrote about his own race, the Malays are not taught to question what is taught to them.[57] This might have contributed to the legalistic, simplistic, and judgmental flavor of Islamism among the Malays.

The conservative stance of the revivalists can be clearly observed through their insistence to uphold certain conservative doctrines and their uncompromising, yet narrow worldview.[58] According to Shamsul, the *dakwah* revivalists, often recruited in their youth, employ "the positivistic scientific paradigms of the West" that give them the "analytic tools for the reinterpretation of Islam in a narrow, legalistic way."[59] With such methodology these revivalists, who are mostly science students, "adopted a narrowly legalistic, black-and-white, conservative position regarding Islam. They see 'Islamic knowledge' or theology in terms of rules, formulae, and equations, a way of categorizing and perceiving the world they have learned from their study of the natural sciences."[60] They adopt a rigid view, judging that "One either practices Islam in a complete way or is an infidel; one either fights for Islam or is irreligious; if a member of an Islamic group, one must be a full-time *dakwah* activist, not merely a sympathizer."[61]

Nevertheless, these simplistic methods are able to articulate "doctrinal precepts of fundamentalist Islamic ideology," combining "theory and practice" that help to popularize the *dakwah* movement.[62] Alatas criticized the revivalist movement as a populist movement that lacks intellectual and religious rigor.[63] In fact, the revivalists prefer public activism to intellectual engagement.[64] The academia is shunned, as the activism-driven revivalists adopt an anti-intellectualism stance, which downplays serious scholarly work.[65] The revivalists

---

57. Asrul, *Malay Ideals*, 171–174.
58. Azhar, *Contemporary Islamic Discourse*, 36.
59. Shamsul, "Identity Construction" 224.
60. Shamsul, 216, 224–225.
61. Shamsul, 216.
62. Shamsul, 219.
63. Azhar, *Contemporary Islamic Discourse*, 42–49.
64. Azhar, 50.
65. Azhar, 51.

selectively follow traditions that suit their agendas.⁶⁶ They are therefore not "embarrassed by blatant and frequent self-contradictions," because they are not trained to think critically.⁶⁷ The lack of reason and intellectual discourse is a constant criticism which is directed toward the conservative Islamists by the moderates such as the IRF.⁶⁸

Followers of Abul A'la Maududi and Sayyid Qutb, the revivalists are "ideologues of the non-dialogue. They do not see any need to engage dialectically with dominant Western thought in open and constructive manner . . . they see the world as a binary of the West versus Islam, where the former is the repository of all negativities."⁶⁹ Subsequently, in their eagerness to propagate Islam, interreligious dialogues are used not to gain mutual understanding but to rebut and defeat other faiths.⁷⁰ Studying of other religions too, is not done with an open, objective, and critical mind, but to prepare one to counter other religions. This is especially true in their zeal to counter Christian evangelism.⁷¹ In short, the revivalists are conservative because they are defensive and exclusivist; they are a mass movement where the learned are in the minority.⁷²

The revivalists are concerned with Christian evangelism, relating it to apostasy among Muslims.⁷³ Anti-Western sentiment is their key characteristic. This contributes to their antagonism toward Christianity. Christianity is considered a threat to Malays, as their numbers are perceived to be increasing.⁷⁴ Asrul Zamani relates such antagonism to fear of the colonists' proselytism efforts.⁷⁵ Asrul's view is typical among the *dakwah* revivalists – associating Christianity as a "Western" cultural force that may erode the Malay culture.

---

66. Azhar, 71.
67. Azhar, 52.
68. Ahmad Fauzi and Che Hamdan, *Middle Eastern Influences*, 10–11.
69. Azhar, *Contemporary Islamic Discourse*, 58–59; Ahmad Fauzi, *Islamisme Dan Bahananya*, 22.
70. Majlis Agama Islam Selangor, *Pendedahan Agenda Kristian*, 120.
71. Azhar, *Contemporary Islamic Discourse*, 59.
72. Azhar, 41. Such a stance is similar to Islamic extremism. See Maqsood Kamil, "Religious Extremism and Christian Response in Pakistan," *Evangelical Review of Theology* 42, no. 1 (2018): 41–56.
73. Azhar, *Contemporary Islamic Discourse*, 41.
74. Asrul, *Malay Ideals*, 25.
75. Asrul, 164.

Some even see Christianity as a subversive Western tool.[76] The Christians are often alleged to attempt to Christianize Malaysia through various subversive plans.[77] There is a fear that with more Chinese embracing Christianity, Malaysia in the future will be dominated by two main rival socioreligious groups – the Muslim-Malays and the Christian-Chinese.[78] As Malay hegemony is juxtaposed with a postcolonial anti-West sentiment, the gulf between the two groups deepens.

Evangelism to the Malays

Mission to Muslims has also been hindered by the legal prohibition for Muslim apostasy.[79] From the Muslims' perspective, legal prohibition for Muslim apostasy is necessary to protect Islam, especially from Christians.[80] Propagating the Christian faith to Muslims is unlawful in some places in Malaysia and generally warned against by the government. Some who were caught doing so were detained under the Internal Security Act (ISA) in 1987.[81] Thus, Malaysian Christians have become reluctant to share their faith to Malays. Furthermore, most Malaysian Christians' understanding of evangelism is limited to verbal proclamation, which leads to a rational response from the hearer in professing the Christian faith. Many non-Christians and even Christian theologians in Malaysia have referred to this method of evangelism as "unethical proselytism," especially as it is often accompanied with some sort of denigration of other religions and cultures.[82] Such methods of evangelism

---

76. Riddell, "Islamization, Civil Society," 174.

77. Furman, "Minorities in Contemporary Islamist Discourse," 11. This follows Egyptian Islamists' attitude toward the Copts. Egypt is also where most of the Malaysian Islamists receive their training.

78. Asrul, *Malay Ideals*, 25–28.

79. Religion matters come under state law, in which Sabah has no provision on the prohibition mentioned. Yet, Muslims' religious matter is under the jurisdiction of Syariah court, which seldom allows conversion. See Zuliza Mohd. Kusrin et al., "Legal Provisions and Restrictions on the Propagation of Non-Islamic Religions among Muslims in Malaysia," *Kajian Malaysia, USM* 31, no. 2 (2013): 1–18; Liow, *Religion and Nationalism*, 141.

80. Amini Amir, "Islamic Revivalism, Religious Freedom," 128.

81. The ISA allows detention without trial. "Internal Security Act (ISA) | HAKAM," *National Human Rights Society*, http://hakam.org.my/wp/tag/internal-security-act/.

82. Rowan, *Proclaiming the Peacemaker*, 184.

Absence of CCS's Mission Engagement with the Malay Muslims   89

are bound to create ethnic tension. So, Christians, in general, refrain from any form of "mission" to the Malays out of fear.[83]

Mission to the Muslims has also suffered from Muslim hostility, reflected in Muslims' attack on evangelism related activities and organizations. The Selangor Islamic Religious Council (Majlis Agama Islam Selangor, or MAIS), in its publication, "Exposing the Christian Agenda," refers to Christianity as the enemy of Islam and Christian evangelism as an insidious effort to hurt Muslims.[84] The book is a reaction to evangelism. Christians are described as deceptive and Muslims are warned not to allow Christians to assume leadership over them.[85] According to the book, the status of Islam in the constitution is unique and higher than other religions, and the protection of Muslims from other "deceptive" religions is clearly provided in the constitution.[86] The book perceives Christian missionary activities to Muslims as strategically planned to defeat Islam openly and subversively.[87] Apostasy in Malaysia, which is the most serious offense in Islam, is related to Christian evangelism.[88] The language used in the book makes plain the resentment of the Muslims toward Christianity in Malaysia. Christians are alleged to have an agenda to establish a Christian nation in Malaysia at the expense of Islam.[89] The book warns the *ummah* of the "10/40 Window movement" and other Christian missions which are under the disguise of humanitarian help.[90] Muslims in Malaysia are also aware of Christian missions that are contextualized.[91] In the book, it is alleged that Christians' efforts to maintain their use of Allah

---

83. Rowan, 183.

84. Majlis Agama Islam Selangor (Selangor Islamic Religious Council), *Pendedahan Agenda Kristian (Exposing the Christian Agenda)* (Shah Alam, Malaysia: Majlis Agama Islam Selangor, 2014), http://www.mais.gov.my/en/. Majlis Agama Islam Selangor, or MAIS is a highly influential Islamic organization in the most affluent state in Malaysia, formed through enactments which endow it with power over all Islamic religious matters except those that come under the Sultan or beyond the enactments which allow it.

85. Majlis Agama Islam Selangor, 16.

86. Majlis Agama Islam Selangor, 17–28.

87. Majlis Agama Islam Selangor, 34–54.

88. Interestingly, it reports that Sabah has the most number of cases of Muslim apostasy among all states in Malaysia, comprising of slightly more than one third of the total number. Majlis Agama Islam Selangor, 32.

89. Majlis Agama Islam Selangor, 59.

90. Majlis Agama Islam Selangor, 67–72.

91. Majlis Agama Islam Selangor, 74–82.

is for the purpose of contextualizing the term in order to make it friendlier and more familiar to Muslims in Malaysia.[92] According to this theory, this will eventually confuse Muslims into accepting Christianity as a friendly religion. The book also warns Malaysian Muslims on the danger of "insider movement" – a movement where new Christian converts are staying within their social-religious network.[93] The insider movement is understood as a strategy by Christians to encourage Muslim apostasy because by remaining within their Muslim social-religious context, the new converts will experience significantly less pressure and danger, making their conversion easier. The book details in technical terms the different levels of insider movement, from "C1 to C6," referring to the movement as cancer in the Islamic society.[94] Even Christians' efforts to be incarnational is noted – Christians "do not force the Malays to attend church but they bring the church to them."[95] With these strategies, the book warns that Malay Christians will increase in Malaysia, especially subversively within the social networks of Muslims.[96] In sum, the Christian agenda is described as a planned strategy to subversively convert Muslims through various contextualized and friendly approaches, in order to "control the political arena."[97]

Christian organizations, which are perceived as related to evangelism, are also targeted. Some Muslims like Azril Mohd. Amin, who mistakenly perceive the "evangelicals" as the primary Christian group that emphasize evangelism, have called for a ban on evangelicalism.[98] Azril, who leads an Islamic NGO, said "the proposal was prompted by the high number of Muslims leaving the faith for Christianity . . . there were some 400 conversion cases before the Syariah courts and if the trend continued, it could have an impact on

---

92. Majlis Agama Islam Selangor, 81.
93. Majlis Agama Islam Selangor, 82.
94. Majlis Agama Islam Selangor, 84–86.
95. Majlis Agama Islam Selangor, 89 (author's translation).
96. Majlis Agama Islam Selangor, 97–100.
97. Majlis Agama Islam Selangor, 107.
98. Azril Mohd. Amin, "Wujudkan Undang-Undang Anti-Evangelicalisme (Make Anti-Evangelicalism Laws)," *Utusan Online*, 15 June 2017, http://www.utusan.com.my/rencana/utama/wujudkan-undang-undang-anti-evangelicalisme-1.493392; Bede Hong, "Outlaw Evangelicalism in Malaysia, Says Islamic Coalition," *The Malaysian Insight*, 15 June 2017, https://www.themalaysianinsight.com/s/5196/.

the country's security."⁹⁹ Regardless of his confusion on "evangelicalism," Azril's concern on the "security" of the country speaks volumes about the Muslims' perception of Christian evangelism. Clearly, they consider evangelism a "threat" to Islam, one of the pillars for Malayness. It is therefore dangerous because without Islam, the Malay identity will be weakened and eventually, their greatest fear – that the Malays will disappear from the face of the earth – will happen. Christians responded by voicing disapproval.[100] NECF, in its statement, rightfully corrects the misconception, explains the Christian's position, and calls for the government to protect the Christian minority. However, both Azril and NECF have different concerns. One focuses on the survival of the Malays and Islam, and the other on stating the facts and safeguarding their constitutional rights.

With all of the sensitivity and hostility, even for those who truly understand the holistic meaning of "witnessing" and being involved in "sensitive evangelism," their witnessing among Malay Muslims must be in secret due to the sentiments and misunderstanding of the Malay society against Christianity.[101] Worse, every time Christians involve themselves in charity or welfare, Muslims are concerned that there is an evangelistic motive behind it. Christianity's motive and contribution to the nation is doubted. In Sabah, the levels of hostility and sensitivity are vastly lower than in the Peninsular. Yet, with legal limitation and Malay hegemony, evangelism to Muslims has become a taboo.

Interfaith Dialogues

Interfaith dialogue between Christians and Muslims in Malaysia remains an exception, especially in Sabah. It is extremely rare and mainly limited to those who are intellectuals.[102] There is no lacking of attempts to organize interfaith dialogue between Muslims and non-Muslims in Malaysia. Christians in Malaysia generally recognize the importance of such dialogue, and Roman

---

99. Asila Jalil, "Azril: Why I Said Christian Evangelicalism Should Be Banned," *The Malaysian Insight*, 21 June 2017, https://www.themalaysianinsight.com/s/5665/.

100. "The Unconstitutional Call – National Evangelical Christian Fellowship Malaysia," *Malay Mail Online*, 16 June 2017, http://www.themalaymailonline.com/what-you-think/article/the-unconstitutional-call-necf-malaysia.

101. Rowan, *Proclaiming the Peacemaker*, 186.

102. Chong, "Modernity, State-Led Islamisation," 263–264.

Catholics have attempted to hold several dialogues.[103] Interfaith dialogue is also supported by CCM and CFM.[104] Theologians such as Batumalai have argued for interfaith dialogue as a way for Malaysian Christians to engage with Muslims.[105]

However, influenced by the *dakwah* movement, Muslims in Malaysia are uninterested in actual dialoguing with Christians. Muslims in Malaysia avoid dialoguing with Malaysian Christians because such act "confers legitimacy on local Christian Movements."[106] There has been very little commitment from the government whenever such dialogues were proposed.[107] An Interfaith Commission (IFC) was once proposed but never materialized during Prime Minister Badawi's time.[108] Protests were held outside of the conference hall attempting to stop the formation of the IFC that intend to explore the implications of Article 11 of the Constitution (on freedom of religion).[109] An international Muslim-Christian interfaith seminar was cancelled three weeks prior to its date in 2007 because of the government's withdrawal of endorsement.[110] Rowan commented, "Recent events have only served to confirm the suspicions of many, that Islam in Malaysia is not serious about inter-faith dialogue."[111] Even Malay intellectuals like Asrul Zamani acknowledge the decline of Muslims' openness to reasoning after it was declared in the twelfth century that the *ijtihad* should be closed and no new interpretation of the Qur'an can surpass those by the earlier scholars.[112]

Dialogues have generally been associated with two other limitations. First, it is limited to intellectuals. It has limited effect with the masses who are often excluded and not trained to dialogue. Moreover, in the case of CCS,

---

103. Riddell, "Islamization, Civil Society," 178.

104. Riddell, 179.

105. Sadayandy Batumalai, *A Malaysian Theology of Muhibbah: A Theology for a Christian Witnessing in Malaysia* (Kuala Lumpur, Malaysia: Seminari Theoloji Malaysia, 1990), 113–130.

106. Riddell, "Islamization, Civil Society," 179, referring to Ng Kam Weng, "Dialogue and Constructive Social Engagement: Problems and Prospects for the Malaysian Church," *Trinity Theological Journal* 5 (1995): 32.

107. Riddell, "Islamization, Civil Society," 179; Sadayandy Batumalai, *Islamic Resurgence and Islamization in Malaysia: A Malaysian Christian Response* (Ipoh, Malaysia: S. Batumalai, 1996), 144–145.

108. Funston, "UMNO," 74–75.

109. Kessler, "UMNO," 154.

110. Rowan, *Proclaiming the Peacemaker*, 175.

111. Rowan, 175.

112. Asrul, *Malay Ideals*, 123.

not many can dialogue with Muslim. In the end, "Hostility, polemics, and misunderstandings remained common among people in the street."[113] Second, as intellectual dialogue focuses on issues, it seldom emphasizes on the emotive and social aspects of those who are involved.

Summary: Limited Missional Engagement with the Malays

CCS have, since the beginning, been monocultural, albeit Westernized. Although they were aware of the need to evangelize, their mission engagement to Muslims has seen a sharp decline since the intensification of Malay hegemony. Furthermore, mission engagement to Muslims has clearly been limited by pressures from the revivalists, legal prohibitions, limitation of evangelism, and ineffective interfaith dialogues. The detachment between Muslims and Christians in Malaysia has reached an alarming state. Islamic revivalism has made the Muslim community "more self-contained where religion became a key consideration for social interaction."[114] The non-Muslims react by placing emphasis "on their own religious identity," resulting in a parallel revivalism among the non-Islam religions in Malaysia since the 1980s.[115] Expectedly, this has resulted in a greater social distance between Muslims and non-Muslims.[116]

Malaysian Christians are concerned about "the growing polarization between Muslims and non-Muslims in the country."[117] However, given the force of Malay hegemony, they have become passive. Their humanitarian and welfare efforts are also being doubted. Restricted in their proselytization activities, Malaysian Christians focus on their religious activities and avoid government interference. Eventually, Christians accept the "status quo limitations" imposed by the government on them.[118] Their functional dhimmitude status is thereby further consolidated.

---

113. Tharwat Wahba, "Dialogues in Egypt: From the Elite to the Street," *Evangelical Interfaith Dialogue, Fuller Theological Seminary* (Fall 2014), http://cms.fuller.edu/EIFD/issues/Fall_2014/Dialogue_in_Egypt.aspx#sthash.Yh1OjPfM.dpuf.

114. Chong, "Modernity, State-Led Islamisation," 231; Riddell, "Islamization, Civil Society," 174.

115. Riddell, 174; Lee and Ackerman, *Sacred Tensions*.

116. Chong, "Modernity, State-Led Islamisation," 231; Riddell, 174.

117. Chong, 231; Riddell, 174.

118. Chong, 228.

Part III

Theological Reflection

CHAPTER 5

Incarnational Mission Defined

This chapter defines incarnational mission and its scope,[1] discussed from the perspective of missional church movement.[2] Ross Langmead, along with others, has helpfully outlined the contour of incarnational mission.[3] However, his research excludes the missional church movement. This chapter aims to present a consolidated concept of incarnational mission based on the various sources within the missional church movement. Langmead's work, among others, will be used to provide comparison and clarifications. This chapter contends that incarnational mission, according to missional church movement, is demonstrated through the church, as it continues the presence of Christ, represents the kingdom of God (kingdom), identifies with people, and submits to God's restoration of his creation through transformation, based on the mission of God (*missio Dei*).[4] The aim of this chapter, ultimately, is to provide a theological basis for CCS to respond to their situation.

---

1. For a comprehensive discussion on "incarnational mission," see Ross Langmead, *The Word Made Flesh: Towards an Incarnational Missiology* (Lanham, MD: UPA, 2004).

2. The "Missional Church Movement" refers to the movement described in, among others, but most significantly, Guder, *Missional Church*. Other works include Alan J. Roxburgh and M. Scott Boren, *Introducing the Missional Church: What It Is, Why It Matters, How to Become One* (Grand Rapids, MI: Baker Books, 2009); Michael Frost, *The Road to Missional, Journey to the Center of the Church* (Grand Rapids, MI: Baker Books, 2011); Craig Van Gelder and Dwight J. Zscheile, *The Missional Church in Perspective: Mapping Trends and Shaping the Conversation* (Grand Rapids, MI: Baker Academic, 2011); Darrell L. Guder, *The Incarnation and the Church's Witness* (Eugene, OR: Wipf & Stock Publishers, 2004); Michael Frost and Alan Hirsch, *The Shaping of Things to Come: Innovation and Mission for the 21st Century Church* (Peabody, MA: Hendrickson Publishers, 2003).

3. Langmead, *Word Made Flesh*.

4. See further definition and explanation on *missio Dei* under "Incarnation as a Model for Mission" in the following sections.

Incarnation, "the Incarnation," and "Incarnational Mission"

Literally, "incarnation" means "in the flesh," or a process of embodiment.[5] "The incarnation," however, is a theological concept. The Chalcedon formulation of Christology stresses the full divinity and humanity of Christ. The incarnation is defined as "the historic act where the eternal Son of God, the second person of the Trinity, without ceasing to be God, took upon himself our human nature and became fully human."[6] Hence, the meaning of incarnation – "becoming flesh" – is considered synonymous with "becoming human."[7] In general, discussions on Christ's incarnation, including that of the missional church's, would involve the Chalcedonian definition.[8]

Discussions of the incarnation need not be overwhelmed by speculations about the hypostatic nature of Christ. Ultimately, "The concept of incarnation . . . cannot explain the unity of God and man in Jesus Christ because it is itself an expression of this unity."[9] Only the result of such unity can be discerned through "Jesus' historical reality."[10] Incarnation can be understood through the essence of such a historical movement while assuming Christ's deity and humanity.[11] This allows incarnation to be defined within the context

---

5. S. Mondithoka, "Incarnation," *Dictionary of Mission Theology: Evangelical Foundations*, ed. John Corrie (Downers Grove, IL: IVP Academic, 2007), 177; Langmead, *Word Made Flesh*, 17.

6. Mondithoka, "Incarnation," 177. Note the trinitarian involvement in the whole process of incarnation (i.e., the incarnation made possible via the Holy Spirit). For a comprehensive definition of the incarnation, see Philip Schaff, *Creeds of Christendom Volume 1: The History of the Creeds – Enhanced Version*, 1st ed. (Christian Classics Ethereal Library, 2009), 46–47.

7. Langmead, *Word Made Flesh*, 27.

8. There are exceptions such as Moltmann, as described by Billings, who questions Moltmann's rejection of two-natures Christology. See J. Todd Billings, "Incarnational Ministry and Christology: A Reappropriation of the Way of Lowliness," *Missiology* 32, no. 2 (2004): 187–201.

9. Wolfhart Pannenberg, *Jesus – God and Man*, trans. Lewis L. Wilkins and Duane A. Priebe, 2nd ed. (Philadelphia: Westminster John Knox Press, 1977), 322. While Pannenberg's opinions on the other notions of Christology may not be found agreeable by proponents of incarnational mission, his emphasis on a "Christology from below" rooted in Jesus' historicity is a much needed balance for the understanding of incarnation.

10. Pannenberg, *Jesus – God and Man*, 323. It is worth noting that Pannenberg's idea of incarnation is one which is extended to resurrection, an event which showed that Jesus is God and with God.

11. Guder, *Incarnation*, 2–3, referring to Karl Barth, "Die Theologie und die Mission in der Gegenwart," *Theologische Fragen und Antworten* (Zollikon: Theologischer Verlag Zurich, 1957),100.

of soteriology and the Trinity.[12] In other words, the meaning of the incarnation should be comprehended teleologically, not just ontologically. Thus, a complete definition of the incarnation includes the motive and effect of Christ's hypostatic nature.

The Motives and Logic of Incarnation

The motives of the incarnation are God's revelation and redemption.[13] Widening the scope of incarnation to its soteriological purpose, Langmead defines the incarnation as the event of "the supreme divinity fully assuming lowly human flesh in a once-for-all self-revelation for the sake of restoring a broken relationship between humanity and God."[14] "The incarnation" refers not only to Christ's hypostatic nature, but also an event or process when God reaches out to creation through the act of self-revelation,[15] and "overcomes the polarity between the divine and human."[16] Through the mysterious incarnation, "God's nature is revealed within the sphere of history in Jesus Christ."[17]

Through incarnation, redemption is made possible. In the Gospel of John, people are called to believe that Jesus Christ is the Messiah and the Son of God through whom one could have eternal life.[18] The incarnation is set in a motive of salvation for humankind, made possible only when God becomes human in Christ, dies a human death, and is resurrected.[19] This movement shows that God has decisively and actively initiated salvation by sending Christ into the world.[20] Hence, the incarnation should not be defined solely by the birth event and hypostatic nature of Jesus Christ, but should be understood as a pivotal part of God's salvific mission for humankind, which was

---

12. John Webster, *Word and Church: Essays in Christian Dogmatics* (Edinburgh: Bloomsbury T&T Clark, 2001), 113–150, 149–150.
13. Mondithoka, "Incarnation," 177.
14. Langmead, *Word Made Flesh*, 17.
15. Guder, *Incarnation*, 1.
16. Langmead, *Word Made Flesh*, 27.
17. Langmead, 27.
18. Langmead, 28.
19. Athanasius was among the earliest to explain the logic of incarnation with a redemptive framework. Athanasius, *On the Incarnation* (Warrendale: Ichthus Publications, 2018); Langmead, 28.
20. Darrell L. Guder, "Missional Church: From Sending to Being Sent," in Guder, *Missional Church*, 186–188; Guder, *Incarnation*, 2, 4.

later accomplished through the cross and the resurrection, and carried on after the ascension, empowered by Pentecost. From an eschatological point of view, the world is still under the effect of the incarnation that marks the inbreaking of the kingdom through the birth of the King.

Incarnation as a Model for Mission

With its soteriological motive and eschatological effect taken seriously, the incarnation has been used as a model for mission.[21] Langmead describes, "God's movement toward creation in enfleshment, from creation throughout history but climactically in Jesus Christ, is the ultimate framework and basis of Christian mission and also the central shaping and empowering factor."[22] He summarizes the essence of incarnational mission into three dimensions – namely, (d1) being patterned on the incarnation/following the example of Jesus, (d2) being enabled by the continuing power of the incarnation/participation in Christ's presence, and (d3) joining the ongoing incarnating mission of God.[23] Note that only d1 concerns methodology, and d2 concerns the ability of the actor of incarnational mission in relation to the presence of Christ. It includes participating with Christ in his imminent redemptive acts, including the transformation of individuals and society. One can associate d2 with ministries through the empowerment of the Holy Spirit. d3 concerns the participation of the mission of God, which is the overarching framework.

Joining in the mission of God (d3) is an essential characteristic of incarnational mission. "Mission of God" is an important concept commonly referred to as *missio Dei*. Following Karl Barth who laid the foundation of

---

21. Since the Second Vatican Council, the Roman Catholics have adopted incarnation as a model for mission. Andrew Walls uses incarnation to explain how the gospel makes itself at home in cultures. The missiological concepts of contextualization and inculturation are all related to the doctrine of incarnation. Most missiologists and contextual theologians advocated the use of incarnation as a model for mission. See Mondithoka, "Incarnation"; Craig Ott, Stephen J. Strauss, and Timothy C. Tennent, *Encountering Theology of Mission: Biblical Foundations, Historical Developments, and Contemporary Issues* (Grand Rapids, MI: Baker Academic, 2010), 97–104; David J. Bosch, *Transforming Mission: Paradigm Shifts in Theology of Mission*, 20th anniversary edition (Maryknoll, NY: Orbis, 2011); Andrew F. Walls, *The Missionary Movement in Christian History: Studies in the Transmission of Faith* (Maryknoll, NY: Orbis Books, 1996), 26; Aylward Shorter, *Toward a Theology of Inculturation* (Maryknoll, NY: Orbis, 1989); Dean S. Gilliland, ed., "Contextual Theology as Incarnational Mission," in *The Word among Us: Contextualizing Theology for Mission Today* (Dallas: Word, 1989), 9–31.

22. Langmead, *Word Made Flesh*, 219.
23. Langmead, 219–220.

this renewed conceptualization of mission,[24] the Willingen Conference of the International Mission Council (IMC) in 1952 defined the meaning of *missio Dei*. Mission was to be understood as the outliving of God's very nature, instead of a movement born out of the church (ecclesio-centric) or the need for the world to be redeemed (based on the need of the world). In Bosch's words, "The classical doctrine on the *missio Dei* as God the Father sending the Son, and God the Father and the Son sending the Spirit was expanded to include yet another 'movement': Father, Son, and Holy Spirit sending the church into the world"[25] – namely, *missio Dei* gives birth to the church and its soteriological purpose. The church is to join God in his mission to redeem the world. "Willingen's image of mission was mission as participating in the sending of God . . . missionary initiative comes from God alone."[26] When the church joins God in his ongoing mission which resembles the act of incarnation – self-emptying, crossing barriers, and reaching out – the church is incarnational. Unlike d1 and to some extent d2, d3 concerns the role of the church/missionary. *Missio Dei* integrates ecclesiology with mission and provides the church an eschatological vision, a characteristic absent in incarnational mission which only exemplifies the other two dimensions. Most of the criticisms against incarnational mission are caused by the ignorance of *missio Dei*, as the following section shows.

The concept of joining the *missio Dei* is important as it denotes involvement in God's process of reaching out to people, which is an act of incarnation. One may argue that the term "incarnational" is unnecessary, but if the scope of the incarnation is widened to its motive and effects, as Langmead does, to participate in God's mission is to join in God's continuous incarnation. Thus, the act of joining itself is an act of being incarnational. Moreover, the church's purpose is to join in God's mission. It was born in the very mission which it is entrusted to continue. To join the mission of God is to be church. *Missio Dei* is also vital in the aspect of eschatology. One can imitate Christ's pattern of mission (d1) and be empowered (d2), but without having a sense of being a part of the *missio Dei* (d3), there is no sense of eschatological direction that points to the full consummation of the kingdom. If God is *still*

---

24. Bosch, *Transforming Mission*, 399.
25. Bosch, 399.
26. Bosch, 399.

working through the church to reach out to God's creation, God is *still* being incarnational and the church that joins God is incarnational.

One final note on joining God's mission is the difference between incarnational mission and incarnational theology. By stating "God's movement toward creation in enfleshment," Langmead includes incarnational theology where incarnation is understood as God's means to embody creation without the need of Christ's salvific work.[27] An extreme version of this "involves a panentheistic view of God in which God continually and by nature reaches out to the universe, not remaining fully transcendent but indwelling creation and becoming embodied in it, particularly in the life of humanity."[28] According to incarnational theology, salvation is through deification, and confession is not required. In general, advocates of incarnational mission reject incarnational theology because it undermines the work of Christ on the cross. However, the motive of God's salvation, and the ultimate model and goal of mission, according to *missio Dei*, is communion.[29] So some level of theosis – that God has become human so human can become divine – is accepted.[30] Anyway, most advocates of incarnational mission consider Christ's saving work on the cross as vital and essential.

On incarnational methodology (d1), Cheong helpfully outlines the different ways in which incarnational mission is understood as missionary method: (p1) direct imitation of Jesus, (p2) insider identification, (p3) contextual translation, and (p4) obedience/discipleship.[31] To Cheong, methodology which employs any one or a mixture of the above (p1- p4) can be considered incarnational. Cheong endorses Langmead's emphasis on seeing incarnation as a "process," instead of just an "event." Supporting d2 and d3, he concludes that incarnation is a viable model for mission as it includes the

---

27. Langmead, *Word Made Flesh*, 20–22.

28. Langmead, 55.

29. Simon Chan, "CVP: The Mission of the Trinity," interview by Andy Crouch, *Christianity Today*, 4 June 2007, https://www.christianitytoday.com/ct/2007/june/11.48.html.

30. Athanasius, *On the Incarnation*. For further reading on theosis, see Vladimir Kharlamov, *Theosis: Deification in Christian Theology*, vol. 2, 1st ed. (Cambridge: James Clarke & Co, 2012); Mark Edwards and Elena Ene D-Vasilescu, eds., *Visions of God and Ideas on Deification in Patristic Thought*, 1st ed. (London: Routledge, 2016).

31. John Cheong, "Reassessing John Stott's, David Hesselgrave's, and Andreas Kostenberger's Views of the Incarnational Model," in *Missionary Methods: Research, Reflections, and Realities*, ed. Craig Ott and J. D. Payne (Pasadena: William Carey Library, 2013), 55.

"continued dynamic in mission."[32] Hence, incarnational mission incorporates methodology (d1) and the other dimensions (d2 and d3) of Langmead. It is the understanding of mission which is "patterned on the incarnation, enabled by the continuing power of the incarnation, and joining the ongoing incarnating mission of God."[33]

Countering Criticisms of Incarnational Mission

To stand as a viable missiology model, incarnational mission needs to answer to at least four groups of critics. First, the suitability of using "the incarnation" as a model for mission is questioned. In Starke's words,

> The doctrine of the incarnation is not necessarily related to the nature of the Son's mission . . . incarnation is fundamentally about mediation, rather than the manner in which Jesus carried himself and interacted with others during his earthly ministry.[34]

McConnell raises a similar question, "I am unsure we really are being sent 'in the same way as Jesus.' Can we really be reducing the incarnation of Christ to the role of 'a missionary model'?"[35] Closely related to this group are those who misunderstand incarnational mission as only methodological (d1).[36] Evidently, they fail to see the scope of incarnational mission, limiting the understanding of incarnation to an event and a theological concept.[37] Contrarily, the nature of Christ's mission is inseparable from the incarnation. The incarnation, once understood from the perspective of *missio Dei*, is God's redemptive movement embodied in Jesus Christ and his ministry, passed on to the church. The church then continues Christ's mission from generation

---

32. Cheong, "Views of the Incarnational Model," 56–57.

33. Langmead, *Word Made Flesh*, 219.

34. John Starke, "The Incarnation Is about a Person, Not a Mission," *The Gospel Coalition*, 16 May 2011, https://www.thegospelcoalition.org/article/the-incarnation-is-about-a-person-not-a-mission/.

35. Mez McConnell, "Why the Divine Incarnation of Jesus Is a Bad Model for Mission," https://20schemesequip.com/why-the-divine-incarnation-of-jesus-is-a-bad-model-for-mission/.

36. Ott, Strauss, and Tennent, *Encountering Theology of Mission*, 103. See how Cheong effectively defends the incarnational model by countering the arguments of this group. Cheong, "Views of the Incarnational Model."

37. A symptom caused by what Bosch called "an underdeveloped theology of the incarnation." Bosch, *Transforming Mission*, 524.

to generation, inheriting the missionary and apostolic nature of the incarnation. Such continuity may encapsulate the dimensions outlined by Langmead. Instead of reducing the incarnation, incarnational mission does the incarnation justice by taking its telos and effects seriously, incorporating the salvation framework and empowerment of God with contextualized methodology.

Second, critics are concerned if incarnational mission is Chalcedonian and whether incarnational mission's characteristic of identification is necessary. This is best illustrated by Billings' criticism.[38] He points out correctly the flaws of Costas's model which is biased toward Liberation Theology. Costas's model is criticized for its departure from Chalcedonian formulation and its lack of realized eschatology. According to Billings, Costas takes the route of Moltmann who denies a two-natures Christology in view of a need for God's passibility to be expressed through the suffering of the Son with those who suffer, which continues till the full coming of the eschaton. Apparently, there is an absence of "transformation" in Costas's model where people experience healing and restoration. Also, missionaries are expected only to identify and be in solidarity with the poor and suffering without offering any solution. In response, Billings offers the "way of lowliness" as the substitute to "incarnational ministry." His version of Christology, while Chalcedonian, is also vivifying. Instead of presenting only a suffering Christ, the redemptive Christ (whose divine nature does not suffer) brings transformation. While Billings's criticism is legitimate, his choice of using Costas's model to denounce incarnational mission or ministry is misleading. First, Costas's model is a subset of Liberation Theology, which should not be confused with incarnational mission. There are others who remain Chalcedonian while applying incarnation as a model of mission. Further, on identification and transformation, there are others, including Langmead and Cheong, who agree with Billings yet hold the incarnational model as legitimate. Indeed, suffering of the Christians – emphasized by Costas's Liberation Theology – is "not redemptive in and of itself."[39] The "way of lowliness" is welcome as a subset of ethical posture for identification. Yet, it falls short as a comprehensive model for mission or ministry. At best, it is only a combination of p2 and p4 of the "patterns" in incarnational mission. There is no consideration of the continuing presence

---

38. Billings, "Incarnational Ministry and Christology."
39. Billings, 196.

of Christ that is made possible by the incarnation (d2) and the incarnation being a part of God's mission (d3).[40] Unlike incarnational mission, it also lacks an overarching framework that connects ecclesiology and eschatology extensively.

Third, some missionaries point out the impossibility of fully identifying with the people. Unlike Christ, they are not naturally incarnated into the cultures of the people group they serve, and the social, economic, and psychological gap between them and the people group is too vast to cross.[41] Yet, the problem is not the incarnational model but the lack of nuanced exposition on the meaning of identification. Many of these issues are dealt with as this discussion progresses, but fundamentally, incarnational mission should not be confused with Christ's incarnation. The term "incarnational" is only an adjective to be used metaphorically.[42] Only God can incarnate because only God can cross the gap between divinity and humanity. Thus, "the primary use of . . . 'the incarnation' in theology is reserved for the action of God."[43] The incarnation is Christ's work "as he steps forth to reveal the Father's will of love and reconciliation, and to effect it."[44] Jesus Christ is "himself the tabernacle of God among men and women, himself the Word of God enshrined in the flesh, and in him that the glory of God is to be seen."[45] Christ is therefore "the subject of the incarnation."[46] The disciples only "participate in Christ's revelatory and redemptive work in a mostly secondary sense."[47] Christ's incarnation as a redemptive move is historic, unique, and perfect; while the church is only incarnational as it is only a community that continues the salvific works

---

40. See a similar approach which emphasizes methodology over essence and overarching framework in Ott, Strauss, and Tennent, *Encountering Theology of Mission*, 103.

41. Ken Baker, "The Incarnational Model: Perception of Deception?," *Evangelical Missions Quarterly* 38, no. 1 (2002), https://missionexus.org/the-incarnational-model-perception-of-deception/.

42. Langmead, *Word Made Flesh*, 19–20.

43. Langmead, 20.

44. Thomas F. Torrance, *Incarnation: The Person and Life of Christ*, ed. Robert T. Walker (Milton Keynes, UK: Paternoster, 2008), 58.

45. Torrance, *Incarnation*, 60.

46. Torrance, 60–61.

47. Cheong, "Views of the Incarnational Model," 53, referring to Andreas J. Kostenberger, *The Missions of Jesus and the Disciples According to the Fourth Gospel: With Implications for the Fourth Gospel's Purpose and the Mission of the Conte* (Grand Rapids, MI: Eerdmans; Lightning Source, 1998), 81.

of Christ's incarnation. These crucial understandings differentiate Christ's unique incarnation from the church's attempt to be incarnational.

Fourth, some critics question the need to "incarnate" into the culture in the incarnational model. McConnell asks,

> Did Jesus enter into this world . . . to "go deep" into our culture? Did he come to hang out with us to get to know us better? . . . Did he need to engage in a bit of cultural homework whilst he was here to get the full picture and be able to bring the gospel home in a meaningful way?[48]

This rejection of cultural identification has been considered by missiologists. From the perspective of mission history, microscopically, Jesus was incarnated or inculturated into human culture – a Jewish culture in a Roman-Hellenistic world. Macroscopically, God has incarnated into humanity (Is this not deep enough?), and such incarnation of the gospel has progressed from one culture to another. This is demonstrated through the missionary movement, where the gospel incarnates itself first from the Jewish to a Hellenistic culture (Acts 15) and then thereon to many other cultures.[49] Missiologists have little problem accepting incarnation as a model for mission because they know every instance of communicating the gospel to a different culture mimics the incarnation. In Bosch's words, "the Christian faith is intrinsically incarnational."[50] Communicating the gospel to a different worldview, whether verbally or through their holistic witness, requires intercultural paradigm shifts. Every meaningful communication of the gospel brings the reality and presence of Christ more tangibly to the people. It is as though Christ and his gospel have gone through incarnation and is being born into a new culture. This continuous missionary movement is considered the effect of incarnation, where the missionaries participate in God's ongoing mission, empowered by the continued power of Christ's presence. Christ may not need any effort to "go deep" in our cultures, but his incarnation is a viable model for intercultural mission. Considering the fluidity of culture and the postmodern context, such "incarnation" is needed for a church that may encounter different subcultures.

---

48. McConnell, "Why the Divine Incarnation."
49. Walls, *Missionary Movement*.
50. Bosch, *Transforming Mission*, 195.

The meaning of "culture" here is no more restricted to a particular people group but includes any subgroups in a community.

Incarnational Mission and the Missional Church

The missional church movement is a movement that attempts to reshape ecclesiology according to God's mission. The concept of "missional church"[51] has its roots in the Gospel and Our Culture Network (GOCN), a movement inspired by the works of Lesslie Newbigin.[52] The missional church is incarnational because of its ecclesiology, which is intertwined with the mission of God.

The Missional Church and *Missio Dei*

A church is missional when it acknowledges that it is spawned by the mission of God, exists for it, and fully participates in it. The missional church bases its entire ecclesiology on the *missio Dei*.[53] It understands that mission is God's initiative, rooted in God's purposes to restore and heal creation.[54] Therefore, the church is not the initiator, forerunner, nor pioneer of mission. Instead, the church is generated by the *missio Dei*.[55] The purpose of its existence is to be "a sent community of people who no longer live for themselves but

---

51. The term "missional church" is certainly definable even though it may come across as ambiguous due to a variety of usages. See Ed Stetzer, "Monday Is for Missiology: What Is the Missional Church? – A New Series," *The Exchange* (blog), 12 October 2015, http://www.christianitytoday.com/edstetzer/2015/october/missional-church-and-its-manifesto.html. For survey, critiques, insights, and suggestions on the movement, see Van Gelder and Zscheile, *Missional Church*.

52. Michael W. Goheen, "Historical Perspectives on the Missional Church Movement: Probing Lesslie Newbigin's Formative Influence," *Trinity Journal for Theology and Ministry* 4, no. 2 (2010): 62–84; Roxburgh and Boren, *Introducing the Missional Church*, 9. The characteristics of incarnational mission were not spelled out explicitly in the work of Newbigin. Yet, it is through Newbigin's thoughts and ideas that most of the incarnational characteristics of the missional church originated. Later proponents of the missional church, such as Guder, utilize the term and concept of "incarnation" more freely and frequently, but their essential ecclesiology is inspired by Newbigin.

53. Frost, *Road to Missional, Journey*, 16.

54. Darrell L. Guder, "Missional Church: From Sending to Being Sent," in *Missional Church: A Vision for the Sending of the Church in North America*, ed. Darrell L. Guder (Grand Rapids, MI: Eerdmans, 1998), Kindle, 4–5.

55. George R. Hunsberger, "Missional Vocation: Called and Sent to Represent the Reign of God," in *Missional Church: A Vision for the Sending of the Church in North America*, ed. Darrell L. Guder (Grand Rapids, MI: Eerdmans, 1998), Kindle, 81. Bosch, *Transforming Mission*, 379–402.

instead live to participate with [God] in His redemptive purposes."[56] In other words, the missional church's identity is found in "the role it plays in God's mission."[57] Mission is not church activity or a part of the church's programs. Instead, it forms the essence and identity of the church.[58] "Missionary activity" is "not so much the work of the church but simply the Church at work."[59] The church is not the sole beneficiary of God's mission and certainly not the purpose and terminal point of God's saving grace. It is used by God to reach out to his creation before the full consummation of the kingdom. This view is consistent in Newbigin's writings and in the missional church movement.

The missional church movement rejects incarnational theology. Its understanding of the incarnation follows Newbigin's "Christocentric *missio Dei*" which stresses the "finality of Christ" – "God has acted decisively and finally in Jesus to reveal and accomplish his redemptive purposes for the whole [of] creation."[60] Like Torrance,[61] the missional church movement accepts an understanding of incarnation that includes a limited theosis,[62] but rejects incarnational theology which undermines Christ's salvific work through the cross and resurrection.

The Missional Church's Incarnational Mission

The missional church embodies incarnational mission. Besides acknowledging its role in *missio Dei*, the missional church recognizes the need to be patterned on the incarnation (d1). In fact, Guder defines incarnational mission as "the understanding and practice of Christian witness that is rooted in and shaped by the life, ministry, suffering, death, and resurrection of Jesus."[63] The missional church also resists the temptation to be "focusing primarily

---

56. Brad Brisco, "Transitioning from Traditional to Missional" (Blue River-Kansas City Baptist Association, 2011), https://blueriver-kansascity.org/wp-content/uploads/2015/07/Transitioning-from-Traditional-to-Missional.pdf.

57. Goheen, "Historical Perspectives," 62.

58. Hunsberger, "Missional Vocation," 81.

59. Van Gelder and Zscheile, *Missional Church*, 32.

60. Michael W. Goheen, "The Significance of Lesslie Newbigin for Mission in the New Millennium," *Third Millennium* 7, no. 3 (2004): 92.

61. Myk Habets, *Theosis in the Theology of Thomas Torrance*, 1st ed. (Farnham, England: Routledge, 2009).

62. Van Gelder and Zscheile, *Missional Church*, 114–115.

63. Guder, *Incarnation*, xii–xiii.

on Christology in the missional conversation" as it tends to "lead the church toward a backward-oriented vision."[64] While emphasizing "imitating what Christ has done in the past," it is aware of the need to discern God's move in the present and in the future.[65] In other words, the missional church movement recognizes the continuing power of the incarnation in the form of Christ's presence and empowerment (d2).[66]

The emphasis of the missional church movement is ecclesiology, which goes beyond acknowledging the church's role in *missio Dei* by also focusing on the continuity of Christ's mission from the perspective of "sent-ness." To Guder, "The church bears a marked resemblance to the incarnation of Jesus . . . It is no accident that the church is called the 'body of Christ.' It continues as an incarnate expression of the life of God."[67] In other words, the missional church's existence is a continuity of Christ's presence, method, and message integrated. Its vocation is incarnational witness – "Jesus Christ as the messenger, the message, and the model for all who follow after him."[68] Christians are called to be disciples who form an apostolic and witnessing community.[69] As God revealed himself through Christ's incarnation "as the One who is and for his creation," the church is sent as "God's people present in the world, with and for the world."[70] This view is a combination of Langmead's dimensions, emphasizing the essence of the church (ecclesiology) in the context of *missio Dei*.

---

64. Van Gelder and Zscheile, *Missional Church*, 118–119.

65. Van Gelder and Zscheile, 118–119.

66. Most of the proponents of the missional church movement emphasize d2. Some, like Frost and Hirsch, are weaker in this area. They consider the missional church incarnational. Their understanding of the missional church does exemplify d3 and greatly emphasizes d1. However, it is a little weak with d2. Frost and Hirsch, *Shaping of Things*, 43. The others in the missional church movement may differ in terms of the details of d1, but in general, much stronger with d2.

67. Guder, "Missional Church," 13–14.

68. Guder, *Incarnation*, 9.

69. Guder, 21–29. The missional church's apostolic nature is often being defined against an attractional approach of outreach by the church or a response to an inward looking, Christendom mindset, as described by Ed Stetzer. Ed Stetzer, *Planting Missional Churches* (Nashville, TN: B&H Publishing Group, 2006), 165; and Frost and Hirsch, *Shaping of Things*, 41. Yet, an anti-attractional and anti-Christendom mindset definition of "apostolic" is not the focus here. Rather, "apostolic" here refers to the "sentness" nature of the church.

70. Guder, *Incarnation*, 9.

The concept of missional church is intertwined with the idea of incarnational mission. As demonstrated, the pattern, power, and participation of God's continuous incarnation are integral in the ecclesiology and ministry philosophy of missional church movement. The missional church takes the essence, the movement, and the overarching framework of incarnational mission seriously, and positions itself as the participating actor in it. "Participation" in the *missio Dei* becomes the basis of its ecclesiology. In other words, the missional church does not just fit in the incarnational model because it has the "pattern," and "power" dimensions of incarnational mission. It is intrinsically incarnational. Incarnational mission is already a part of its ecclesiology.

Yet, while the essence of incarnational mission exemplified through Langmead's three dimensions is encapsulated in the missional church movement, the missional church expresses incarnational mission with its own emphases. Especially, the missional church stresses the importance of kingdom ethics and transformation. The missional church's understanding of incarnational mission has a stronger emphasis on eschatology akin to the concept of the kingdom that has "already arrived but not yet fully consummated" in the New Testament.[71] Langmead presents an overview of how incarnational mission looks like. In the missional church movement, the role of the church as the instrument of God's incarnational mission is further delineated. The church's essence as a new community in the new kingdom and its role of pointing to the hope of transformation and new humanity are highlighted. All these are integrated with the dimensions and methodology of the incarnational mission. In fact, through the expression of the missional church, the essence and methodology of incarnational mission are demonstrated through the praxis of the local church.

The following sections explore the incarnational nature of the missional church through the three areas of its expression. These areas are intertwined with the essence and patterns of incarnational mission. First, the missional church witnesses for Christ by continuing Christ's presence in the world. Second, it represents the kingdom, and third, it identifies with people.

---

71. George Eldon Ladd, *A Theology of the New Testament*, rev. subsequent edition (Grand Rapids, MI: Eerdmans, 1993).

The Missional Church Is Christ's Continuous Presence in the World

The missional church considers itself the continuity of Christ in two aspects. First, it considers its essence as the continuity of Christ's presence. Second, Christ's presence is demonstrated through his ministry principles.

The Church as the "Body"

The missional church is incarnational as it continues Christ's presence in the world. It carries the effects of the incarnation through the presence and power of Christ. The missional church inherits Newbigin's understanding that Christians are a continuity of God's story; they live out Jesus's story and live in it until it becomes their own.[72] On this foundation, Newbigin develops a Christocentric *missio Dei* where the church would continue the Son's mission in God's salvific story: "as the Father has sent me, I am sending you" (John 20:21).[73] In fact, the birth of the church is for the continuity of Christ's incarnational presence in this world, as both his "body" and the instrument for his continuous mission in the world through the Holy Spirit.[74] Biblical references such as John 1:14 are related to the Old Testament concept of tabernacle – the meeting place between God and his people.[75] Through the incarnation, the true glory of God, manifested in Christ, takes "residence" in humanity.[76] Like Christ, the church is to show the world the glory of God. The church is the continuity of Jesus (God) in the world, a tangible "flesh" which would stay (residence). To Guder, unless the world sees and is engaged with the Word

---

72. Lesslie Newbigin, *The Gospel in a Pluralist Society* (Grand Rapids, MI: Eerdmans, 1989), 151.

73. Lesslie Newbigin, *The Open Secret: An Introduction to the Theology of Mission*, rev. ed. (Grand Rapids, MI: Eerdmans, 1995), 47–48; Michael W. Goheen, *"As the Father Has Sent Me, I Am Sending You": J. E. Lesslie Newbigin's Missionary Ecclesiology* (Zoetermeer: Boekencentrum, 2000), 126–127, 162.

74. A collapse of Christology into ecclesiology must be avoided. The church needs to be distinctly identified apart from Christ, who is unique and fully divine and holy. The incarnation of Christ must be distinguished from the incarnational nature of the church.

75. D. A. Carson, *The Gospel according to John* (Grand Rapids, MI: Eerdmans, 1991), 123–124.

76. Carson, *Gospel according to John*, 127–128.

through the church, incarnation is incomplete.⁷⁷ In other words, in the context of missional church, Christ's presence is experienced through the church.⁷⁸

Imitation and Discipleship as Christ's Continuous Ministry

Tangibly, Christ's presence continues today through the practice of the church. The church is understood as the continuity of Jesus's work in this world, sent for its salvation.⁷⁹ The church should imitate Christ because imitation of Christ is integral to being incarnational, just as the acts of Christ (words and deeds) are integral to his incarnation. Specifically, the missional church sees itself as a continuity of Jesus's preaching, teaching, and healing.⁸⁰ The continuity of Jesus's ministry after his ascension was clearly described as incarnational by Newbigin, followed by the proponents of the missional church such as Hunsburger and Guder.⁸¹ They consider the call of discipleship key to the church not just as a faithful response to Jesus's call, but also to continue Jesus's ministry in the world according to the way of Jesus.⁸² Those who follow Jesus integrate word and deed in mission just as Jesus did.⁸³

Such continuity of Christ's presence today through imitation is based on ministry principles (Cheong's p4). Some missionaries reject this aspect of incarnational mission because they find it impossible to fully imitate Christ.⁸⁴ This is because they only focus on a superficial imitation of Jesus (Cheong's p1) instead of following his ministry principles. Jesus's principle of ministry

---

77. Guder, *Incarnation*, 5–6. Guder's statement is dangerously close to collapsing Christology into ecclesiology; but, it does represent the general position of the missional church movement.

78. The emphasis here is how others may encounter Christ through the church instead of the speculation on how Christ is actually present in the church.

79. Lois Barrett, "Missional Witness: The Church as Apostle to the World," in *Missional Church: A Vision for the Sending of the Church in North America*, ed. Darrell L. Guder (Grand Rapids, MI: Eerdmans, 1998), 132; Hunsberger, "Missional Vocation," 103–104.

80. Barrett, "Missional Witness," 132–141.

81. Guder being influenced by John Mackay. Daryl L. Guder, "Incarnation and the Church's Evangelistic Mission," *International Review of Mission* 83, no. 330 (1994): 421.

82. Guder, "Incarnation," 421.

83. Langmead, *Word Made Flesh*, 49–51.

84. Berdine Van den Toren-Lekkerkerker and Benno Van den Toren, "From Missionary Incarnate to Incarnational Guest: A Critical Reflection on Incarnation as a Model for Missionary Presence," *Transformation* 32, no. 2 (2015): 81–96; Harriet Hill, "Incarnational Ministry: A Critical Examination," *Evangelical Missions Quarterly* 26, no. 2 (1990), https://missionexus.org/incarnational-ministry-a-critical-examination/.

is rooted in his ethics, demonstrated through his humility and suffering at the cross, summarized by Yoder as "servanthood replaces dominion" and "forgiveness absorbs hostility."[85] Following Jesus is to follow these ministry principles, not merely the forms of his ministry. Participating in Christ is inseparable with being the body of Christ "because it shares in the sufferings of Christ."[86] In conclusion, to continue Jesus's ministry in the world, Christians are to operate according to the ethics of Christ, which emphasizes servanthood and forgiveness. The result of such following goes beyond shallow imitation of Christ that focuses only on the way he conducted his earthly life.

The Missional Church Represents the Kingdom of God

To the missional church, incarnational mission cannot be understood apart from its relationship with the kingdom. The inauguration and in-breaking of the kingdom began through the incarnation. The continuous presence of Christ today must be understood as the presence of the king, with the church as the representative of the kingdom. Embracing a realized, albeit not yet fully consummated kingdom is key to demonstrate the kingdom as an incarnational reality today. Further, the missional church continues the incarnational mission of God by witnessing to the world the nature of a new humanity, which is redeemed and restored. It lives in the world incarnationally with a new life governed by the ethics of the kingdom.

The Kingdom and New Humanity

The missional church is aware that it is "spawned by the reign of God and directed toward it."[87] As a community, it models the forthcoming fulfillment of God's kingdom.[88] It is "the provisional representation . . . of humanity justi-

---

85. John Howard Yoder, *The Politics of Jesus*, 2nd ed. (Grand Rapids, MI: Eerdmans, 1994), 131. True discipleship or Christian ethics, Yoder argued, lies not in the superficial imitation of Christ of the St. Franciscan way, which he stressed was absent "in the apostolic writings." Yoder, *Politics of Jesus*, 132.

86. Barrett, "Missional Witness," 129.

87. Hunsberger, "Missional Vocation," 98–99.

88. Hunsberger, 81–82, 100–104.

fied in [Christ],"[89] the "harbinger of the new humanity that lives in genuine community," and "a form of companionship and wholeness that humanity craves."[90] The world would see a new hope of humanity through a church that breaks racial and cultural barriers.[91]

The kingdom is neither separated from the church nor equated to the church.[92] The church is a "hermeneutic of the gospel" which, having tasted the first fruit of the Holy Spirit (Acts 1), is experiencing the foretaste of the kingdom and living by the gospel.[93] It is a subset and definite part of the kingdom of God.[94] The scope of the church's mission is extended to where God's reign is, which includes every aspect of humanity and creation.[95] Knowing this scope prevents the church from confining the gospel within the private lives of Christians while ignoring the public realm.

Through the incarnation, "Jesus' humanity reveals what God intends his people to be and to become."[96] Through Christ's humanity, hope is secured, and through the church that is constantly undergoing sanctification, the world sees the hope of transformation. Hence, the missional church's witnessing is incarnational because the process of sanctification it experiences shows God's intention of sanctifying humanity. In short, "The church is to be an imperfect but perfecting social incarnation of God's inbreaking reign of love and reconciliation, joy and freedom, peace and justice."[97] Thus, the church demonstrates a "new humanity, fully immersed in creation and human culture, while at the same time undistorted by sin and estrangement."[98] It represents God's reign as God's community, servant, and messenger.[99] The missional church

---

89. "Missional ecclesiology is also a representational ecclesiology." Barth, *Church Dogmatics*, IV/ 1, 643, as quoted in Van Gelder and Zscheile, *Missional Church*, 107.

90. Hunsberger, "Missional Vocation," 100–104.

91. Hunsberger, 100–104.

92. Goheen, *As the Father*, 175.

93. Goheen, 176; Newbigin, *Gospel in a Pluralist*, 227.

94. Newbigin, 107; Goheen, *As the Father*, 175–176.

95. Lesslie Newbigin, "Church as Witness: A Meditation," *Reformed World* 35 (1978): 6; Goheen, *As the Father*, 175; Newbigin, *Gospel in a Pluralist*, 138.

96. Guder, *Incarnation*, 16.

97. Inagrace T. Dietterich, "Missional Community: Cultivating Communities of the Holy Spirit," in *Missional Church: A Vision for the Sending of the Church in North America*, ed. Darrell L. Guder (Grand Rapids, MI: Eerdmans, 1998), Kindle, 158.

98. Van Gelder and Zscheile, *Missional Church*, 139–140.

99. Hunsberger, "Missional Vocation," 102–103.

is simultaneously participating in both "culture/world and God's redeeming activity, so that the world can see and experience provisionally but powerfully the new humanity that God is bringing forth through the Spirit."[100]

Kingdom Ethics Incarnated

The missional church submits to God's reign and subscribes to kingdom ethics. The church is a community of believers under a different authority.[101] The ethics of the kingdom is an inseparable part of incarnational mission.[102] The continuity of Jesus's ministry and the incarnating presence of Christ naturally embodies the ethics of Jesus. As representative of the kingdom, the church's submission to the rule of the kingdom takes precedence over the rule or patterns of the world. The church is "to embody the reign of God by living under its authority," thus showing forth God's tangible reign in human and social form.[103] It is a Holy Nation among the nations.[104] Besides, as active agent and instrument, the church holds the divine reign's authority and asserts the authority of the kingdom in the world as a prophetic voice.[105]

The Missional Church Identifies with the People

One of the key characteristics of the missional church and incarnational mission is the emphasis on identification. Identification means being in solidarity with the people and their situation, while respecting and accepting their cultures. The practice of identification in incarnational mission, expressed through the missional church, is governed by a set of practical principles.

---

100. Van Gelder and Zscheile, *Missional Church*, 139–140.

101. Lesslie Newbigin, *Foolishness to the Greeks: The Gospel and Western Culture* (Grand Rapids, MI: Eerdmans, 1986), 124.

102. Guder, *Incarnation*, 5, 33–46; Langmead, *Word Made Flesh*, 49–51.

103. Hunsberger, "Missional Vocation," 103–104.

104. Barrett, "Missional Witness," 117.

105. Hunsberger, "Missional Vocation," 103–104. For peace and justice as demonstrations of kingdom ethics, see Frost, *Road to Missional, Journey*, 104–110.

Solidarity with Others and Their Situation

Incarnational engagement with people begins with solidarity. Being "in the flesh," Christ's incarnation enables him to identify with humanity.[106] The unceasingly holy Christ entered the sinful world to redeem it.[107] Through incarnation, Christ's solidarity with humanity is demonstrated, as Torrance describes,

> in becoming flesh the Word penetrated into hostile territory, into our human alienation and estrangement from God . . . he became all that we are in our opposition to God in our bondage under law – that is the amazing act of gracious condescension in the incarnation, that God the Son should assume our flesh, should enter a human experience under divine judgment.[108]

The incarnation "embodies an act of profound identification with the entire human race."[109]

Following the example of Christ, an incarnational church does not stay remote from sin, tragedy, and suffering of the people, but humbles itself to serve them.[110] It considers seriously the human condition, which includes all aspects of human sinfulness and wellbeing. Thus, incarnational mission includes entering society and initiating "relational identification" with others.[111] The church that is involved is to enter into "concrete acts of solidarity and accompaniment" – "If God loves us in Christ, so that God identifies with us relationally in a posture of humility, then we are to share this same love with our neighbors."[112] The medium, which is the church, is "entirely the message." Through identification, people are reached "in all ways possible without compromising the truth of the gospel itself."[113]

Identification should be applied to all missions in all contexts because it reflects "that primal act of identification that was an intrinsic part of Christ's

---

106. Mondithoka, "Incarnation," 177.
107. Mondithoka, 177.
108. Torrance, *Incarnation*, 61.
109. Frost and Hirsch, *Shaping of Things*, 36.
110. Mondithoka, "Incarnation," 178.
111. Van Gelder and Zscheile, *Missional Church*, 115.
112. Van Gelder and Zscheile, 115.
113. Frost and Hirsch, *Shaping of Things*, 37.

incarnation."[114] If Jesus was not docetic, having been a genuine part of the organic life in a given community, the church should also have a "real and abiding incarnational presence" through identification with the people it engages with.[115] Christ's incarnation brought his tangible, physical, and relational presence into the world. So, Christ's presence through the church must also be tangibly felt and experienced in the community. Hence, missional approaches are shaped via "dialogue and engagement with the contexts."[116] The church is to enter the local community and "sit with the people to enter and be shaped by their narratives."[117] It should imitate the early church, to "reenter our neighborhoods, to dwell with and to listen to the narratives and stories of the people."[118] This shall not be done to attract others to churches, but as a natural expression of incarnation – "a way of life."[119]

Respect and Acceptance of Others' Culture

Identification includes immersing into people's culture and situations to empathize and stand in solidarity with them.[120] Such identification follows Christ's incarnation, which is "the most spectacular instance of cultural identification in human history."[121] The church must identify with the culture to be relevant to a context. It follows the example of Jesus who incarnated into a particular culture. In fact, a local church "always takes particular form, shaped according to the cultural and historical context in which it lives."[122] So, the missional church rejects cultural imperialism, where churches impose various cultural forms of their faith unto others.[123] Instead, incarnational mission means "people will get to experience Jesus on the inside of their culture

---

114. Frost and Hirsch, 38.
115. Frost and Hirsch, 39.
116. Roxburgh and Boren, *Introducing the Missional Church*, 84.
117. Roxburgh and Boren, 85.
118. Roxburgh and Boren, 85–86.
119. Roxburgh and Boren, 85–86.
120. Guder, "Missional Church," 13.
121. Willowbank Report, 1978, quoted in Ott, Strauss, and Tennent, *Encountering Theology of Mission*, 100.
122. Guder, "Missional Church," 13–14.
123. Frost and Hirsch, *Shaping of Things*, 38.

(meaning systems) and their lives because of [the Church's] embodying the gospel in an incarnationally appropriate way."[124]

Therefore, it is paramount that the church be incarnationally involved with the daily lives of the people. While engaging with the people, the church must be attentive to "the values and meanings that underlie the surface activities of the neighborhood."[125] Such respect, acceptance, and "sitting with" replicates Christ's incarnation, where he "came to pitch his tent beside ours."[126] The purpose is not only gaining new knowledge about the culture, but also an opportunity to discern the guidance of the Spirit, while seeing the people and their cultures through God's lenses.[127]

The Practice of Identification

The practice of identification, which includes solidarity with people and acceptance of their culture, is the logic that governs incarnational mission. The acts of continuing Christ's ministry and manifesting kingdom ethics alone do not equal to being incarnational unless there is an attempt to communicate the gospel meaningfully. Even the right message and godly messengers do not guarantee an incarnational mission unless there is an attempt to be relevant. Being relevant here means being able to carry the meaning of the gospel faithfully while being understood by the people who receive it.

The church, however, cannot identify with others like Jesus did. Being incarnational is different from being incarnated. Christ's incarnation remains a unique, hypostatic, historic event. The Word incarnated into humanity that he created. Christ condescended himself to be with those he created and became one of them.[128] The church certainly cannot incarnate like Christ did as it is neither the Creator nor has any status to condescend from. The church is incarnational simply because it is called to represent Christ and the kingdom, and for that reason it identifies with others as a redeemed community. The

---

124. Frost and Hirsch, 40.
125. Roxburgh and Boren, *Introducing the Missional Church*, 86, 89.
126. Roxburgh and Boren, 86, based on their interpretation of John 1:14
127. Roxburgh and Boren, 86.
128. Torrance, *Incarnation*, 65; Webster, *Word and Church*, 138.

church must therefore, like Christ, remain "holy" and yet willing to identify with the people.[129]

However, identification with people does not bring salvation to them; neither can it bring salvation to the church involved. This is a constant critique directed toward Liberation Theology.[130] Following Jesus's example of identifying with the poor is undoubtedly incarnational, as it continues Jesus's ministry for the poor and with the poor. The danger is when such imitation of Christ becomes the goal of missions. Often, the means to salvation is conflated with solidarity with the poor. Identifying with the poor and suffering becomes so prominent in some theologies to the extent that the Christian mission is reduced to mere identification with the oppressed.[131]

Indeed, identification with people in itself is not equal to missions. Solidarity and identification with the marginalized themselves do not bring salvation, lest it becomes a kind of "salvation by works." Though the church may intend to love others genuinely as God loves them, the church's love is imperfect. The church, as imperfect human beings, cannot do what Christ did, but they can testify what Christ has done, and what Christ can do for others. The goal for identification is to identify with the people in a context while imitating Christ's apostolic movement and ministry principles. In other words, the continuity of Christ's ministry is in the form of witnessing.

So, one does not need to become poor to be with the poor; nor does one need to become a member of another ethnicity to identify with the other ethnicity.[132] The church is incarnational, but it does not and cannot "incarnate." The church's role is only to witness the presence of Christ as the harbinger of the kingdom while carrying the message verbally and holistically.

---

129. For the relationship between culture and faith and the tension between them, see Walls, *Missionary Movement*, 3–15.

130. Billings, "Incarnational Ministry."

131. See Billings' criticisms on Moltmann and Costa. Billings, "Incarnational Ministry"; Orlando E. Costas, *Christ Outside the Gate: Mission Beyond Christendom* (Eugene, OR: Wipf & Stock, 2005).

132. Some of the critiques of incarnational mission are: Baker, "Incarnational Model"; Hill, "Incarnational Ministry"; Van den Toren-Lekkerkerker and Van den Toren, "From Missionary Incarnate."

Transformation and Human Flourishing

Any reference to Christ's incarnation is incomplete without including its purpose, which is transformation. Those who consider the incarnation by only referring to the birth of Jesus Christ often emphasize "creation at the expense of redemption, and incarnation without the cross and resurrection. It implies that the saving purpose of the incarnation is accomplished simply by God becoming human, regardless of what happened next."[133] This "incarnational theology" is the belief that salvation rests in the embodiment of God with his creation without an emphasis on repentance and transformation. Referring to James Dunn, Langmead denounces this as unbiblical.[134] Quoting Jean Daniélou, Langmead concludes that "incarnational mission based on 'getting alongside' and 'identifying' has only taken the first step; it also needs to bring good news, challenge others and lead to transformation."[135] Thus, incarnation must not be understood as merely Jesus's birth, life, and teaching, but also includes his death and resurrection.[136] It includes repentance and transformation as both its motive and outcome.

Value and Transformation of Humanity

The incarnation of Christ necessarily entails the transformation of humanity. The teleological aspect of humanity in the context of eschatology must not be neglected. Salvation is not just personal, but also involves the whole of humanity, which has a destination. The destiny of humanity is in turn, related to its purpose of existence. God's creation is therefore the basis for the teleology of humanity. Salvation is the restoration of God's design for humanity. The kingdom of God, which will ultimately be consummated, will fully realize such restoration.[137] This puts Christ's incarnation and its relationship with humanity in context.

---

133. Langmead, *Word Made Flesh*, 18.

134. Langmead, 18, referring to James D. G. Dunn, "Incarnation," in *The Anchor Bible Dictionary*, ed. David Noel Freeman (New York: Doubleday, 1992), 3:404; James D. G. Dunn, *Unity and Diversity in the New Testament: an Inquiry into the Character of Earliest Christianity*, 2nd ed. (London: SCM, 1990), 223.

135. Langmead, *Word Made Flesh*, 18, referring to Jean Daniélou, *The Salvation of the Nations* (Notre Dame, IN: University of Notre Dame Press, 1962), 33.

136. Langmead, *Word Made Flesh*, 19.

137. Webster, *Word and Church*, 265.

Through incarnation, Christ "fully identified with us in our humanity . . . to redeem us and transform us into his glory (Heb 2:14). The incarnation is the ultimate expression of the immanence of the transcendent Creator God, who, without ceasing to be holy, entered into the sinful world to make human beings holy and to enable them to participate in his glory."[138] Further, in his resurrection, "Christ took his transformed humanity with him into eternal glory."[139] These statements endorse the value, potential, hope, and future of humanity. Surely, even prior to the full consummation of the kingdom, humanity can be redeemed to its glory, albeit not in its fullest potential.

Related to transformation is the concept of human flourishing, which also plays a vital role in giving necessary credential and rationale for the restoration of the social dimension of the gospel in incarnational mission. There would be no need to restore the social dimension of the gospel if human beings and their activities – commonly grouped and coined as their "culture" – are negligible in mission. As a fabric of meanings for a group of people, culture is vital for ensuring the wellbeing of the community concerned.[140] Theologically, the concept of shalom is related to the kingdom.[141] The missional church, which represents the kingdom, would also bring shalom to the people around it.[142] By embodying and carrying the shalom, it means a church brings God's goodness to its context. This is an act of ensuring human flourishing, which also echoes the nature of the missional church that offers the world hope in humanity and a vision of the common good.[143] It offers, then, not just the "mystical" dimension but also the "prophetic." In Volf's words,

---

138. Mondithoka, "Incarnation," 177.

139. Mondithoka, 177.

140. Culture is not the enemy, sin is. On culture, see Clifford Geertz, *The Interpretation Of Cultures* (New York, NY: Basic Books, 2008). On culture-faith relation, see Walls, *Missionary Movement*.

141. Paul Keeble, *Mission with: Something Out of the Ordinary* (Watford, UK: Instant Apostle, 2017), Kindle, pt. 1. Johannes C. Hoekendijk was the first to relate shalom to mission. Shalom is the reign of God proclaimed, lived, and demonstrated, as the true peace of God is experienced holistically and communally. Sunquist, *Understanding Christian Mission*, 139–140.

142. "I believe in the Church which is a function of the Apostolate, that is, an instrument of God's redemptive action in this world . . . The Church is nothing more (but also nothing less!) than a means in God's hands to establish shalom in this world." Sunquist, *Understanding Christian Mission*, 139–140, quoting Johannes C. Hoekendijk, "Call to Evangelism," *Ecumenical Review of Mission* 39 (1950): 167–175.

143. Hope, unlike that of Moltmann, is to be expressed in progress.

As a prophetic religion, Christian faith will be an active faith, engaged in the world in a noncoercive way – offering blessing to our endeavors, effective comfort in our failures, moral guidance in a complex world, and a framework of meaning for our lives and our activities. To be engaged in the world well, Christians will have to keep one thing at the forefront of their attention: the relationship between God and a vision of human flourishing.[144]

Volf's proposals echo those of the incarnational mission. He urges Christians to engage in the world "with their whole being."[145] Such engagement must also cover "all dimensions of a culture."[146] So ultimately, a proper understanding of humanity, and its need for flourishing and transformation, becomes an integral part of the incarnational mission. For only with such theological bases, incarnational mission finds its eschatological context.

Submission to God in Transformation

Transformation is God's prerogative. The missional church acknowledges that God is sovereign, active, and leading ahead of his church.[147] The church is vital to God's plan as the representative of the kingdom that serves the purpose of God's reign.[148] Yet, a church that submits to *missio Dei* must also be faithful to the gospel that is sovereign and has a life of its own.[149] God is understood "to already be present and active in the world, with the church being responsible for discovering what God is doing and then seeking to participate in that."[150] Hence, mission activities are based on the mission of

---

144. Miroslav Volf, *A Public Faith, How Followers of Christ Should Serve the Common Good*, Reprint ed. (Grand Rapids, MI: Brazos Press, 2011), 54.

145. Volf, *Public Faith*, 96.

146. Volf, 98.

147. Van Gelder and Zscheile, *Missional Church*, 31.

148. Hunsberger, "Missional Vocation," 100.

149. Theology Working Group, "The Whole Church Taking the Whole Gospel to the Whole World," *Lausanne Movement*, 1 June 2010, https://www.lausanne.org/content/twg-three-wholes.

150. Van Gelder and Zscheile, *Missional Church*, 31, citing the 1967 WCC publication, World Council of Churches, *The Church for Others: Two Reports on the Missionary Structure of the Church* (Geneva: World Council of Churches, 1967); also in Ad Gentes, as described in Stephen B. Bevans and Roger P. Schroeder, *Constants in Context: A Theology of Mission for Today* (Maryknoll, NY: Orbis Books, 2004), Kindle, chap. 9.

God in the world, instead of the church's effort to extend itself.[151] The church is therefore not "the purpose or goal of the gospel, but rather its instrument and witness."[152]

Subsequently, submission to God's sovereignty enables the church to focus on witnessing instead of speculating the outcome of evangelism. The church is not to expect a mechanistic, causal reaction from its evangelism, but submit patiently to God's transformative work in the people that it evangelizes to. The result of evangelism is not defined by a "bounded set."[153] A bounded set approach uses some criteria to determine who is "in the Kingdom" and who is not. The missional church is inclined to the centered set that defines members of the church as those who focus on Jesus and direct their lives toward being more intimate with him.[154] Hence, instead of being occupied with delineating the criteria of a bounded set, the missional church aims to focus on pointing others to Jesus and nurturing a new relationship between new believers and God.

Summary: The Shape of Incarnational Mission

To conclude, incarnational mission takes the form of a movement by the missional church, is based on the *missio Dei*, and expressed through the church's engagement with the world by continuing Christ's presence, representing the kingdom, and identifying with people. The sociopolitical and cultural dimensions are included as arenas for witnessing. The value of this holistic nature of mission rests in the recognition of the teleology of humanity as God's worthy creation. Hence, incarnational mission must result in transformation. Yet, the church should only concern itself with its witnessing because transformation is the work of God. Instead of speculating the outcome of evangelism, the church should embrace incarnational mission and faithfully engage with its surrounding communities and their cultures.

---

151. Hunsberger, "Missional Vocation," 81–82.

152. Guder, "Missional Church," 4; Van Gelder and Zscheile, *Missional Church*, 33.

153. Paul G. Hiebert, *Anthropological Reflections on Missiological Issues* (Grand Rapids, MI: Baker Academic, 1994), 106–136.

154. Frost and Hirsch, *Shaping of Things*, 47–51, 206–210.

CHAPTER 6

Restoring Incarnational Mission among the Chinese Christians in Sabah

With incarnational mission as a theological framework, CCS can restore their political identity, commitment to nation-building, and mission with Malay Muslims. This chapter explains how incarnational mission should form the basis for CCS's political identity and nationalism. It also surveys how incarnational mission may restore the missing social dimension of the gospel among the CCS. Lastly, incarnational mission is argued as the theological basis for Malaysian Christians and CCS to engage with the Malays faithfully and effectively.

Embracing an Incarnational and Malaysian Identity

Incarnational mission provides the theological means for CCS to resolve their unsettled political identity. CCS's political identity, much like their understanding of nationalism, is the product of liberal democracy. There is little evidence that the formation of such political identity has gone through sufficient theological deliberation. There is a clear absence of missional and incarnational identity among the CCS. A critique on the present CCS's political identity is necessary for its reconstruction to take place.

The Absence of Missional and Incarnational Identity

Official CCS documents and teachings have never acknowledged *missio Dei* or incarnational mission.[1] CCS retain an older, colonial understanding of "mission."[2] The official reports of the Anglican Diocese's mission committee, for example, have consistently referred to "mission" as an activity of the church. In the Anglican Church in Sabah, years of sending ordinands to theological studies at Bible colleges and seminaries heavily influenced by American Evangelicalism have resulted in an annihilation of the incarnational sacrament in its liturgy.[3] This is evident in the absence of the Anglo-Catholic incarnational theology.[4] Other CCS, apart from the Roman Catholics, suffer similar weaknesses. The Basel Church has no explicit teaching on missional ecclesiology, as revealed in their Chinese General Council monthly bulletins from 2010 to 2017 and other publications.[5] Without incarnational mission

---

1. The lack of theological understanding of an incarnational mission is evident from a review of the various available literatures in the churches studied. The literature review is limited to official documents, especially policy related documents such as general meetings reports and key meetings minutes. Some newsletters and other official church documents are also included. Interviews and surveys are not conducted. Though the published literatures may not articulate CCS theology directly, their theological concepts can be derived and interpreted accurately from the writings and reports. As official publications or reports, these documents have institutional significance and often direct the theology of the church.

2. This is consistent in all the available records – Synod Reports, Clergy and Pastor Conferences from as early as the 1950s, and the publications of the Anglican Diocese of Sabah including the following: Boughton, *Sabah Anglican Diocese*; Koo, *Diocese of Sabah*; Kay Keng Khoo, ed., *Diocese of Sabah Silver Jubilee, 1962–1987* (Kota Kinabalu, Malaysia: Anglican Diocese of Sabah, 1987); Kay Keng Khoo, ed., *All Saints' Cathedral Parish Diamond Jubilee, 1911-1986* (Kota Kinabalu, Malaysia: Anglican Diocese of Sabah, 1986); Luke H. S. Chhoa, *Short Reflections of the Third Bishop of Sabah* (Kota Kinabalu, Malaysia: The Anglican Diocese of Sabah, 2000); Luke H. S. Chhoa, *Renewal, Breakthrough and Growth* (Kota Kinabalu, Malaysia: The Anglican Diocese of Sabah, 1986); Michael Green, *Asian Tigers for Christ: The Dynamic Growth of the Church in South East Asia* (London: SPCK Publishing, 2001).

3. John E. William, "Mission Strategy 1911-1985 with Particular Reference to the Period 1972-1985," in *All Saints' Cathedral Parish Diamond Jubilee, 1911-1986*, ed. Kay Keng Khoo (Kota Kinabalu, Malaysia: Anglican Diocese of Sabah, 1986), 23.

4. For Anglican incarnational theology, see Charles Gore, *Lux Mundi: A Series of Studies in the Religion of the Incarnation* (Eugene, OR: Wipf and Stock Publishers, 2009), digital. For relationship of incarnational theology and incarnational mission, see Langmead, *Word Made Flesh*, 18, 182–187.

5. "Basel Church Chinese General Council Monthly Bulletin Archive," *The Basel Church of Malaysia Chinese General Council*, http://cgcnews.bccmchinese.org/; Wong, "The Basel Christian Church and 130 Years of the History of Sabah: A Survey"; Tsen, *History of the Basel Christian Church*; De Lai Zhang, "The History of Early Hakka Migration in Sabah," *Malaysian Journal of Humanities and Social Sciences* 3, no. 1 (2014): 1–9; Thomas Tsen Lip Tet, "Pastoral Care amidst the Multicultural Context of a Lutheran Church – Basel Christian Church of

or *missio Dei* related in their policies and teachings, CCS lack the missional vocation that undergirds the awareness to live incarnationally.

A Critique on Liberalism as the Basis for Christian Identity in Malaysia

The absence of an incarnational identity among the CCS has contributed to the uncritical acceptance of liberalism as the normative basis for their political identity. CCS defend their Chinese and Christian identities by advocating multiculturalism, and they have, in the process, utilized constitutionalism. However, both constitutionalism and multiculturalism are based on liberalism, and must be rejected as the foundation for Christian political theology and identity.[6]

Common criticisms against liberalism among political theologians are categorized into four areas.[7] First, political theologians reject liberalism's ethical orientation, which is devoid of "the ethical telos or the good."[8] Next, they reject liberalism's understanding that individuals are autonomous and free. Third, they refuse to accept the individual as the sole basis of unit for the government, the state, and civil society. Finally, they are skeptical of liberalism's abstract and universal claims, as they stress the importance of "particularity and historicity." The "aspirations of human rights," for example, may "arise from philosophically dubious perspectives such as individualism and universalism."[9]

Song summarizes the above into two main problems, with the problem of ethics being one and the other three grouped together. Song attributes the problem of ethics as the problem of the absence of the Transcendent. He calls the second problem the centrality of the will, which to Song, is an expression of self-interest of individuals with the freedom defined by liberalism. From a Christian perspective, individuals in liberalism, in their fallen state, perceive

---

Malaysia: A Proposal for a Theological Model of Contextual Pastoral Care in a Diverse Christian Community of Malaysia" (PhD thesis, St. Paul, MN: Luther Seminary, 2006).

6. Both multiculturalism and constitutionalism are based on constitutional liberalism. Robert Song, *Christianity and Liberal Society* (Oxford: Oxford University Press, 2006), Kindle, chap. 2.

7. Elizabeth Phillips, *Political Theology: A Guide for the Perplexed* (London: Bloomsbury Academic, 2012), Kindle, 109.

8. Phillips, *Political Theology*, 109.

9. Phillips, 109.

an incomplete "reality," allowing freedom of their will to be disguised as their chief virtue.[10]

From a slightly different perspective, Stanley Hauerwas's criticism against liberalism is also divided into two parts. First, liberalism has misplaced "the location of authority in the individual," and second, "the establishment of self-interest as the foundation of the social order."[11] Again, the first criticism of Hauerwas is related to the centrality of the will. The second criticism of Hauerwas relates the individuality of liberalism with ethics. Like Song, he questions the focus on self-interest, which resulted from the individual "self" succumbed to its own free will. In sum, political theologians have in general identified the lack of ethical telos and the problem of self-interest as the two main theological problems. Obviously, these two problems are detrimental to the forming of Christian political theology, especially an incarnational one.

An Incarnational Political Theology

Incarnational political theology is political theology assessed and constructed from the perspective and purpose of incarnational mission. Political theology analyzes and critiques political arrangements from God's perspective.[12] It includes considerations on how God would want the church to be involved in the arrangement of power in society. Since incarnational mission is based on *missio Dei*, an incarnational political theology should begin with God's interest rather than human self-interest.

The liberal understanding of individual freedom, its autonomous nature, and the assumption that it is the basic unit of society, resulted in the typical liberal phenomenon of individualism. Self-interest becomes the natural tendency of individuals in the absence of values and ethics, and it is expressed

---

10. Song, *Christianity and Liberal Society*, chap. 7.

11. Phillips, *Political Theology*, 112; see also Stanley Hauerwas and William H. Willimon, *Resident Aliens: Life in the Christian Colony*, Expanded, anniversary ed. (Nashville, TN: Abingdon Press, 2014), Kindle; Stanley Hauerwas, "The Church and Liberal Democracy: The Moral Limits of a Secular Polity," in *A Community of Character: Toward a Constructive Christian Social Ethic*, 1st ed. (Notre Dame, IN: University of Notre Dame Press, 1991), Kindle, chap. 4; Stanley Hauerwas, "A Christian Critique of Christian America (1986)," in *The Hauerwas Reader*, ed. John Berkman and Michael Cartwright (Durham, NC: Duke University Press Books, 2001), 459–480.

12. Peter Scott and William T. Cavanaugh, eds., *The Blackwell Companion to Political Theology*, 1st ed. (Malden, MA: Wiley-Blackwell, 2004), 1.

through the worship of freedom. This has been the driving force of the liberal states, spawning capitalism and the free market.

However, self-interest cannot be the foundation for Christian life; neither should it be the starting point for political theology. For incarnational mission, its main concern is the "interest of God" because *missio Dei* sets the agenda for the church. Since the missional church's vocation is derived from *missio Dei*, Christians' political identity too, must pledge its first allegiance to the *missio Dei*. Christians should understand that their primary identity in the whole business of how God orders the powers in this world is as the representatives of God who seek his interest. Their incarnational identity should direct their political relationships in this world. As they engage with politics, their concerns are no more on their own interests but God's.

Since the church is incarnationally representing the kingdom, it must exhibit kingdom ethics. Christians should relate to the state as incarnational representatives of the kngdom. The church "does not philosophize about a future world; it demonstrates the working of the coming kingdom within this one. Through the authorization of the Holy Spirit it squares up to civil authority and confronts it."[13] Newbigin too advocated a "public faith" which openly challenges the sociopolitical endeavors of the society.[14] On this, Yoder offers an understanding of church-state relation, which is based on an ethicist perspective. Much like Hauerwas, Yoder sees the church's primary responsibility as to seek full restoration to the standard of the kingdom instead of "attacking" the power structure of the present world.[15] This means, the ethics of the kingdom are on display in the eyes of the world, without needing to be actively drafted in any national policy.[16] Instead of Christianizing the society, the church can effectively testify for Christ through its ethics, even as a minority in a pluralist society.[17] This differs from the social gospel,

---

13. Oliver O'Donovan, *The Desire of the Nations: Rediscovering the Roots of Political Theology* (Cambridge, UK: Cambridge University Press, 1999), 217. On this, O'Donovan agrees with Yoder, though they disagree on how the church should relate to the state. O'Donovan approves the Christendom's political arrangement, while Yoder disapproves of it.

14. Jeppe Bach Nikolajsen, *The Distinctive Identity of the Church: A Constructive Study of the Post-Christendom Theologies of Lesslie Newbigin and John Howard Yoder* (Eugene, OR: Pickwick, 2015).

15. Yoder, *Politics of Jesus*, 150–151.

16. Nikolajsen, *Distinctive Identity of the Church*, 194.

17. Nikolajsen, 192.

which puts its locus and first priority in reforming societal system to create an earthly utopia.[18] Contrarily, for incarnational political theology, personal ethics, repentance, transformation of the believers, and the church's witness take precedence. Thus, as a minority under Malay hegemony, CCS should continue their refrainment from direct political involvement. Instead of "Christianizing" the government, they should focus on their incarnational identity as representatives of the kingdom and its ethics.

Yet, prioritizing kingdom ethics and refraining from direct political involvement does not mean a retreat from the public life. With incarnational mission, CCS shall now find their political identity first in their missional and incarnational identity. When Christians rediscover their incarnational identity, they recover their apostolic nature. Self-interest is replaced with mission. The political identity of Christians is for the world, not the self. Hence, the church's life is to be constituted to reflect "God's radical gift-giving for the sake of the world."[19] In true incarnational fashion, the church is "to become as Christ is: for others – and that means ultimately not for the church but for the world."[20] Both "God and church are pointed in a single direction with a single purpose: towards the world in fulsome graced blessing."[21] By breaking free from liberalism, CCS should refuse to be utilitarian and story-less, but demonstrate their commitment for the country. Instead of accommodation or separation, they may adopt Volf's political theology that focuses on engagement, based on a positive understanding of incarnation. In Volf's words, "properly understood Christian identity is not reactive but positive; the center defines the difference, not fear of others, either of their uncomfortable proximity or their dangerous aggressiveness."[22] CCS would incarnationally identify with the local context as Malaysians, while they uncompromisingly witness for the inaugurated kingdom and involve in political engagement with a renewed, incarnational identity.

---

18. Walter Rauschenbusch, *A Theology for the Social Gospel* (Nashville, TN: Abingdon Press, 1990).

19. Brad East, "An Undefensive Presence: The Mission and Identity of the Church in Kathryn Tanner and John Howard Yoder," *Scottish Journal of Theology* 68, no. 3 (2015): 329.

20. East, "Undefensive Presence," 330.

21. East, 330.

22. Volf, *Public Faith*, 95.

Restoring CCS's Incarnational Identity as Malaysians

Incarnational mission gives theological reasons for CCS to embrace their Malaysian identity. As a subset of the Chinese community, CCS share the same resentment against Malay hegemony. However, an incarnational identity requires CCS to dissociate themselves from such sentiments and begin to identify with the Malays and the state. The struggle to build a "Malaysian Malaysia" need not be compromised, but the basis and means of achieving it must change. Instead of grounding their political identity on liberal ideas, they should adopt an incarnational identity and commit to nation-building with the purpose of witnessing for Christ. With incarnational identity, CCS would not be directed by a modernist, charismatic ethos that relegates Christians to a group of non-committed citizens whose focus is on self-interest. Instead of adopting a liberal outlook that focuses on championing for their own rights, CCS would embrace an incarnational identity that demonstrates servanthood and forgiveness.

Being incarnational includes the awareness of being the representative of the kingdom. Hwa Yung stresses the importance for Malaysian Christians to embrace their kingdom identity both as "Christ's body" and as local members of their society in Malaysia.[23] Hwa suggests that Christians in Malaysia should be aware of their kingdom identity without discarding their cultural identity.[24] Referring to the Malaysian Christians, Hwa reminds that

> like the incarnate Christ, our present citizenship of God's Kingdom is lived out within a specific society and culture. All that is good and true within our particular culture is affirmed and accepted by God who created these things in the first place. Hence there is a need for us to recover a clear sense of confidence in them . . . when we truly discover or recover our Christian identity, then the missionary efforts that come from such a discovery will be really effective and fruitful. So long as we are not

---

23. Rowan, *Proclaiming the Peacemaker*, 192–193; Hwa Yung, "Kingdom Identity in Christian Mission," *Mission Round Table – The Occasional Bulletin of Mission Research* 4, no. 2 (December 2008): 2–12.

24. Hwa, "Kingdom Identity," 3.

clear about our own Christian identity, our mission will be less than what it should and could be.[25]

An incarnational identity also allows a church to be a missional presence that identifies with the context. CCS shall commit to Malaysia as citizens – regardless of which nationalism they advocate – and stay on incarnationally to be missionaries. In other words, CCS are truly "local," being at the same time the light and salt for Malaysia. While having a different nation-of-intent, they remain in Malaysia not because the context suits their needs or fulfills their requirements. Instead, they choose to remain in a hostile context, and be "at home." In short, CCS should embrace their Malaysian identity as an incarnational identity. This will result in incarnational presence, which is genuine, rooted locally, and long-lasting.

Restoring the Missing Social Dimension of the Gospel among CCS

Incarnational mission would also restore CCS's social involvement and nation-building. As depicted in chapter 3, Malay hegemony has distanced CCS from the main national discourse. Civil negotiation of the CCS has experienced limitations. As they resolve their confused Malaysian identity with an incarnational identity, CCS may also restore their social involvement and recommit incarnationally to nation-building.

Eschatological and Soteriological Reductionisms

Social detachment of CCS described in chapter 4 is the result of eschatological and soteriological reductionisms. Eschatological reductionism is the reduction and distortion of the "eschatological shaping of the gospel."[26] The sense of God's kingdom manifested through the church has been reoriented to "an individualistic emphasis on the second coming" and the resurrection of the body is replaced by the "Hellenistic concept of the immortality of the

---

25. Hwa, 3.

26. Darrell L. Guder, "The Church as Missional Community," in *The Community of the Word: Toward an Evangelical Ecclesiology*, ed. Mark Husbands and Daniel J. Treier (Downers Grove, IL: IVP Academic, 2005), 118–119.

soul."²⁷ The focus on the reign of God has been shifted to the future. Salvation is misunderstood as attaining immortality after death instead of being a part of the kingdom in the present. Human flourishing is neglected.

A related problem is "soteriological reductionism," which means salvation has been reduced to individual salvation, especially about maintaining the well-being of individual believers. A church affected by soteriological reductionism loses its missional vocation in the face of individual believer's benefits. The church then is "construed as essential for individual blessedness."²⁸ This has become the basis for developmentalism described in chapter 4.

Hwa attributes the root of churches' social detachment in Malaysia to dualism. To Hwa, the ministry of some churches has been divided into the physical and social, outer realm and the private, inner, "spiritual" realm. This is due to the uncritical adaptation of platonic dualism in Christian theology.²⁹ Salvation is "not only for the 'soul' but also for the whole person."³⁰ However, a church which is influenced by dualism will only focus on the soul, neglecting the other aspects of humanity. It lacks "adequate understanding of Christian responsibility to human physical and social needs," and their theology and ethics "tend to be pietistic and personal, emphasizing personal holiness in private lives rather than social righteousness and responsibility in public life."³¹

Actually, "Jesus' message was the inbreaking reign of God, and the early church confessed Him as the one who . . . brings that reign into human reality. He is enthroned and He rules as Savior and Lord, witnessed to by His Church through the empowering of the Holy Spirit."³² In a typical missional church, Christian vocation is understood as "not merely to individual 'savedness,' but to the service of God's mission to bring healing to the nations."³³ Christian witness is apostolic. The church is not a safe enclave "walled off from the world."³⁴ Instead, it is intended to be a community that "lives its message publicly, transparently, vulnerably . . . an assembly set apart to do

---

27. Guder, "Church as Missional Community," 119.
28. Guder, 118.
29. Hwa, *Beyond AD 2000*, 35.
30. Hwa, 35.
31. Hwa, 37.
32. Guder, "Church as Missional Community," 118–119.
33. Guder, 125–126.
34. Guder, 125–126.

public business in view of the watching world."[35] No church can claim to be incarnational unless it witnesses for Christ in public through its tangible sociopolitical presence. By public, it means the church shall be involved in the welfare of the community, engaging with the civil society.

The Diminishing Public Presence of CCS

In general, CCS suffer soteriological reductionism and eschatological reductionism typical of the modern, evangelical churches.[36] A survey of all the monthly bulletins of the Basel Church Chinese General Council from 2010 to 2017 reveals such a pattern.[37] The emphasis on the salvation of souls is prominent while the imminent manifestation of the kingdom through Christians' involvement in the society is neglected. An under-realized eschatology often prevails. The sense of "radical and transforming anticipation, of living hope that profoundly shapes the 'now' of the corporate Christian witness" is absent. The eschatological "now," which gives urgency for a corporate witness has been gradually "reoriented to an individualistic emphasis on the second coming at the end of time."[38] Eschatological reductionism causes CCS to lose their identities as representatives of the imminent kingdom. Hence, CCS neglect their social responsibility, as their focus is only on the individuals and the future. This betrays the meaning of being missional, which goes beyond individualistic salvation and limited eschatology, but also includes addressing social ills as well as locating God's kingdom now, not only in the future. The importance of championing social justice and speaking for the deprived in the present age fades in the shadow of a truncated evangelism. This is evident in CCS's silence during the rampant Islamization under Mustapha and Harris.

Related to this is the underdeveloped theology of human flourishing. Human flourishing has never been a part of the agenda among CCS apart from the Roman Catholics. Church involvement in politics, if any, has always concerned the welfare of the church as an institution, rather than the welfare of all people. There have been efforts to contribute to society and nation-building, especially through education, with mission schools as the prime

---

35. Guder, 126, referring to John Howard Yoder, *Body Politics: Five Practices of the Christian Community before the Watching World* (Nashville: Discipleship Resources, 1992, 1997).

36. Guder, 114–128.

37. "Basel Church Chinese General Council Monthly Bulletin Archive."

38. Guder, "Church as Missional Community," 119.

example. Yet, human flourishing is seldom considered in CCS's theological formulation concerning their sociopolitical involvement.

In the larger context of Malaysia, the need for churches to move from private faith to public relevance and public theology has long been acknowledged. Goh urges the highly privatized Malaysian Christians to "come out of their shells."[39] Their private stance, stresses Goh, is detrimental to their public testimony. The church should "exercise a more caring attitude to issues of national interest and take its rightful place as salt and light."[40] Only by developing theological reflection on key national issues can Malaysian churches project Christian perspectives on national issues, so that the nation would know the Christians' stance.[41] There has been no lacking of Christians' attempts to be sociopolitical participants in Malaysia. However, if ever the Malaysian churches have had any involvement in politics, their participation has been crippled by shallow theology that causes inconsistent practices.[42] Christians in Malaysia remain private in their faith as they are under the deception of developmentalism, enjoying short term economic freedom at the expense of long-term civic rights.

Hwa suggests two ways in which Malaysian Christians can resolve their privatized faith.[43] First, the church should emulate the model of the early church doing good to all people (Gal 6:10), and loving others as themselves (Mark 12:31).[44] Second, Hwa argues that the church will need to develop a comprehensive theology of social engagement.[45] Hwa is aware of the threat of Muslim nationalism, and is critical of the churches in Malaysia, which he describes as

> locked into a Western dualistic theology and unbiblical worldview, dazed and overawed by the changes around . . . yet serenely comfortable in our middle-class existence, Christians

---

39. Goh, "Church and State in Malaysia," 20.
40. Goh, 20.
41. Goh, 20.
42. Lau, "Intimating the Unconscious," 10.
43. With experiences as a pastor, principal of a theological seminary, and a bishop of one of the largest denominations in Malaysia, Hwa's assessment of the Malaysian churches holds great credential.
44. Hwa, *Beyond AD 2000*, 38.
45. Hwa, 39.

have generally withdrawn from the world, like a tortoise into its shell. But could it be that we are lulling ourselves into a sleep of death while the world rolls by?[46]

He stresses the importance of developing a theology for sociopolitical engagement. Only then, the church can show that Christ is relevant and only then the church can make "a significant contribution to the building of a nation that is godly, righteous and just."[47] However, formulation of a sustainable theological framework for the above cannot be accomplished without dealing with the specific situation of Malay hegemony. There has been very little deliberation on the matter of political identity, meaning of good works, and suggestions for Christian social ethics in the context of Malay hegemony.

Not only has the church failed to witness to the world the holistic gospel that is relevant to all, but in Malaysia the church has also been misunderstood. It has become parochial and has disengaged with the larger society. The pseudo-evangelical and charismatic zeal of Christians in Malaysia, which has resulted in some level of revivalism, has been documented by various sources.[48] Yet, what is more alarming is the disparity between church numerical growth and sociopolitical influence.[49]

Embracing the Social Dimension of Incarnational Mission

The remedy for the above would be the outworking of incarnational mission, which includes human flourishing. As the continuous presence of Christ in the form of his body and the representatives of the kingdom, the church understands the fullness of its theology of salvation and eschatology. Salvation is not limited to the private lives of Christians. The goodness of God's grace and God's reign should shape the society that CCS belong to. Their representation of the kingdom will be one that gives hope for the future and instigates transformation in the present. The restoration of the social dimension of

---

46. Hwa, 40.
47. Hwa, 40–41.
48. See Lee and Ackerman, *Sacred Tensions*.
49. As Hwa observes, "Christianity has grown rapidly throughout the Majority World, especially since the end of the Second World War. Yet its social and political impact on the nations does not appear to be commensurate with the numerical growth of the church." Hwa Yung, "The Gospel and Nation-Building in Emergent Nations: An Evangelical Agenda," in *Mission in Context: Explorations Inspired by J. Andrew Kirk*, ed. John Corrie and Cathy Ross (Oxford: Routledge, 2016), Kindle.

the gospel among the CCS will revitalize them to witness to others around them, not just through a pietistic spirituality or rationalistic proclamation of truth but through relationship and the demonstration of kingdom ethics. There will be no separation of the sacred and the secular. Developmentalism would be rejected as CCS incarnationally coalesce their private faith with their social context.

Identification in Civil Negotiations

Incarnational mission also would reinvigorate CCS's civil negotiation by either changing their ways of public negotiations or directing them to alternatives of public negotiations. With a renewed, incarnational identity, CCS would approach civil negotiation not as individuals claiming their liberal rights, but as servants of God who are willing to forgive.[50] They identify with the "others" incarnationally and respect their culture. They would avoid unnecessary public negotiations, and turn to other forms of social engagement that allow them to better express their incarnational identification and kingdom ethics. A restored social dimension of CCS mission would form the theological basis for such social engagement.

Restoring Incarnational Witnessing among the Chinese Christians in Sabah

Restoration of incarnational mission among CCS includes establishing a theological basis to witness to Malay Muslims in the context of Malay hegemony. CCS need to be incarnational to engage Malays in a meaningful way. The limited understanding of evangelism and the theologies surround it must be addressed. A more robust theology of witnessing should be reinstated for incarnational mission to take place.

Limited Evangelism and the Absence of Missional Strategy to the Malays

The absence of incarnational mission among CCS has been manifested through the deficiency in their theology of witnessing and evangelism.

---

50. For Lau's argument on unconditional forgiveness as the "singularity of the church," see Lau, "Intimating the Unconscious," 236–278.

Personal evangelism is understood and carried out as communicating the gospel message through verbal proclamation by targeting individuals, aiming for confessions. Witnessing Christ through other means is neglected.

This deficiency is due to both soteriology and eschatological reductionisms. The objective of evangelism, usually only in the form of proselytism, is to gain more converts and enlist them into the church.[51] The new converts' decision to believe is considered as sufficient "requirement" to become a part of the "Kingdom," which in this case, the "Kingdom" is "going to heaven after their death." The kingdom is pushed to the future and its imminence is lost, and salvation is misunderstood as only the salvation of the soul, safeguarded for a future destiny.

Suffering from the dichotomization and the reductionism above, CCS lose the full meaning of evangelism. Evangelism should be the act of "introducing Jesus Christ to others and inviting them to become partakers in his Kingdom."[52] Yet, with only verbal proclamation and a focus on conversion, the relational aspect of evangelism is often neglected. Instead of introducing Jesus, CCS tend to judge others and call them to repent, focusing only on converting others to a "religion."

Incarnational Mission through Witnessing

As an instrument participating in God's mission, the missional church's main job is to introduce the grace of God.[53] Hunsberger reminds that the church's primary duty is not to build or extend itself institutionally, but to proclaim the grace of God that allows sinners to "receive" the gift of salvation and "enter" into the kingdom.[54] As the beneficiary of the grace of salvation, the church's responsibility is to invite and welcome others as "co-pilgrims" in the journey of being the community of God.[55]

---

51. Bosch distinguishes evangelism from proselytism and church extension. Bosch, *Transforming Mission*, 424–425.

52. Sunquist, *Understanding Christian Mission*, 312.

53. James W. Gustafson, "The Integration of Development and Evangelism," *Missiology* 26, no. 2 (1998): 131–142.

54. Hunsberger, "Missional Vocation," 93, 95.

55. William J. Abraham gives a compelling development of a theology of evangelistic ministry as "initiation into the Kingdom," (*The Logic of Evangelism* (Grand Rapids MI: Eerdmans, 1989)), as cited in Hunsberger, "Missional Vocation," 97.

According to Newbigin, the church represents those who were already reconciled with God and charged with the responsibility to witness to the rest of the human family.[56] Those reconciled are not witnessing due to legalistic obligation, but doing so because they are promised the gift to witness.[57] This gift is through the Holy Spirit, the first fruit (Rom 8:23) and the guarantee (2 Cor 1:22; Eph 1:12). Such deposit or foretaste is also a sign of the kingdom, witnessing the presence of God's kingdom through the presence of the church. So, whoever is chosen is blessed not with merely being a part of the kingdom, but more importantly, is blessed with the gift to bear witness for the kingdom.

So, in witnessing, there should not be any categorization of inclusivist, exclusivist, or pluralist. These categories are the result of soteriological reductionism which reduces the understanding of salvation to mere personal blessedness, expressed in the strict delineation of "who is in" and "who is out" of the kingdom based on culturally limited terms and human perceptions.[58] How others come to know Jesus is God's prerogative and a mystery beyond human categories. The reasoning and "coherent story" of how someone mysteriously came to faith may only come to light afterwards.[59] Newbigin breaks from the conventional classification of the above categories. He is inclusive when it comes to the possibility of salvation of non-Christians apart from explicit faith in Christ, but rejects that other religions play a part in it, and is hence exclusive.[60] The missional church movement too rejects these categories. It prefers the use of "bounded, fuzzy and centered sets" to illustrate the relation between Christ and those who have come to know him. The fact remains that witnessing concerns the church's faithfulness in holistically and faithfully presenting the gospel through being the representatives of the kingdom, rather than speculating who is "saved" merely based on the available doctrinal codes.

---

56. Goheen, *As the Father*, 168–170; Goheen, "Significance of Lesslie Newbigin," 90; Newbigin, *Gospel in a Pluralist*, 84–85.

57. Newbigin, "Church as Witness," 5–6.

58. Samuel Wells, *Incarnational Mission: Being with the World* (Grand Rapids, MI: Eerdmans, 2018), 84–86.

59. Sunquist, *Understanding Christian Mission*, 313. See chapter 10 of Sunquist's book for clarification of the meanings of evangelism and witnessing.

60. Goheen, "Significance of Lesslie Newbigin," 92.

As God is the initiator and the completer of his mission and the church only his instrument, people are saved by God's grace and the church's utmost duty is witnessing. The outcome of evangelism is not the prerogative of the church. It is God who adds people to the church through ways that often go beyond verbal proclamation and rational process. The missional church understands that ultimately, it is the "centered set" approach of witnessing which fits into the biblical teaching of God's sovereignty. Personal encounter with God, repentance, and the individual believer's transformation remain crucial in the "centered set" approach. Yet how each person's journey of salvation unfolds is not speculated, as it is the prerogative of God. Hence, in incarnational witnessing, one submits to God's timing and method for the conversion process to take place, relying on God's power and accepting its mysterious nature. This distinguishes incarnational witnessing from the social gospel that places the locus of the gospel in its version of social engagement that is based on activism. Although the social gospel movement emphasizes the social aspect of the gospel and solidarity with the people, it has a false optimism in the ability of humanity to defeat social ills without the atoning power of the cross and reliance on God.[61] Consequently, it also undermines proclamation, repentance, and believers' personal relationships with God. Incarnational witnessing, on the other hand, maintains the primacy of these aspects of the gospel, while emphasizing God's sovereignty and grace.

By restoring to a fuller understanding of God's sovereignty and his grace in his mission, CCS's perspective on evangelism and mission should undergo fundamental change. Instead of the old church-centric mindset, CCS should embrace incarnational mission. They would focus on identification instead of outcome. This allows the church to break free from a business-minded, modernist way of doing missions.[62] The church's renewed focus on blessing the community releases it from the unnecessary burden of producing

---

61. The social gospel's eschatology is postmillemial and it denies substitutionary atonement. According to the social gospel, the church should continue the struggle of the realized kingdom Jesus initiated against the "evil kingdom" perpetuated by structural social sins. See chapters 18 (on eschatology) and 19 (on atonement) in Rauschenbusch, *A Theology for the Social Gospel*.

62. John William Drane, *The McDonaldization of the Church: Spirituality, Creativity, and the Future of the Church* (London: Darton Longman & Todd, 2000); James F. Engel and William A. Dyrness, *Changing the Mind of Missions: Where Have We Gone Wrong?* (Downers Grove, IL: IVP Books, 2000).

conversions. Such understanding is vital for CCS in the context of witnessing to Muslims. If CCS are the faithful and gracious witnesses for Jesus, God, in his sovereignty, and not the church, will convict and convert people. Instead of operating from the old controlling mindset, CCS must be sensitive to God's leading in its context and seek to participate in what God is doing among the Muslims.[63]

Thus, building a long-term, genuine, and meaningful relationship is as important as the acts of evangelizing, discipling, or teaching. Referring to evangelism in an honor-shame culture, Georges and Baker describe their mission as "completing people's honor, socially and spiritually."[64] Likewise, CCS should approach the Malays who operate with honor-shame culture by honoring them. In the context of honor-shame culture, the church administers social honor and at God's appointed time, the unbelievers will receive "eternal honor," which is God's saving grace.[65] Likewise, by being honoring and authentic companions, CCS can help others to know God and establish an authentic relationship with God.

In conclusion, the ultimate theological solution to the restrictions of evangelism among Malay Muslims is incarnational mission. The incarnation was not merely proclamation. It was a holistic, unreserved outpouring of God to humanity. It produces not a gospel reduced to proclamation by word and judged by confessions. An incarnational approach introduces Christ through identification. The endeavor of witnessing ends at witnessing itself and not at winning a convert. In CCS's context, legal prohibitions will not hinder the encounter between Christ and the Muslims. The primary duty for the church is to be good witnesses that continue the presence of Christ, representing the kingdom and identifying with Muslims.

Summary: Incarnational Identification

Incarnational mission provides CCS an incarnational political identity that resolves their identity crisis that has resulted from the clash of nationalisms.

---

63. Lesslie Newbigin, "Recent Thinking on Christian Beliefs: VIII. Mission and Missions," *Expository Times* 88, no. 9 (1977): 261, as quoted in Hunsberger, "Missional Vocation," 99.

64. Jayson Georges and Mark D. Baker, *Ministering in Honor-Shame Cultures: Biblical Foundations and Practical Essentials* (Downers Grove, IL: IVP Academic, 2016), Kindle, chap. 8.

65. Georges and Baker, *Ministering in Honor-Shame*, chap. 8.

By embracing their incarnational identity as representatives of the kingdom, CCS may recover the fullness of incarnational mission by living out the ethics and expressions of the kingdom in the present, effectively eliminating eschatological and soteriological reductionism. The restored social dimension would eradicate CCS's developmentalism, restore their social responsibility, and motivate CCS to reengage with nation-building. By recovering the fullness of their theology of witnessing, CCS's incarnational mission would find their expression through identification. However, restoring CCS's incarnational mission only rectifies their theology. To engage with Malays and the Malaysian sociopolitical context, CCS need a practical solution, which the following chapter addresses.

Part IV

Proposed Application

CHAPTER 7

Social Engagement as a Preferred Means for Incarnational Mission

This chapter contends that social engagement is theologically and strategically suitable for CCS to apply incarnational mission in the context of Malay hegemony. The first part of this chapter outlines different approaches of social engagement. It is determined that Samuel Well's approach of "being with" fits the theological tenets of incarnational mission. The second part of this chapter argues that social engagement is strategically suitable in the Malaysian sociopolitical situation. Finally, this chapter explains how social engagement can be practically applied by CCS.

Christian Social Engagement in Malaysia

Christians in Malaysia and Sabah acknowledge the importance of social engagement but lack a comprehensive theological framework. Social engagement has been the subject of various theological reflections.[1] However, these reflections are based on a liberal tradition that tends to advocate Western liberal democracy uncritically instead of developing a robust political

---

1. Sadayandy Batumalai, *A Prophetic Christology for Neighbourology* (Kuala Lumpur, Malaysia: Seminari Theologi Malaysia, 1986); Batumalai, *Malaysian Theology of Muhibbah*; C. Sadayandy Batumalai, "The Task of Malaysian Theology," *Inter-Religio* 13, (Summer 1988); Hwa Yung, *Mangoes or Bananas?: The Quest for an Authentic Asian Christian Theology*, 2nd rev. ed. (Oxford: Regnum, 2014), Kindle; Ng, "Christian Social Vision."

theology.² Indeed, there is "an inadequate theological understanding of social engagement."³

An Incarnational Approach of Social Engagement

Social engagement that CCS practice should demonstrate the characteristics of incarnational mission. Various theological approaches are related to social engagement. Yet, not all are based on incarnational mission. Wells' approaches are an exception.

Approaches of Social Engagement

Wells outlines four approaches or "types" of social engagement – namely, the mission of "working for," "working with," "being for," and "being with." By "working for," Christians assume an authoritative and skilled position, and work for those who are in depravity.⁴ The deprived are defined "by their deficit; if they have capacities, these are seldom noticed or harnessed."⁵ The "working with" approach focuses on partnership alongside the needy. The helpers engage the needy "in their own redemption, rather than deciding and operating for them."⁶ Like "working for," this model does aim to resolve some targeted problems, but its primary goal is to harness a collective effort from the beneficiaries in the process. The result and the skills involved are secondary to long-term partnership.⁷ In the "being for" approach, the helper

---

2. For example, Ng's suggestions, such as that of applying the concept of "covenant" by Michael Walzer, presuppose a society which accepts Western liberal tradition where individual right is honored and Hobbs' idea of social contract is assumed. Ng, "Christian Social Vision," 4. The Roman Catholics, on the other hand, have the benefit of a range of theologies since Vatican II that is based on incarnation. The concept of inculturation, evangelization that includes both proclamation and social actions, has been the norm in Roman Catholicism. It is however uncertain if any contextual approach which considers the Malay culture seriously has been developed.

3. Rowan, *Proclaiming the Peacemaker*, 146.

4. Samuel Wells, *A Nazareth Manifesto: Being with God*, 1st ed. (Malden, MA: John Wiley & Sons, 2015), Kindle, 23.

5. Samuel Wells, *Incarnational Ministry: Being with the Church* (Grand Rapids, MI: Eerdmans, 2017), Kindle, 153–159.

6. Wells, *Nazareth Manifesto*, 23.

7. Wells, *Incarnational Ministry*, 159–165.

does not encounter the needy at all. There is no active pursuit of the needy person's interests through "working" or "with."[8]

The "being with" model is where the helpers and the deprived are "equally involved, and the engagement only proceeds if they both continue to be so."[9] It focuses not on "work," but "on stillness, on disposition, on letting the . . . person take the decisive steps and identify the significant issues."[10] Problem solving is not the focus. Acknowledging that most problems in life cannot be resolved through the encounter, this model believes the helper should focus on empowering the deprived through accompanying them, while they attempt to resolve their own problem.[11] The helper would celebrate and enjoy those who are in need. Instead of being judgmental, they recognize the potential of every person.[12] Vitally, the "being with" approach "seeks to model the goal of all relationships: it sees problem-solving as a means to a perpetually deferred end, and instead tries to live that end – enjoying people for their own sake."[13]

Wells' approaches for social engagement are incarnational.[14] He advocates identification by stating that, "We cannot understand, listen to, be taught by, or receive grace from people unless we inhabit their world which we see as valuable for its own sake."[15] He endorses the value of cultures, believing that there is much that Christians may learn from them.[16] Although Well's manifesto lacks an ecclesiological dimension and borders on incarnational theology, the "being with" model, which he himself advocates, corresponds to the criteria of incarnational mission outlined in this study.[17]

---

8. Wells, *Nazareth Manifesto*, 23.
9. Wells, 23.
10. Wells, 23.
11. Wells, *Incarnational Ministry*, 165–174.
12. Wells, 165–174.
13. Wells, 165–174. Keeble similarly stresses the importance of "being with," in his model of "mission-with." See Keeble, *Mission With*, Part 1.
14. Wells, *Nazareth Manifesto*, 27–28.
15. Wells, 29.
16. This is expounded by Wells through the language of grace. Wells, 28.
17. Wells' affirmation of the value of culture, at times, sounds overly optimistic. Wells, 29.

Social Engagement as an Outworking of Incarnational Mission

A "being with" social engagement demonstrates the characteristics of incarnational mission through its emphasis on the imminence of God's presence. Wells concludes that the "being with" model is "the most faithful form of Christian witness and mission, because being with is both incarnationally faithful to the manifestation of God in Christ and eschatologically anticipatory of the destiny of all things in God."[18] Through incarnation, "God is with us" (Matt 1:23) and the Word *is* living *with* us (John 1:14). The words "with" and "is" describe that God is with us now.[19] While the working-for models focus on solving the problems in the world, being-with approaches are "inclined to perceive creation as a gift to be enjoyed."[20] The importance of human flourishing is assumed. Indeed, social engagement that adopts the "being with" approach is incarnational. It exhibits the apostolic movement of incarnation, the presence of Christ, the imminence of the kingdom, and the practice of identification.

Sociopolitical Reasons for Social Engagement

Social engagement is the preferred means to the incarnational mission pf the CCS because it can operate in the sociopolitical context of Malay hegemony while remaining faithful to God's mission. An incarnational social engagement focusing on "being with" the people can help CCS to identity with Muslims. It is an alternative to civil negotiation and a better way of witnessing.

Social Engagement as a Means to Identify with the Malay Muslims' Culture

Social engagement creates social space for CCS to identify with the Malay culture. Unlike Indian Christians who face oppression due to Hindu nationalism, CCS must engage Malay nationalism as a different religious *and* cultural group. CCS do not have the advantage of Indian Christians who share the

---

18. Wells, 23–24.
19. Wells, 3, 7.
20. Wells, 23–24.

same culture with Hindu nationalists.[21] To CCS, an intentional and incarnational effort to understand Malay culture is vital.

The Malays consider themselves the most tolerant people on earth and confess that they would avoid conflict whenever possible.[22] They also consider an unexpected or sudden move as disrespectful because gracefulness is a virtue.[23] This is in contrast with the Chinese who are known to be efficient, especially in business. The Malays are also sensitive to others' perception of themselves.[24] They are shy and not assertive, thus they are often passive and sometimes lack confidence.[25] Correspondingly, the Malay way of criticism is indirect and done by using various similes, sayings, metaphors, figures of speech, folklore, hyperbole, proverbs, and myth.[26] This is due to the Malays' unwillingness in "reprimanding others directly for fear of repercussions and for the reason of not wanting to cause hurt onto others."[27] The Malays recognize that they are more emotional than other ethnicities.[28] Priority is given to the feelings and reputation of those involved when they are confronted with a problem.[29] Securing one's reputation or honor (*nama*) is a means to secure an individual's rank in Malay society. This cultural trend typical of the Malay is still in play today.[30] The pursuit of a good name has caused the Malays to value social reputation over financial status and progress. This, to the pride of Malays, differentiates them from the Chinese whom they despise as pursuing industry.[31]

---

21. Indigenized Indian Christianity is common today. Oddie, "Indian Christians," 353–354. Christian ashram – an effective means to social engagement in the form of indigenous Hindu-patterned community under a guru, was possible in the Indian context as both the Christians and the Hindus share a common culture. M. M. Thomas, *The Acknowledged Christ of the Indian Renaissance* (London: SCM Press, 1969), 332.
22. Asrul, *Malay Ideals*, 150–152.
23. Asrul, 179.
24. Asrul, 181.
25. Asrul, 182.
26. Asrul, 187.
27. Asrul, 186.
28. Asrul, 189.
29. Milner, *The Malays*, 205.
30. Milner, 129.
31. Milner, 239.

By "being with" the Malays, CCS will be able to understand, respect, appreciate, and identify with the Malay culture. CCS may learn from the approach of Matteo Ricci.[32] One of Ricci's greatest gifts

> was a capacity to delight in the company of others. He was able to accomplish so much ... engage pastorally in theological debates with some of the brightest Buddhists of his day, and joyfully welcome thousands of inquisitive scholars to his home – because of the mutual support and companionship of his friends ... the vast majority of his friends were Chinese: the scholars, officials and local people he talked with on his travels and in the marketplace. To recall Ricci's exploits, it is necessary to remember his company of friends.[33]

The core of Ricci's missiology is the belief that one must first befriend others before one introduces Christ, and the essential way to show one's friendliness is by the acceptance of others' culture.[34] It is this attitude which incarnational identification through social engagement looks like, and only with such an attitude would CCS be able to meaningfully and successfully engage with the Malays. CCS's solidarity with the Malays is essential to the Malays' acceptance of CCS, so both the witnessing of CCS and the proclamation of the gospel may have a social space to take place. Similarly, any political negotiations with the Malays would be made easier with identification, especially when there is established relationship built through social engagement.

A confrontational attitude is to be avoided when relating to Malay Muslims, as Malays value indirectness, humility, being accommodating, and politeness.[35] Repeatedly, Muslims in Malaysia have accused Christians

---

32. Samuel Hugh Moffett, *A History of Christianity in Asia,* vol. 2: 1500-1900 (Maryknoll, NY: Orbis Books, 2005), 105–142.

33. Jeremy Clarke, "When West Met East: Matteo Ricci's Cross-Cultural Mission to China," *America Magazine – The Jesuit Review,* 10 May 2010, https://www.americamagazine.org/issue/736/article/when-west-met-east.

34. James V. Schall, "Matteo Ricci's 'Maxims' and Friends – Catholic World Report," *The Catholic World Report,* 19 June 2015, https://www.catholicworldreport.com/2015/06/19/matteo-riccis-maxims-and-friends/. For detailed academic treatment of the subject, see Ana Carolina Hosne, "Friendship among Literati. Matteo Ricci SJ (1552–1610) in Late Ming China," *Transcultural Studies* 1 (2014): 190–214.

35. Suryani Awang, M. Maros, and N. Ibrahim, "Malay Values in Intercultural Communication," *International Journal of Social Science and Humanity* 2, no. 3 (2012): 201–205.

of "challenging their sensitivity."[36] This phrase can only be understood when one acknowledges that among the Malays, there is no separation of objective discussion and personal feelings. Questioning or interpreting the status of Islam in the constitution, in Malay psyche, is not a legal issue but a personal attack. Likewise, evangelism is not just about propagating of a religion but a challenge or attack to the dignity of the Malays. Yet, with incarnational attitude, one can approach the Malays sensitively and indirectly. With loving motive, humility, respect, honor, gentleness, and politeness, CCS may initiate conversations and make contacts. With that, CCS must enter the realm of Muslims, just like Christ entered the realm of humanity.

An Alternative to Civil Negotiation in Nation-Building

Instead of focusing on justice or "just society" which CGA have been emphasizing in their civil negotiation, CCS may focus on building a collective culture, which could only be achieved through social engagement, particularly one which is incarnational. Chinese civil negotiations fail because they focus on protecting their rights. Not only that, these negotiations are offensive to Malays; they only focus on one dimension in the development of a multicultural society – namely, justice and liberal rights. This has further caused Malays to associate Western liberalism with Christianity. Moreover, since they regard Christians as *dhimmi*, they do not agree with the interpretation of rights according to the Christians. Meanwhile, political negotiation concerns power struggles and is often carried out by interest-based and sectarian organizations, hence damaging interethnic relations. Often, it incorrectly projects the image that the Christians seek to Christianize Malaysia. Instead, social engagement that includes both social service and social action would focus on relationship and social ethics, which are crucial for the formation of a collective "Malaysian" culture.

Furthermore, civil negotiations have been ineffective because of the different worldview and culture of Malay Muslims. Civil negotiations, often done in public, risk damaging the reputation of the Malays concerned. Civil negotiations are also often confrontational and project a hostile image of the party that makes the appeals. Social engagement, with its non-confrontational stance, emerges as a preferred means to narrowing cultural differences.

---

36. Majlis Agama Islam Selangor, *Pendedahan Agenda Kristian*, 119.

Civil negotiations that aim to champion CCS's rights are still necessary, but not without the support of social engagement. In the absence of incarnational social engagement, identification will be missing and civil negotiation risks distancing CCS further from the Malays who do not operate with the same worldview.

Practically, CCS should not let the debate about constitutionalism and multiculturalism dominate their encounter with Muslims. Law alone cannot guarantee their constitutional right in the context where the constitution has been modified and interpreted according to the ideology of Malay hegemony. Instead, social engagement is a better way to negotiate their position. Since being incarnational requires Christians to see beyond the existing channels and avenues to "enter into the others," so instead of relying on the political structure for democracy and civil society, CCS may seek to relate directly to the people through social engagement.

A kind of social engagement that connects people at the ground level is social service. Muslims have high regard for the various charity and welfare works of Christians in Malaysia, considering them as effective and admirable, but they are fearful of the influence of the Christian faith they represent.[37] An example of Christian social service is in the form of "diakoinonia spirituality," where connections are made and maintained by Christians to a community in distress through "social relief and development efforts."[38] Samuel helpfully outlines six areas and possibilities where Christians can engage the community – empowerment, services, development, prevention, intervention, and rehabilitation. Examples that correspond to incarnational mission here are services such as support homes, development such as economic development, intervention such as advocacy, and rehabilitation involving care provision and treatment.[39]

For all these, the preferred approach of social engagement remains one, which is "being with" the people. They should go beyond the "working for" and "working with" model. To Lau, "A better approach . . . is for hostile

---

37. Asrul, *Malay Ideals*, 61.

38. Wilfred J. Samuel, "Diakoinonia Spirituality: A Paradigm for Transformation and Empowerment in Practicing Redemptive Christian Social Action," in *Theology and Practice, Contextual Reflections from Asia*, ed. Weng Kit Cheong (Kota Kinabalu, Malaysia: Sabah Theological Seminary, 2013), 316–325.

39. Samuel, "Diakoinonia Spirituality," 320–321.

communities to *find solidarity in suffering*, in the shared anxiety and pain both parties have experienced, albeit differently."[40] This creates amicable social space, a preferred way of engagement compared to civil negotiation that champions one's rights and relies on reasoning. Social services are neutral from sectarian politics or religious allegiance because parties involved are handling common issues. It deals with the masses, not the elites. Thus, social engagement is the practical way for people who advocate both Muslim nationalism and Chinese nation-of-intent to meet at the ground level, without needing to take sides, but to build authentic relationship in the process of engagement.[41]

Social engagement is also the preferred means for Christians to nurture their sense of belonging in Malaysia. Working out "concrete, compassionate ways within the wider community, can serve to strengthen a commitment among Christians to the nation."[42] Rowan acknowledges the potential of social engagement at the ground level among the masses. "In small ways," he opines, "local church communities can plant 'mustard seeds' – acts of social concern in the local community – that contribute to the goal of national unity and *bangsa* Malaysia."[43] Furthermore, through social services, Christians endorse human flourishing and incarnationally demonstrate kingdom ethics. Christians, being the "salt and light" of the world, bring shalom to their society.

A collective culture may also be developed through social engagement, which joins different ethnicities together in social services and social actions. Ownership of this collective culture is shared by all parties as they contribute to it. This is how a country's shared national identity can be formed. In Parekh's words, "while cherishing their respective cultural identities, members of different communities also share a common identity not only as citizens but as full and relaxed members of wider society, and form part of a freely negotiated and constantly evolving collective we."[44] Through the collective culture, members of such society "are likely to feel sufficiently committed

---

40. Lau, "Intimating the Unconscious," 27.
41. Yapp, "'Copyright' Controversy," 155–156.
42. Rowan, *Proclaiming the Peacemaker*, 178.
43. Rowan, 178.
44. Parekh, *Rethinking Multiculturalism*, 238.

to it to live with their differences and not to want to harm its well-being."⁴⁵ With social engagement, CCS will have an avenue to further develop their shared identity even though they may remain deeply rooted in their respective cultures. The process may take time and there will be misunderstandings and frictions, but these are necessary for consolidation and formation of a commonly shared culture. The key is to provide a practical framework for the creation of a space for collective culture in a multicultural society to develop its shared national identity.

Social Engagement as Witness to Muslims in Malaysian Legal Context

Social engagement is also the practical expression of incarnational witness to Muslims. Christians in Malaysia are aware of the risks of propagating the gospel to Muslims. Hence, they knowingly exclude the Malay community from evangelism.[46] Yet, there have been little indication that Christians in Malaysia have developed other alternatives to remain faithful to their mission amid such legal limitation.

With social engagement, witnessing can take place because evangelism is not limited to verbal proclamation. Rejecting eschatological and soteriological reductionism, the incarnational church expands its theology of witnessing. It takes seriously the imminence of God's presence and his kingdom, acknowledging that it is God through the work of the Holy Spirit who convicts people. The kingdom is also more than personal salvation. So, CCS that adopt such an incarnational stance will go beyond simply propagating their "religion." Through social engagement, they find an alternative to engage with Malays beyond personal evangelism.[47]

Witnessing incarnationally through social engagement is crucial because of the hostility that Muslims harbor against Christians and their evangelism. It has been discussed earlier that evangelism – whether openly, contextually, or through the insider movement – have all been considered offensive

---

45. Parekh, 238.

46. Rowan, *Proclaiming the Peacemaker*, 141.

47. This is compatible with the Lausanne Covenant which stresses that evangelism and social responsibility are not mutually exclusive. Lausanne Covenant 1974, point 5, "The Lausanne Covenant," 1 August 1974, https://www.lausanne.org/content/covenant/lausanne-covenant.

to Muslims.[48] They have become more defensive with Christians. In the case where evangelicals are accused of attempting to evangelize Muslims in Malaysia, Christians' response is again based on constitutionalism and multiculturalism. This will only perpetuate the cycle of misunderstanding. Lack of cultural sensitivity would also further distance the disputing groups. Championing the right of evangelism alone will only be counterproductive and should not be the sole strategy for mission in the context of Malay hegemony. Social engagement, on the other hand, does not bring along with it a confrontational manner that is culturally and religiously offensive to Malay Muslims. Its aim is not to proselytize but love. It creates a social space for Christ to be introduced in person. It submits to God's leading and does not see conversion as its prerogative or goal because conversion is the act of God, while witnessing is the duty of the church. Instead of focusing on "work," by "being with" Muslims Christians enjoy the relationship and acknowledge God's goodness in them. Incarnational mission through such social engagement is not subversive like the insider movement. This is consistent with John Stott who rejects any ulterior motive in Christian social engagement. Stott sees social engagement as a natural outcome of Christian love.[49] He rejects using social engagement as a means to evangelism or regarding it as an aspect of proclamation (in the form of a "visible preaching" or "tangible" manifestation of the gospel). Accordingly, this includes the rejection of the social gospel that has the motive of social reform in its version of social engagement. Following Stott, if social engagement is authentic and has no other agenda, CCS should simply and naturally "be with" others and be faithful witnesses who are filled with God's love. Social engagement then becomes a natural space for witnessing to happen. Grounded in incarnational mission, love would be CCS's motive and social engagement its expression.

Through social engagement that focuses on "being with" and identification, CCS may incarnationally bring Christ's presence and the imminence of kingdom ethics into the Malay community. This witnessing does not replace proclamation by words, but it provides first a space for interaction, then the

---

48. Majlis Agama Islam Selangor, *Pendedahan Agenda Kristian*.

49. John Stott, *Christian Mission in the Modern World* (Downers Grove, IL: IVP Books, 2009), 30–32. Stott uses "social action," but his meaning coincides with social engagement or what the Lausanne Covenant calls social responsibility, "The Lausanne Covenant," 1 August 1974, https://www.lausanne.org/content/covenant/lausanne-covenant.

opportunity for the good news to be "demonstrated and described."[50] As explained in chapter 6, this is by no means leaning toward social gospel that undermines the cross, personal encounter with God, and repentance. Unlike social gospel which identifies the locus of the gospel in social action and its goal in social reform, social engagement is merely the space for witnessing to take place. Adopting the "being with" approach, social engagement is not goal-oriented and expects no return.[51] Under the pretext of *missio Dei*, submission to God is prioritized over one's own desired outcome. How life-sharing and friendly encounters in social engagement unfolds is God's prerogative.

Furthermore, with a clear incarnational Malaysian identity, CCS's social engagement with Muslims demonstrates a God and his people that love Malaysia and, more importantly, love Malay Muslims. Instead of having to constantly defend themselves, with good relationship and testimonies, soon it will be others who would testify for Malaysian Christians.

Dialogue as the Practice of Social Engagement

Dialogue is a practical means to incarnational mission in the form of social engagement.[52] Dialogue does not compromise the gospel, yet it ensures that the gospel is presented in God's humble way.[53] Dialogue is a way to engage with others while discerning the timing for prophetic acts.[54] It nurtures one's submission to God's timing of transformation.

To use dialogue as a means for social engagement, CCS may be the providers of social services or social actions. Alternatively, CCS may engage with Malay Muslims through partnership in social services or social actions. Siaw-Fung Chong, in his attempt to propose ways for non-Muslim indigenes to engage with Malay Muslims, advocates partnership in social services and

---

50. Sunquist, *Understanding Christian Mission*, 321.

51. On "no return," see John Stott, *Christian Mission in the Modern World* (Downers Grove, IL: IVP Books, 2009), 31.

52. Batumalai, *Malaysian Theology of Muhibbah*, 113–130; Stephen B. Bevans and Roger P. Schroeder, *Prophetic Dialogue: Reflections on Christian Mission Today* (Maryknoll, NY: Orbis Books, 2011), 59–60.

53. "Bold humility," Bosch, *Transforming Mission*, 501; "prophetic dialogue," Bevans and Schroeder, *Prophetic Dialogue*, 61.

54. Bevans and Schroeder, *Prophetic Dialogue*, 55.

social actions.⁵⁵ This is similar to Wells' proposal where partnership and participation are applied as ways to "being with."⁵⁶

According to Chong, partners in social engagement can "meet each other on multiple podiums – humanitarian concerns, ethno-cultural identity, religious customs, theology, and legal-political positions."⁵⁷ Humanitarian needs are undoubtedly the "greatest common concern" for indigenous Sabahan Christians and Malay Muslims, and Chong believes that efforts must be made to ensure that their cooperation is carried out objectively, free from the ethnoreligious conflicts.⁵⁸

For CCS, a similar approach can be applied. They may partner with Malay Muslims to help the deprived. In the process, they witness for Christ incarnationally. So, social engagement here happens in two places simultaneously. On the one hand, CCS engage with deprived Malay Muslims and on the other hand, they engage with their partners who are also Malay Muslims. Either way, they encounter individuals in person by being with them. Meanwhile, Christ is represented not in the context of religion but through the presence of his disciples.⁵⁹

However, social engagement through partnership may not work naturally between different ethnicities due to past experiences and prejudices. It is well known that mere institutional arrangement, normally through civil organizations, has had little racial integration. For example, civil societies and associations have in general failed to bring different ethnic groups together. Organizations such as Lion's Club and Rotary Club have experienced a limited degree of ethnic integration.⁶⁰ Generally, "more non-Malays than Malays . . . associate with each other in benevolent organizations since people formed some of these social cliques around these bases."⁶¹ The Malays, however, prefer Malay organizations, such as Islamic groups and political

---

55. Siaw Fung Chong, "'Can Allah and Tuhan Not Be One?': Overcoming Issues and Challenges of Muslim-Christian Relations among Malaysian Bumiputera Christians," Spring 2016.
56. Wells, *Incarnational Mission*, 15.
57. Chong, "Can Allah and Tuhan?," 17.
58. Chong, 17.
59. Wells, *Incarnational Mission*, 97.
60. Timothy P. Daniels, *Building Cultural Nationalism in Malaysia: Identity, Representation and Citizenship* (New York, NY: Routledge, 2013), Kindle, 165–166.
61. Daniels, *Building Cultural Nationalism in Malaysia*, 174.

parties.[62] Furthermore, as described in chapter 4, Malay Muslims are suspicious of Christian humanitarian and welfare works, often associating them as Christians' covert methods to evangelize. A more detailed and robust delineation is needed to determine what actual types of dialogue must be involved.

To this end, Chong stresses the need to categorize dialogues into different groups. Chong bases his categorization on the types of dialogues proposed by En-Yu Thu. According to Thu, there are four types of dialogues.[63] The dialogue of life concerns the interaction between people out of necessary interactions in their daily lives. The dialogue of discourse, on the other hand, encourages the parties involved to "probe in-depth knowledge of each other."[64] This kind of dialogue is comparatively technical and complex. It requires "open attitudes and humane approaches."[65] The aim is to "create a community of conversation or a community of heart and mind across religious and racial barriers."[66] The dialogue of spirituality concerns the spiritual. Parties involved would learn each other's worldview, values, and life experiences as they seek ways to enrich each other.[67] The dialogue of action is "an interaction founded on deeds of assistance and concern."[68]

Chong then develops three principles for social engagement in the form of dialogue. First, engagement must be carried out specifically, pinpointing sectors of concern.[69] Chong develops sectors of concern, which are divided into engagements relating to humanitarian works, ethnocultural identity, religious customs, theology, and legal-political position. To him, dialogues should be carried out within these sectors. This is to frame the engagement within a manageable objective.

Next, Chong stresses the importance of both the dialogues of life and action, stating that they "could effectively build up mutual trust and understanding toward meaningful dialogues of discourse and spirituality at a more

---

62. Daniels, 174.

63. En Yu Thu, *Ethnic Identity and Consciousness in Sabah: A Christian Perspective* (Kota Kinabalu, Malaysia: Sabah Theological Seminary, 2010), 198–199. Batumalai has a very similar categorization, see Batumalai, *Malaysian Theology of Muhibbah*, 114.

64. Thu, *Ethnic Identity and Consciousness*, 198–199.

65. Thu, 198–199.

66. Thu, 198–199.

67. Thu, 198–199.

68. Thu, 198–199.

69. Chong, "Can Allah and Tuhan?," 18.

in-depth stage."⁷⁰ Thus, engagement is better if it begins with these dialogues before the engagement progresses into "more sensitive areas."⁷¹ Chong argues, "Before dealing with the anxieties of differences in ethno-cultural, religious, and political issues, it is advisable to achieve mutual trust through cooperation in humanitarian [work] and customs which will promote trust and affection. In other words, strengthen relational ties before dealing with difficult issues."⁷² Chong's idea is reflected in the lives of the common people, as the experience of Egypt shows:

> While the old form of dialogue between elite scholars and religious leaders remains, recent events have added something new. Now ordinary Christians and Muslims in the streets of the nation's cities, towns, and villages have become engaged in a daily dialogue. Having discovered each other, they now eat together, protect each other's homes, and talk about their faiths. This has helped to foster a more open and secure environment in which people can live and work together while pursuing the common good. This democratization of dialogue tends to focus on practical issues of common concern, and it sometimes results in joint action. If it continues, perhaps it will lead to more intentional daily interaction between Muslim and Christian neighbors.⁷³

Similarly, Paul F. Knitter also advocates the "dialogue of action."⁷⁴ Such dialogue does not replace theological dialogue, but it provides a "more effective place to start, or a more practical arena in which to carry on discussions about beliefs and spirituality."⁷⁵ Hence, a new incarnational and missional engagement is possible. To Knitter, such "practical priority . . . is not just ethical – to keep inter-religious dialogue from becoming a tea party; it is also methodological or hermeneutical – to enable inter-religious dialogue to deal with the complexities and obstacles in really *understanding* and *empathizing*

---

70. Chong, 18.
71. Chong, 18.
72. Chong, 18.
73. Tharwat Wahba, "Dialogues in Egypt: From the Elite to the Street."
74. Paul F. Knitter, "Inter-Religious Dialogue and Social Action," in *The Wiley-Blackwell Companion to Inter-Religious Dialogue*, ed. Catherine Cornille (Chichester, UK: John Wiley & Sons, 2013), 124.
75. Knitter, "Inter-Religious Dialogue," 133.

with someone who comes from a totally different world."[76] The "reality of unnecessary suffering" tends to unite followers of different religious communities. Varying in their doctrines and experiences, people of different faiths may, "in differing ways and to differing degrees, feel the necessity of offering some kind of response to the sufferings that drench the human condition."[77] For CCS, they may join with Muslims to participate in such social action.[78]

Concerning the people involved, "engagement should be conducted among the relevant subgroups of particular sector of concern to avoid misconceived generalization that might produce unnecessary distress."[79] Common individuals operate from within their own cultural preferences and are susceptible to ethnocentric and political sentiments. These elements will affect their partnership with others, hampering friendship and goodwill, and damaging their participation.[80] So, more technical issues related to complex and sensitive sectors of concern must be carried out by those who are familiar with the sector. Often, experts are the ones required for a certain sector. For example, dialogue under the sector of legal-political position should be carried out by community and political leaders, intellectuals, and professionals.[81]

Chong also utilizes Burbules's categorization of virtues and emotions for dialogue. Burbules considers dialogue as essentially a social relation, instead of mere "communicative form of question and answer." He considers dialogue an engagement, which involves the virtues and emotions of concern, trust, respect, appreciation, affection, and hope.[82] In dialogue, one relates with the other and identifies with the other's emotions. The totality of this combination of commitment, empathy, and identification is called "concern."[83] Next, "trust" enables parties involved in dialogue to believe in one another and the good will of the dialogue. For trust to develop, parties involved must learn to trust before demanding trust. Eventually, trust will cease to be an issue in

---

76. Knitter, 133, italics added by author.
77. Knitter, 133.
78. Knitter, 134.
79. Chong, "Can Allah and Tuhan?," 18–19.
80. Chong, 18–19.
81. Chong, 18–19.
82. Nicholas C. Burbules, *Dialogue in Teaching: Theory and Practice* (New York: Teachers College Press, 1993), 35–41.
83. Burbules, *Dialogue in Teaching*, 36. This corresponds to Wells' "presence" and "attention" combined. Wells, *Incarnational Mission*, 14.

the relationship. Parties involved in dialogue would also take risks to allow trust to grow in their relationship, and in the process, learn to courageously expose themselves.[84] Another emotional factor in dialogue is "respect." Respect sustains a relation because it overcomes all differences and compels one to humbly learn from another regardless of differences in background.[85] It prevents assertion of authority and exploitation. Another factor is "appreciation," which grows naturally in dialogue.[86] It should be encouraged because appreciation improves connectedness of conversation and quality of dialogue.[87] As dialogue is commonly entered with an expectation, hope inevitably follows. So, it is vital to keep dialogue alive, amid times of difficulty.[88] In sum, Chong incorporates Burbules's emotional factor for dialogue while referring to Besley and Peters.[89] As an educationist, Chong helpfully integrates dialogue for education to social engagement. Combining the thoughts of Thu and Burbules, Chong proposes a model – The Multiple Plenary Model for Interfaith and Intercultural Relations (see table 1 on the following page).[90]

With its focus on "being with" and considering its other incarnational attributes, social engagement, which this present work suggests, belongs to the first category – the humanitarian sector of concern. The approach of dialogue in this section emphasizes the incarnational presence of Christians in the common social, educational, economic, and welfare sectors where they are simply a part of the community. As Christian humanitarian and welfare organizations are deemed suspicious by the Muslims, Christians should take every opportunity to engage with Muslims informally and genuinely through their involvement in various activities in the society. Instead of organizing their own, CCS may join existing humanitarian or welfare services. They may simply choose "being with" the Muslims who are already there, instead of only "working with" or "working for" them. "Being with" that includes stillness, incarnational presence, and insider identification, is the antidote to the

---

84. Burbules, *Dialogue in Teaching*, 37–38.
85. Burbules, 38–39.
86. "Delight" and "enjoyment" in Wells, *Incarnational Mission*, 14–15.
87. Burbules, *Dialogue in Teaching*, 39–40.
88. Burbules, 40–41.
89. Tina (AC) Besley and Michael A. Peters, "Intercultural Understanding, Ethnocentrism and Western Forms of Dialogue," *Analysis and Metaphysics; Woodside* 10 (2011): 89–90.
90. Chong, "Can Allah and Tuhan?," 19.

suspicion caused by activism. "Humanitarian" here is not limited to formal humanitarian activities such as social services. It includes the necessary interactions of people in their daily lives. For example, the daily encounter with each other in workplaces or in the market. This "Dialogue of Life" is the most effective and suitable dialogue for CCS in the context of Malay hegemony. With "Dialogue of Life," the results would be emotive in nature, involving affection, trust, and concern. These are values that an incarnational mission, expressed through identification with the people, would pursue.

Table 1. The Multiple Plenary Model for Interfaith and Intercultural Relations

	Sector of Concern	Dialogue Approach	Relevant Subgroups	Anticipated Results
Greater common concern	Humanitarian – social and economic development, education, welfare, etc.	Life and action	Individuals, local community	Affection, trust, concern
	Ethnocultural identity	Life, action, discourse	Individuals, local community, intellectuals	Respect
	Religious customs	Life, discourse	Individuals, local community, religious experts, intellectuals, professionals	Respect, appreciation
	Theology	Discourse, spiritual	Religious experts, intellectuals, professionals	Respect, appreciation
	Legal-political position	Action, discourse	Community and political leaders, intellectuals, professionals	Hope

This table, while originally developed for indigene Christians and Malay Muslims, is applicable to the CCS.

Dialogue of action is especially relevant in social action. Through social engagement, CCS might engage with Muslims through meaningful partnership and genuine relationships. CCS must avoid the mistake of Indian Christians who stayed indifferent to the noncooperation and civil disobedience movement led by Gandhi.[91] In recent years, many Malaysian Christians have responded to the call to speak out for Clean and Fair Election (BERSIH). They have also spoken against corruption and actively involved in ending the sixty-year rule of Barisan Nasional and UMNO through electoral democracy. It is a kind of social action where dialogues happen among the masses. CCS must not miss such strategic opportunities to engage with the Malay majority.

By "being with" the people and identifying with them through dialogues of life and action, CCS incarnationally created a space for the gospel to be conveyed through their witness. Social engagement becomes the sphere for faithful witnessing. It eliminates suspicion and prejudice, opens closed doors, and "gain[s] a hearing for the Gospel."[92] Unlike tools or methods for evangelism, social engagement is incarnational – a natural expression of the presence of Christ through his church. It may not begin naturally, but it certainly can be developed through action. As the church involves in social engagement, it will become more naturally incarnational. Strategically, by focusing on the "humanitarian" sector, CCS avoid problems related to civil and public negotiation. Civil and public negotiations belong to sectors of concern that suffer limitations due to Malay hegemony. Civil negotiations are under the "legal-political position" sector. Interfaith dialogue belongs to the "theology" sector. These sectors of concern are important, but they do not result or intend to result in affection, trust, and concern. Instead, due to the clash of nationalisms, these encounters have created unnecessary bitterness. They are also limited to experts, professionals, and intellectuals. While these groups often hold moderate views, they do not represent the majority. Their influence in the wider society is also uncertain.

Summary: Incarnational Mission in Practice

Social engagement is the preferred expression of incarnational mission because it encapsulates incarnational identification through its emphasis on relational and emotive aspects. This characteristic is especially obvious when

---

91. Oddie, "Indian Christians," 363.
92. "LOP 21 – Evangelism and Social Responsibility."

social engagement is practiced through the "being with" approach and via dialogues. As a result, social engagement demonstrates its unique suitability for the Malay hegemony context, being the alternative to stereotypical civil negotiations and means to identify with Malay Muslims. Subsequently, it paves the way for CCS to remain faithful in their witnessing to Malay Muslims. Dialogue of life and action is considered the best practice among all the approaches of social engagement. It embodies the characteristics of incarnational mission and the qualities to overcome the various obstacles CCS face in the context of Malay hegemony.

Summary and Conclusion

This study has argued that social engagement is the preferred means for incarnational mission in the context of Malay hegemony. The following sections summarize the arguments presented in this study. Finally, a two-fold conclusion marks the end of this study.

Summary

This work begins with a description of the ministry context of the CCS by highlighting that their cultural and historical background did not prepare them for Malay hegemony. Arriving as immigrants, CCS had a monocultural beginning. They lacked integration with other cultures. Yet, CCS eventually committed to British North Borneo as their new home. They gradually but effectively relinquished their immigrant identity in the period between the end of the Second World War and 1963. British colonists and missionaries from the West enjoyed a corporative and amicable relationship with CCS, as CCS too had been encouraged by various immigration and governance policies of the British. Settling down as citizens of British North Borneo and with their affinity with the British, their reluctance to participate in the formation of Malaysia is understandable. The formation of Malaysia, and then the intrusion of Malay hegemony, resulted in the antagonism of the CCS toward Malay Muslims.

The Malays, on the other hand, experienced a process of ethnogenesis that saw Islam taking an increasingly important role. Instigated by the foreigners' presence – especially the Chinese and the British – Malay self-determination eventually leaned toward Islam as the bedrock of their nationalism. This process took place at the expense of Malay royalty, which by the nineteenth century, had lost much of its prestige, respect, and influence. As Islamism joined forces with the *bangsa* movement, a tension between two forces between Malay-Islam and foreigners (Chinese and British) was formed prior to Malaya's independence in 1957.

The independence of Malaya was followed by differences in the interpretation of the country's constitution, with the Malay interpreting it as supporting Malay nationalism, and non-Malay, Malaya (and later, "Malaysia") nationalism. With Singapore that supported Malaysian nationalism expelled, and after the riot of 13 May 1969, Malay nationalism dominated all policies in Malaysia. Under the emergency rule and the powerful force of the Malay fundamentalists, Malay nationalism was legitimized and promoted as the defining philosophy for nation-building. The NEP created Malay supremacy through economic affirmative action and Islamic values were incorporated into a deliberately planned national culture policy.

As Malay nationalism became the dominant nationalism, the Chinese attempted to challenge it with Malaysian nationalism. While struggling to integrate into the main Malaysian nation-building process, Malaysian Chinese, including the CCS, refused to compromise their cultural distinctness. Enculturation to Malay culture and Islam are rejected. They would persist with a cultural identity, which is not only distinct from Malay Muslims, but an antithesis to Islamist ideology. Meanwhile, Christians are victimized as they are accused as a threat to Islam.

When Malay nationalism evolved into Malay hegemony, the clash of nationalisms intensified. Having traditionally shunned Islam, the Chinese resentment toward Malay hegemony increased, causing them to hold on to their version of nationalism more tightly. For CCS, Malay nationalism robbed them of North Borneo where they enjoyed equality and religious freedom. Now they are considered a dhimmitude. Their reluctance to actively participate in nation-building is understandable because Malaysia today is not the one that they envisioned. The commitment of Malaysian Chinese and CCS to the country has been shaken, and their "Malaysian" identity too, is unsettled by the clash of nationalisms.

As Malaysian Chinese advocate Malaysian nationalism through political and civil negotiation, CCS too have been engaged in various civil negotiations. It has been proven over the years that the effectiveness of their negotiations is limited. Meanwhile, as there is no apparent comprehensive and overarching theological basis for political engagement, the Malaysian Chinese and CCS have been adopting liberalism as their political theory. Their multiculturalism and constitutionalism are fundamentally expressions of liberalism, albeit often being decorated with ad-hoc Christian ideas and scriptural references.

Meanwhile, CCS's missional engagement to Muslims has been interrupted. With greater restriction on evangelism, there is no clear theology or strategy on how CCS may remain faithful in their duty to witness to Muslims. So, the CCS suffer from two detachments today. First, they are detached from nation-building. Their citizenship and political identity, devoid of a nationalism that they envision and hope for, do not give them reason to commit to the country. Second, their missional engagement with Muslims is limited by Malay hegemony. These are the ministry challenges that the CCS face in their context.

This study then argues for incarnational mission as a theological framework that CCS should adopt to resolve their two "detachment" problems. To be incarnational corresponds to being missional. An incarnational mission includes the primacy of *missio Dei*, the continuous presence of Christ in the life of the church, the kingdom's imminence effects of ethics and hope, and identification with people. Application of incarnational mission is explored in chapter 6. CCS's reliance on liberalism as the basis for their political identity is critiqued and rejected. An identity based on an incarnational political theology is proposed. Through this renewed identity, CCS would base their struggle on the *missio Dei*, bringing the presence of Christ and the shalom of the new kingdom with them, as they identify with the very group that rejects their nationalism and treats them as *dhimmi*. As a minority, Christians may tend to retreat into their ghettos and cease to engage with the dominant sociopolitical and religious forces that at times persecuted them. Yet, as they restore their incarnational identity and mission, CCS should confidently engage with their sociopolitical surroundings.

The restoration of incarnational mission in CCS will also equip them with a holistic theology of evangelism that recognizes the importance of witnessing and God's prerogative in mission. This allows the CCS to engage Malay Muslims confidently and purposefully, with the intention to witness for Christ. All in all, CCS's sociopolitical and mission engagements should be incarnational because they operate on the basis of *missio Dei* and a missional ecclesiology. These theological reflections in chapter 6 connect incarnational mission with the ministry challenge that CCS face. As the problems of identity and theology of CCS are now resolved, social engagement is proposed to be the application that carries out CCS's incarnational mission in practical terms.

Conclusion

The conclusion of this study can be described in two interconnected points. Social engagement is the preferred means for incarnational mission in the context of Malay hegemony because of the following two arguments.

First, social engagement is the preferred practice for incarnational mission as it fulfills the characteristics of incarnational mission, especially in the form of "being with." Social engagement is also a true character of the missional church with its social dimension restored. Social interaction in a foreign realm is a basic criterion of incarnation. Social engagement encapsulates this motive and effect of incarnational mission as it carries with it the presence of Christ through the life of the church, kingdom ethics and hope, and identification with the people – all based on the concept of *missio Dei*.

Incarnational mission is needed because it is the theology that can restore CCS's political identity, social responsibility, and concept of witnessing. It is incarnational mission that gives CCS a purpose and identity to be "incarnated" in Malaysian society. Through incarnational mission too, CCS find a theological basis to engage with their sociopolitical context with a holistic understanding of the gospel. A renewed identity and sociopolitical involvement would deliver them from a self-centric spirituality that is devoid of missional vocation and the ethics of the kingdom. Moreover, only with incarnational mission, would CCS find impetus to identify and stand in solidarity with people. Only with these characteristics of incarnational mission would a holistic understanding of evangelism be developed, where the social dimension of evangelism, particularly witnessing, is not neglected.

Specifically, incarnational mission is the antidote for theological reductionism and an incomplete understanding of the gospel. Its first contribution to CCS would be the restoration of a missional ecclesiology based on the *missio Dei*. Much of Malaysian and Sabah Christians' concerns are focused on how to survive as Christian institutions. This work suggests that the church's identity is missional instead of being limited to "religious institutions." The focus is not survival but faithfulness to the *missio Dei* in this context incarnationally, as Malaysians and as witnesses to Malay Muslims.

Second, social engagement is also the preferred option for mission in the sociopolitical context of Malay hegemony. As an expression of incarnational mission, social engagement is the means to identify with Malay Muslims and their culture. It carries the characteristic of incarnational identification.

It opens doors and opportunities for natural and genuine relationships to flourish. It is also an alternative to participation in nation-building, considering the various limitations of civil negotiation. Even the limitations to propagate the Christian faith cannot stop social engagement from witnessing to the gospel of Christ among Muslims. Social engagement eliminates the "hostile" image of Christianity in Malaysia, which to the Muslims, is only another religion trying to convert them. Social engagement, with a holistic understanding of evangelism that does not compromise the essence of gospel proclamation, allows a sustained, loving, and genuine relationship to provide a space for Jesus to be introduced through witnessing. Understanding the logic of *missio Dei*, CCS may submit the outcome of such witnessing to God. The gospel, then, is neither reduced to verbal confession, nor restricted to the institutional church; but the focus will be on Christ's presence and the imminence of the kingdom in the community. Furthermore, with the poor and deprived around the church, social engagement is not only an effective way to witness for Christ through identification, but the natural expression of the incarnational mission that concerns those who are in need.

Strategically and practically, social engagement can be carried out through dialogues. This study identifies dialogue of life and dialogue of action as the forms of dialogue that best represent the incarnational, "being with" social engagement. The dialogue of life is especially suitable. Through common concerns and daily interactions, witnessing becomes a part of life and this also builds a strong relational foundation for effective civil negotiation. Also, equally strategically, CCS might inspire the KDM and other Christians in the Peninsular to be incarnationally involved in social engagement. Minority Christian communities that face hegemonic oppression elsewhere might also consider the proposal of this work. Christian mission continues amid hegemonic oppression, for God's incarnational mission continues through his Church that brings hope. CCS and other minority churches must enter into the various uncertainties they face incarnationally and courageously through social engagement. For "the fear of Caesar" must not obscure "the wonder of God."[1]

---

1. Wells, *Incarnational Mission*, 201.

Epilogue

This epilogue is added as a response to the developments in Malaysia after the completion of this work. This work was originally a dissertation completed in October 2018. A new political alliance that includes parties which support "Malaysian Malaysia" and moderate Islam overthrew UMNO and its allies in May 2018. Yet, this alliance, known as Pakatan Harapan (PH) or Alliance of Hope, was toppled in less than two years. A new government (formed by Perikatan Nasional, PN, or National Alliance) was formed by a coalition of Malay leaders across all Malay political parties and a few other parties representing the minorities. Old enemies such as UMNO and PAS partnered with the main Malay parties and splinter groups from the PH to form PN, purportedly to defend the Malays and Islam that are "under threat." Again, Malay hegemony is proven to be resilient and formidable.[1] A few incidents from 2018 to 2020 further strengthen the case.[2]

Rejection of Multiculturalism

In November 2018, under the new, supposedly moderate PH government, Malaysia withdrew a pledge to ratify the International Convention on the Elimination of All Forms of Racial Discrimination (ICERD), allegedly

---

1. Some have begun to use the term "Malay-Muslim hegemony," and concede to its supremacy although stating its demise at first (prior to the 2020 coup). See Mohamed Nawab Mohamed Osman and Edmund Terence Gomez, "Breaking Malay-Muslim Hegemony – Patronage, Factionalism and Feuds in the 14th Malaysian General Election," *The Round Table* 109, no. 2 (2020): 116–125.

2. Surely, the sociopolitical changes that took place were the result of political struggles with vested interests, but again, without needing to assess how genuine some of these Islamic rhetoric are, one can still discern the rationale and ideological traces of Malay hegemony within.

"following backlash from groups who fear it could dilute privileges for majority ethnic Malays."[3] ICERD resolves

> to adopt all necessary measures for speedily eliminating racial discrimination in all its forms and manifestations, and to prevent and combat racist doctrines and practices in order to promote understanding between races and to build an international community free from all forms of racial segregation and racial discrimination.[4]

Apparently, the ICERD is claimed to be against Article 153 of the Malaysian Constitution which gives special privileges and status to the Malays. Ratifying ICRED also means a betrayal of the "social contract" between Malays and non-Malays.[5] The failure of the PH government to ratify ICERD is a setback for Malaysian nationalism and a victory to Malay nationalism. It is another indication of the influence of Malay hegemony and the rejection of multiculturalism.

The PH government's failure to harness support from the majority Malay Muslims is also related to their perception of multiculturalism. The Malay parties that partner with the Democratic Action Party (DAP) were accused of collaborating with the "enemy of Malays and Islam." DAP is a secular party that fights for Malaysian Malaysia. Cooperation with DAP is seen as a sign that Anwar Ibrahim, the de facto leader of the PH has succumbed to "liberal political ideology."[6] Anwar is accused of being "liberal" because he is open to discuss about multiracialism and liberalism.[7] The situation is aggravated by

---

3. "Why Malaysia Backpedalled on ICERD Ratification," *NST Online*, 2018, https://www.nst.com.my/news/nation/2018/11/434078/why-malaysia-backpedalled-icerd-ratification.

4. UN Human Rights Office of the High Commissioner, "International Convention on the Elimination of All Forms of Racial Discrimination," *OHCHR*, https://www.ohchr.org/en/professionalinterest/pages/cerd.aspx.

5. "Why Malaysia Backpedalled on ICERD Ratification."

6. Malaysiakini, "Pengertian liberal menurut Anwar (The Definition of Liberal according to Anwar)," *Malaysiakini*, 2020, https://www.malaysiakini.com/news/520053.

7. Anwar was the only key Malay leader who was not invited to the Malay Dignity Congress, attended by literally all Malay leaders, including heads of political parties. See Mohamed Nawab and Gomez, "Breaking Malay-Muslim Hegemony," 122; Adib Povera and Arfa Yunus, "Five Resolutions Presented at Malay Dignity Congress," *NST Online* (Shah Alam, Malaysia, 6 October 2019), online edition, https://www.nst.com.my/news/nation/2019/10/527514/five-resolutions-presented-malay-dignity-congress; Mahathir Mohamad, "Orang Melayu tidak percaya Anwar sebab tubuh Parti Liberal (Malays Distrust Anwar because He Establishes Liberal Party),"

the fact that Anwar's party is a part of Liberal International, a clear sign of its departure from the main Malay hegemony narrative.[8] Three times since 1998, the political experiment of cooperation between the Islamists and secularists led by Anwar has failed.[9] Every association with parties that support multiculturalism has been punished.

Rejection of Moderate Islam

The collapse of the PH government also signifies, to some extent, the rejection of moderate Islam in Malaysia. Amanah and the People's Justice Party (Parti Keadilan Rakyat, PKR) which epitomize moderate Islam were rejected. The moderates do not necessarily support Malaysian-Malaysia, but at least they are more willing to work as equal partners with the non-Muslims. Their defeat signifies a significant setback to the non-Muslims. The defeat is not just a rejection of inclusiveness *(Islam Rahmatan lil-Alamin)*, but also the rejection of *maqasid Sharia* and *fiqh Malaysia* ("interpretation of Islamic jurisprudence within a Malaysian context"). Those who hold these views are marginalized and even persecuted.[10]

After the defeat of the PH government, its supporters have reverted to a more aggressive stance, acting as harsh critics of the new PN government. While this change might be politically motivated, it has renewed the old competition of pushing one another to be more "Islamic." Amanah members, for example, have since been critical of the PN government on Islamic matters, forcing the PN government to implement policies and laws which are

---

interview by Baharom Mahusin et al., *Sinar Harian*, 12 March 2020, https://www.sinarharian.com.my/article/73526/BERITA/Nasional/Orang-Melayu-tidak-percaya-Anwar-sebab-tubuh-parti-liberal. Conservative and Salafism-oriented Muslims have accused Anwar as supporter of liberalism and multiculturalism over the years. AIDC, "Anwar Ibrahim & Projek Islam Liberal Malaysia?," *AIDC* (blog), 18 April 2009, http://aidc-editor.blogspot.com/2009/04/anwar-ibrahim-projek-islam-liberal.html. The AIDC site is clearly biased against Anwar, but it does provide some hints to credible sources such as Anwar Ibrahim, "Universal Values and Muslim Democracy," *Journal of Democracy* 17, no. 3 (2006): 5–12. PAS' accusation is especially pertinent. Muhammad Mujahid Ir Hj Mohammad Fadzil, "Liberalism Yang Terancang," *Harakahdaily*, 4 February 2020, https://harakahdaily.net/index.php/2020/02/04/liberalism-yang-terancang/.

8. "Parti Keadilan Rakyat (PKR)," *Liberal International*, https://liberal-international.org/members/pkr_malaysia/.
9. Ahmad Fauzi, *Islamisme Dan Bahananya*, 22.
10. Ahmad Fauzi, 24.

deemed to be more "Islamic." A recent example is the call for a blanket ban on alcohol sale and manufacturing.

Discussion on dhimmitude was brought to the open when PH was in power. One of the state mufti's open accusation of DAP as *kafir harbi* (infidels who belong to the realm of war) was reexplored and received endorsements from other Islamic scholars.[11] *Kafir harbi* are understood as non-believers who constantly oppose divine revelation and need to be subdued or conquered.[12] Unlike the *dhimmi*, these are infidels who are excluded in the realm of Islam and are outrightly enemies of Islam. DAP was deemed *kafir harbi* because of their constant opposition to the implementation of Islamic law in Malaysia and their secular agenda.[13] The use of *kafir harbi* implies the legitimacy of another related concept – the dhimmitude. The minister in the prime minister's Department for Religious Affairs, Mujahid Yusof Rawa disagreed, arguing that dhimmitude and the category of *kafir harbi* are only relevant in the context of Islamic rule in the past where the world was perceived as divided into *dar al-Islam (Darul Islam)* and *dar al-Harb (Darul Harb)*. These categories are not relevant in a nation-state governed by a constitution.[14] Since *jizya* is not paid, Mujahid Yusof Rawa argues there is no dhimmitude. Others have since refuted Mujahid's arguments by stressing the symbolic nature of the *jizya*.[15] The absence of *jizya* does not change the requirement for non-Muslims to

---

11. "Mufti Anggap Tak Salah Rujuk Bukan Islam Sebagai 'Kafir' (Mufti Consider Referring Non-Muslims 'Kafir' Appropriate)," *MYNEWSHUB*, 5 March 2019, https://www.mynewshub.tv/utama-sensasi/mufti-anggap-tak-salah-rujuk-bukan-islam-sebagai-kafir/; Bernama, "No Retraction or Apology over Kafir Statement Says Pahang Mufti," *NST Online* (Kuantan, Malaysia, 27 June 2016), https://www.nst.com.my/news/2016/06/155157/no-retraction-or-apology-over-kafir-statement-says-pahang-mufti.

12. John L. Esposito, ed., "Kafir," in *The Oxford Dictionary of Islam* (Oxford University Press, 2003), https://www.oxfordreference.com/view/10.1093/acref/9780195125580.001.0001/acref-9780195125580-e-1229; Mohammad-Reza Djalili, Elizabeth Keller, and Matthew Gray, "Dār Al-Ḥarb," *The Oxford Encyclopedia of the Islamic World*, Oxford Islamic Studies Online, http://www.oxfordislamicstudies.com/opr/t236/e0177.

13. "Mufti Anggap Tak Salah Rujuk Bukan Islam Sebagai 'Kafir' (Mufti Consider Referring Non-Muslims 'Kafir' Appropriate)."

14. Nur Hasliza Mohd Salleh, "Mujahid- Jangan Ada Lagi Gelaran Kafir Harbi, Zimmi (Mujahid – Don't Use the Terms 'Kafir Harbi, Dhimmi')," *Free Malaysia Today*, 24 July 2018, https://www.freemalaysiatoday.com/category/bahasa/2018/07/24/mujahid-jangan-ada-lagi-gelaran-kafir-harbi-zimmi/; Yayasan Dakwah Islamiah Malaysia, "Tiada Lagi Gelaran Kafir Harbi, Zimmi Dalam Sistem Kewarganegaraan (No More Kafir Harbi, Dhimmi Titles in System of Citizenship)."

15. Muhammad Firdaus, "Kafir Harbi-Zimmi Perlu."

submit to Islamic rule. In fact, the Islamic worldview that consists of *dar al-Islam* and *dar al-Harb* and the obligation of *jihad* are nonnegotiable. The heart of the issue is the need for the Muslims to rise up and defend the sovereignty of Islam. Muslims who are not overly concerned with the terms agree with the underlying rationale of those who use the polemic terms of *kafir* and *harbi*.[16] In any case, while it is not normally discussed in the open, the concept of dhimmitude is deeply rooted in Malaysia. Moderates such as Mujahid may refer to technical difficulties to refute the possibility of dhimmitude in the "modern" state of Malaysia. Yet, this just implied that if an "Islamic" state is established, dhimmitude is technically valid. Again, one must remember, most moderates in Malaysia are only Islamists who take the gradual and long-term approach toward the full implementation of Islamism.

Non-Muslims under Malay Hegemony

A few incidents illustrate the plight of the non-Muslims even during the time of the purportedly moderate PH government. First, the attempt by the Ministry of Education to introduce Jawi writing to vernacular primary schools. This enraged the non-Muslims, especially the CGA, represented by the Dong Jiao Zhong.[17] Their response was direct: "We are not anti-Jawi or anti-Malay or anti-Islam. There is no issue if students are asked to learn all cultures. But we don't want to see the gradual Islamization of Chinese schools and the marginalization of [the Board of Directors]."[18] This statement reveals the sentiment of fear. Apart from their concern of Islamization, the attempt of the Ministry to bypass the school board signifies a hegemonic attitude toward the minorities. In other words, this is another case of Malay hegemony attempting to obliterate multiculturalism.

Second, fear and reactions toward Christians' alleged threats to the country and Islam continue. The enforced disappearance of a Christian pastor by state agents made headlines and shook the Christian community in 2017. Pastor Raymond Koh was suspected of proselytizing Muslims through the

---

16. Muhammad Firdaus.

17. United Chinese School Committees Association of Malaysia, UCSCAM, and The United Chinese School Teachers' Association of Malaysia, UCSTAM.

18. Wah Foon Ho, "Feature: Spotlight on Jawi Issue," *The Star Online*, 22 December 2019, https://www.thestar.com.my/news/focus/2019/12/22/feature-spotlight-on-jawi-issue.

NGO he founded, Harapan Komuniti.[19] Even with all the evidence and involvement of human rights NGOs, there has been little progress from the investigation even during the PH government's term. The failure of civil negotiation is evident. This incident demonstrates the sensitivity of Malaysian Muslims toward evangelism. Meanwhile, the DAP was again accused of attempting to "Christianize" Malaysia. Muslim NGOs have successfully utilized this false accusation to influence the Malays, making DAP a liability to the Malay parties in the PH government.

Third, the appointment of non-Muslims in key government positions has triggered waves of disapproval from the conservatives. In the context of Malay hegemony, key leadership positions of the country must be reserved for Muslims. Religion instead of meritocracy determines one's qualification as a leader. The appointment of Christians, such as Richard Malanjum, as chief justice, Tommy Thomas as attorney general, and Liew View Keong as de facto law minister enraged certain Muslim groups. Allegedly, "the legal rights of Muslims are now under threat following the appointments of non-Muslims into top legal positions in the country."[20] This is yet another expression of Malay hegemony, operating with the same Islamic worldview that gives birth to the concept of dhimmitude. With this worldview, only Muslims are qualified to assume key leadership positions in the government.

Conclusion

Obviously, Malay hegemony has intensified albeit with a change to a purportedly more moderate government after the 14th General Election (GE14) in

---

19. "The pastor was at the center of controversy in 2011 after Harapan Komuniti was accused by the Selangor Islamic Religious Department (Jais) of proselytizing Muslims, following a raid at a thanksgiving and fundraising dinner at the Damansara Utama Methodist Church. Later, a box containing two bullets and a note in Malay written in blood red threatening his life was sent to his house." "An Agonising Wait for Hubby's Return | Daily Express Online – Sabah's Leading News Portal," http://www.dailyexpress.com.my/news.cfm?NewsID=116851; Stephanie Sta Maria, "Harapan Komuniti Receives Death Threat," *Malaysia Today*, 27 August 2011, https://www.malaysia-today.net/2011/08/27/harapan-komuniti-receives-death-threat/.

20. Adib Povera and Arfa Yunus, "Five Resolutions Presented at Malay Dignity Congress"; Zurairi A. R., "Claiming 'Christian' DAP in Control of Dr M, Umno Man Plans Parliament Protest," *Malay Mail*, 12 July 2018 (Kuala Lumpur, Malaysia), https://www.malaymail.com/news/malaysia/2018/07/12/claiming-christian-dap-in-control-of-dr-m-umno-man-plans-parliament-protest/1651529.

2018. Political uncertainty will remain for the foreseeable future. Much is unpredictable. With the diminishing space for civil society, the avenue to negotiate Malaysian nationalism is fading. The Christians in Malaysia may also have limited freedom or space to proclaim their Christian message. Yet, when words are restricted or absent, the dialogue of life continues. What is certain is the need for Christians to be incarnational and to be faithful to God's mission. "Dialogue of Life" will enable them to witness for Jesus faithfully and effectively.

I hope the content of this book can make a case for practical theology and incarnational mission. Considering the fact that the use of hegemonic power on minorities is happening in many parts of the world today, some may find the theological and practical ideas in this book useful in their context. Christians that are under a hegemonic power that forces a different nationalism on to them may find this work particularly relevant. Even Christians who are constantly struggling against cultural hegemony, such as secularism, may identify with this work. Hopefully, they will also find some insights here.

Bibliography

"About Us – Christian Federation of Malaysia (CFM)," 2018. https://cfmsia.org/about-cfm/.

"About Us – G25 Malaysia." *G25 Malaysia*, https://www.g25malaysia.org/about-us-1.

Abu-Munshar, Maher Y. "In the Shadow of the 'Arab Spring': The Fate of Non-Muslims under Islamist Rule." *Islam and Christian-Muslim Relations* 23, no. 4 (2012): 487–503.

———. *Islamic Jerusalem and Its Christians: A History of Tolerance and Tensions*. London: Tauris Academic Studies, 2007.

"An Agonising Wait for Hubby's Return | Daily Express Online – Sabah's Leading News Portal." http://www.dailyexpress.com.my/news.cfm?NewsID=116851.

Ahmad Fauzi Abdul Hamid. *Islamisme Dan Bahananya: Cabaran Besar Politik Malaysia Abad Ke-21* (Islamism and Its Discontents: A Major Challenge to Twenty-First Century Malaysian Politics), Siri Syarahan Umum Pelantikan Profesor. Penang, Malaysia: Universiti Sains Malaysia, 2018.

Ahmad Fauzi Abdul Hamid and Che Hamdan Che Mohd Razali. *Middle Eastern Influences on Islamist Organizations in Malaysia: The Cases of ISMA, IRF and HTM*. ISEAS Publishing, 2016.

AIDC. "Anwar Ibrahim & Projek Islam Liberal Malaysia?" *AIDC* (blog), 18 April 2009. http://aidc-editor.blogspot.com/2009/04/anwar-ibrahim-projek-islam-liberal.html.

Amini Amir Abdullah. "Islamic Revivalism, Religious Freedom and the Non-Muslims in Malaysia: A Preliminary Discussion." *Pertanika* 11, no. 2 (2003): 119–134..

Ananthi Al Ramiah, Miles Hewstone, and Ralf Wölfer. *Attitudes and Ethnoreligious Integration: Meeting the Challenge and Maximizing the Promise of Multicultural Malaysia*. Kuala Lumpur: CIMB Foundation, January 12, 2017.

Anwar Ibrahim. "Universal Values and Muslim Democracy." *Journal of Democracy* 17, no. 3 (2006): 5–12.

Arkoun, Mohammed. "Locating Civil Society in Islamic Context." In *Civil Society in the Muslim World: Contemporary Perspectives*, edited by Amyn B. Sajoo, 35–59. London: I. B. Tauris in association with The Institute of Ismaili Studies, 2004.

Asila Jalil. "Azril: Why I Said Christian Evangelicalism Should Be Banned." *The Malaysian Insight*, 21 June 2017. https://www.themalaysianinsight.com/s/5665/.

"Asri: You Can't Simply Label Non-Muslim Citizens 'Kafir Harbi.'" *Free Malaysia Today*, 24 June 2016. http://www.freemalaysiatoday.com/category/nation/2016/06/24/asri-you-cant-simply-label-non-muslim-citizens-kafir-harbi/.

Asrul Zamani. *The Malay Ideals*. Kuala Lumpur: Golden Books Centre, 2002.

Athanasius. *On the Incarnation*. Warrendale: Ichthus Publications, 2018.

Azeem Fazwan Ahmad Farouk. "The Limits of Civil Society in Democratising the State: The Malaysian Case." *Kajian Malaysia, USM* 29, no. 1 (2011): 91–109.

Azhar Ibrahim. *Contemporary Islamic Discourse in the Malay-Indonesian World: Critical Perspectives*. Petaling Jaya, Malaysia: Strategic Information and Research Development Centre, 2014.

Azril Mohd Amin. "Wujudkan Undang-Undang Anti-Evangelicalisme (Make Anti-Evangelicalism Laws)." *Utusan Online*, 15 June 2017. http://www.utusan.com.my/rencana/utama/wujudkan-undang-undang-anti-evangelicalisme-1.493392.

Baker, Ken. "The Incarnational Model: Perception of Deception?" *Evangelical Missions Quarterly* 38, no. 1 (2002): 81–96. https://missionexus.org/the-incarnational-model-perception-of-deception/.

Barnard, Timothy P., ed. *Contesting Malayness: Malay Identity Across Boundaries*. Singapore: NUS Press, 2004.

Barrett, Lois. "Missional Witness: The Church as Apostle to the World." In *Missional Church: A Vision for the Sending of the Church in North America*, edited by Darrell L. Guder, 110–141. Grand Rapids, MI: Eerdmans, 1998.

"Basel Church Chinese General Council Monthly Bulletin Archive." *The Basel Church of Malaysia Chinese General Council*. http://cgcnews.bccmchinese.org/.

Batumalai, Sadayandy. *Islamic Resurgence and Islamization in Malaysia: A Malaysian Christian Response*. Ipoh, Malaysia: S. Batumalai, 1996.

———. *A Malaysian Theology of Muhibbah: A Theology for a Christian Witnessing in Malaysia*. Kuala Lumpur, Malaysia: Seminari Theoloji Malaysia, 1990.

———. *A Prophetic Christology for Neighbourology*. Kuala Lumpur, Malaysia: Seminari Theologi Malaysia, 1986.

———. "The Task of Malaysian Theology." *Inter-Religio* 13 (Summer 1988): 1–17.

Bauer, Walter. *A Greek-English Lexicon of the New Testament and Other Early Christian Literature*, edited by Frederick William Danker. 3rd edition. Chicago: University of Chicago Press, 2001.

Bernama. "No Retraction or Apology over Kafir Statement, Says Pahang Mufti." *NST Online*. Kuantan, Malaysia, 27 June 2016. https://www.nst.com.my/news/2016/06/155157/no-retraction-or-apology-over-kafir-statement-says-pahang-mufti.

Besley, Tina (AC), and Michael A. Peters. "Intercultural Understanding, Ethnocentrism and Western Forms of Dialogue." *Analysis and Metaphysics; Woodside* 10 (2011): 81–100.

Bevans, Stephen B., and Roger P. Schroeder. *Constants in Context: A Theology of Mission for Today*. Maryknoll, NY: Orbis Books, 2004. Kindle.

———. *Prophetic Dialogue: Reflections on Christian Mission Today*. Maryknoll, NY: Orbis Books, 2011.

Bienz, H. "Short History of the Borneo Basel Self-Established Church, Usually Called the Basel Mission, in North Borneo." *Journal of the Malaysian Branch of the Royal Asiatic Society* 39, no. 1 (209) (1966): 166–168.

Billings, J. Todd. "Incarnational Ministry and Christology: A Reappropriation of the Way of Lowliness." *Missiology* 32, no. 2 (2004): 187–201.

Bosch, David J. *Transforming Mission: Paradigm Shifts in Theology of Mission*. 20th anniversary edition. Maryknoll, NY: Orbis, 2011.

Boughton, Gordon. *Sabah Anglican Diocese Golden Jubilee History 2012*. Kuala Lumpur: The Anglican Diocese of Sabah, 2012.

Bradley, C. Paul. "Communal Politics in Malaysian Borneo." *The Western Political Quarterly* 21, no. 1 (1968): 123–140.

Branson, Mark L., and Juan F. Martinez. *Churches, Cultures and Leadership: A Practical Theology of Congregations and Ethnicities*. Downers Grove, IL: IVP Academic, 2011. Kindle.

Brisco, Brad. "Transitioning from Traditional to Missional." Blue River-Kansas City Baptist Association, 2011. https://blueriver-kansascity.org/wp-content/uploads/2015/07/Transitioning-from-Traditional-to-Missional.pdf.

British North Borneo Chartered Company. *British North Borneo Company Charter*. Ithaca, NY, 1878. http://archive.org/details/cu31924078409665.

Burbules, Nicholas C. *Dialogue in Teaching: Theory and Practice*. New York: Teachers College Press, 1993.

Carson, D. A. *The Gospel according to John*. Grand Rapids, MI: Eerdmans, 1991.

Chan, Geok Oon, and Boon Hock Lim. "The Mission to Reclaim Mission Schools." *Berita NECF* (November-December 2008): 10–11.

Chan, Simon. "CVP: The Mission of the Trinity." Interview by Andy Crouch. *Christianity Today*, 4 June 2007. https://www.christianitytoday.com/ct/2007/june/11.48.html.

Cheah, Boon Kheng. *Malaysia: The Making of a Nation*. Singapore: Institute of Southeast Asian Studies, 2002.

Cheong, John. "Reassessing John Stott's, David Hesselgrave's, and Andreas Kostenberger's Views of the Incarnational Model." In *Missionary Methods: Research, Reflections, and Realities*, edited by Craig Ott and J. D. Payne, 39–60. Pasadena: William Carey Library, 2013.

Chhoa, Luke H. S. *Renewal, Breakthrough and Growth*. Kota Kinabalu, Malaysia: Anglican Diocese of Sabah, 1986.

———. *Short Reflections of the Third Bishop of Sabah*. Kota Kinabalu, Malaysia: The Anglican Diocese of Sabah, 2000.

Chi, Melissa. "Be Brave like ISIL Fighters, Najib Tells Umno." *Malay Mail*. Kuala Lumpur, Malaysia, 24 June 2014. https://www.malaymail.com/s/693209/be-brave-like-isil-fighters-najib-tells-umno.

Chin, James. "Forced to the Periphery: Recent Chinese Politics in East Malaysia." In *Malaysian Chinese: Recent Developments and Prospects*, edited by Hock Guan Lee and Leo Suryadinata, 109–124. Singapore: Institute of Southeast Asian Studies, 2012.

———. "From Ketuanan Melayu to Ketuanan Islam: UMNO and the Malaysian Chinese." In *The End of UMNO?: Essays on Malaysia's Dominant Party*, edited by Bridget Welsh, 171–212. Petaling Jaya, Malaysia: Strategic Information and Research Development Centre, 2016.

Chin, James, and Andrew Harding, eds. *50 Years of Malaysia: Federalism Revisited*. Singapore: Marshall Cavendish International, 2015.

Chin, Simon. "St. James' Church – 97 Years in Kudat." In *Diocese of Sabah Silver Jubilee, 1962-1987*, edited by Kay Keng Khoo, 70–73. Kota Kinabalu, Malaysia: Anglican Diocese of Sabah, 1987.

Chong, Eu Choong. "Modernity, State-Led Islamisation and the Non-Muslim Response: A Case Study of Christians in Peninsular Malaysia." School of Social Sciences, University Sains Malaysia, 2010. https://www.academia.edu/6751048/Modernity_State-led_Islamisation_and_the_non-Muslim_Response_A_case_study_of_Christians_in_Peninsular_Malaysia.

———. "The Christian Response to State-Led Islamization in Malaysia." In *Religious Diversity in Muslim-Majority States in Southeast Asia: Areas of Toleration and Conflict*, edited by Bernhard Platzdasch and Johan Saravanamuttu, 290–320. Singapore: Institute of Southeast Asian Studies, 2014.

Chong, Siaw Fung. "'Can Allah and Tuhan Not Be One?': Overcoming Issues and Challenges of Muslim-Christian Relations among Malaysian Bumiputera Christians," Spring 2016. https://www.academia.edu/25430894/_CAN_ALLAH_AND_TUHAN_NOT_BE_ONE_OVERCOMING_ISSUES_AND_

CHALLENGES_OF_MUSLIM-CHRISTIAN_RELATIONS_AMONG_ MALAYSIAN_BUMIPUTERA_CHRISTIANS.

Chuah, Osman Abdullah @ Hock Leng. "Methodology of Da'wah to the Non-Muslim Chinese in Malaysia: A Preliminary Observation." *Ulum Islamiyyah, The Malaysian Journal of Islamic Sciences* 5, no. 1 (2006): 65–93.

"A Church after God's Own Heart – Leaflet Introducing the Methodist Church in Malaysia." The Methodist Church in Malaysia, 2017.

Clarke, Jeremy. "When West Met East: Matteo Ricci's Cross-Cultural Mission to China." *America Magazine – The Jesuit Review*, 10 May 2010. https://www.americamagazine.org/issue/736/article/when-west-met-east.

Cobbold, Cameron. "Report of the Commission of Enquiry, North Borneo and Sarawak, 1962." In *The Birth of Malaysia: A Reprint of the Cobbold Report, the I.G.C. Report and Malaysia Agreement*, edited by James Kim Min Wong, 10–119. Kuching, Malaysia, 1962.

Connor, Walker. "Ethnic Nationalism as a Political Force." *World Affairs* 133, no. 2 (1970): 91–97.

———. "The Timelessness of Nations." *Nations and Nationalism* 10, no. 1–2 (2004): 35–47.

Costas, Orlando E. *Christ Outside the Gate: Mission Beyond Christendom*. Eugene, OR: Wipf & Stock, 2005.

Daniels, Timothy P. *Building Cultural Nationalism in Malaysia: Identity, Representation and Citizenship*. New York, NY: Routledge, 2013. Kindle.

DeBemardi, Jean. "Chinese in Southeast Asia." *Encyclopedia of World Cultures*. Vol. V, *East and Southeast Asia*, 74–75.

Dietterich, Inagrace T. "Missional Community: Cultivating Communities of the Holy Spirit." In *Missional Church: A Vision for the Sending of the Church in North America*, edited by Darrell L. Guder, 142–182. Grand Rapids, MI: Eerdmans, 1998. Kindle.

Diocese of Kota Kinabalu. *Diocesan Organizational Pastoral Plan, 1998–2004*. Kota Kinabalu, Malaysia: DOPP Core Group, 1997.

"Don't Create Trouble, 'Allah' Exclusive to Muslims, Former Home Minister Tells Churches." *Malaysia Today*, 10 July 2014. http://www.malaysia-today.net/2014/07/10/dont-create-trouble-allah-exclusive-to-muslims-former-home-minister-tells-churches/.

Drane, John William. *The McDonaldization of the Church: Spirituality, Creativity, and the Future of the Church*. London: Darton Longman & Todd, 2000.

East, Brad. "An Undefensive Presence: The Mission and Identity of the Church in Kathryn Tanner and John Howard Yoder." *Scottish Journal of Theology* 68, no. 3 (2015): 327–344.

Edwards, Mark, and Elena Ene D-Vasilescu, eds. *Visions of God and Ideas on Deification in Patristic Thought*. London: Routledge, 2016.

Engel, James F., and William A. Dyrness. *Changing the Mind of Missions: Where Have We Gone Wrong?* Downers Grove, IL: InterVarsity Press, 2000.

Esposito, John L., ed. "Fatwa." *The Oxford Dictionary of Islam*. New York, NY: Oxford University Press, 2003. http://www.oxfordislamicstudies.com/article/opr/t125/e646.

———, ed. "Kafir." *The Oxford Dictionary of Islam*. Oxford University Press, 2003. https://www.oxfordreference.com/view/10.1093/acref/9780195125580.001.0001/acref-9780195125580-e-1229.

Farish A. Noor. "Muslim Nationalism in Southeast Asia." *Oxford Islamic Studies Online*. http://www.oxfordislamicstudies.com/article/opr/t343/e0042.

Federspiel, Howard M. "Modernist Islam in Southeast Asia: A New Examination." *The Muslim World* 92, no. 3–4 (2002): 371–386.

Freedman, Amy L. "Civil Society, Moderate Islam, and Politics in Indonesia and Malaysia." *Journal of Civil Society* 5, no. 2 (2009): 107–127.

Frost, Michael. *The Road to Missional, Journey to the Center of the Church*. Grand Rapids, MI: Baker, 2011.

Frost, Michael, and Alan Hirsch. *The Shaping of Things to Come: Innovation and Mission for the 21st Century Church*. Peabody, MA: Hendrickson, 2003.

Funston, John. "UMNO – From Hidup Melayu to Ketuanan Melayu." In *The End of UMNO?: Essays on Malaysia's Dominant Party*, edited by Bridget Welsh, 11–146. Petaling Jaya, Malaysia: Strategic Information and Research Development Centre, 2016.

Furman, Uriah. "Minorities in Contemporary Islamist Discourse." *Middle Eastern Studies* 36, no. 4 (2000): 1–20.

Geertz, Clifford. *The Interpretation of Cultures*. New York, NY: Basic Books, 2008.

Gellner, Ernest. *Conditions of Liberty: Civil Society and Its Rivals*. London: Penguin Books, 1994.

George, K. M. "Historical Development of Education." In *Commemorative History of Sabah, 1881–1981*, edited by Anwar Sullivan and Cecilia Leong, 467–490. Kota Kinabalu, Malaysia: Sabah State Government, Centenary Publications Committee, 1981.

———. "The Contributions of Mission Schools to the Development of the Church and the State of Sabah." In *Diocese of Sabah Silver Jubilee, 1962–1987*, edited by Kay Keng Khoo, 26–31. Kota Kinabalu, Malaysia: Anglican Diocese of Sabah, 1987.

Georges, Jayson, and Mark D. Baker. *Ministering in Honor-Shame Cultures: Biblical Foundations and Practical Essentials*. Downers Grove, IL: IVP Academic, 2016. Kindle.

Gill, Graeme. *The Nature and Development of the Modern State*. 1st edition. NY: Palgrave Macmillan, 2003.

Gilliland, Dean S., ed. "Contextual Theology as Incarnational Mission." In *The Word Among Us: Contextualizing Theology for Mission Today*, 9–31. Dallas: Word, 1989.

Goh, Daniel P. S., Matilda Gabrielpillai, Philip Holden, and Gaik Cheng Khoo, eds. *Race and Multiculturalism in Malaysia and Singapore*. London: Routledge, 2009.

Goh, Keat Peng. "Church and State in Malaysia." *Transformation* 6, no. 3 (1989): 16–20.

Goheen, Michael W. *"As the Father Has Sent Me, I Am Sending You": J. E. Lesslie Newbigin's Missionary Ecclesiology*. Zoetermeer: Boekencentrum, 2000.

———. "Historical Perspectives on the Missional Church Movement: Probing Lesslie Newbigin's Formative Influence." *Trinity Journal for Theology and Ministry* 4 no. 2 (2010): 62–84.

———. "The Significance of Lesslie Newbigin for Mission in the New Millennium." *Third Millennium* 7, no. 3 (2004): 88–99.

Gore, Charles. *Lux Mundi: A Series of Studies in the Religion of the Incarnation*. Eugene, OR: Wipf & Stock, 2009. Digital.

Green, Michael. *Asian Tigers for Christ: The Dynamic Growth of the Church in South East Asia*. London: SPCK, 2001.

Griffith, Sidney H. "Review of the Decline of Eastern Christianity under Islam: From Jihad to Dhimmitude, Seventh-Twentieth Century." *International Journal of Middle East Studies* 30, no. 4 (1998): 619–621.

Griffith, Sidney H. *The Church in the Shadow of the Mosque: Christians and Muslims in the World of Islam*. Princeton, NJ: Princeton University Press, 2008.

Guder, Darrell L., ed. *Missional Church: A Vision for the Sending of the Church in North America*. Grand Rapids, MI: Eerdmans, 1998.

———. "Missional Church: From Sending to Being Sent." In *Missional Church: A Vision for the Sending of the Church in North America*, edited by Darrell L. Guder, 1–17. Grand Rapids, MI: Eerdmans, 1998.

———. "The Church as Missional Community." In *The Community of the Word: Toward an Evangelical Ecclesiology*, edited by Mark Husbands and Daniel J. Treier, 114–128. Downers Grove, IL: IVP Academic, 2005.

———. *The Incarnation and the Church's Witness*. Eugene, OR: Wipf & Stock, 2004.

Guder, Daryl L. "Incarnation and the Church's Evangelistic Mission." *International Review of Mission* 83, no. 330 (1994): 417–428.

Gustafson, James W. "The Integration of Development and Evangelism." *Missiology* 26, no. 2 (1998): 131–142.

Habets, Myk. *Theosis in the Theology of Thomas Torrance*. Farnham, UK: Routledge, 2009.

Harper, Susan Billington. *In the Shadow of the Mahatma: Bishop Azariah and the Travails of Christianity in British India*. 1st edition. Grand Rapids, MI: Routledge, 2000.

Hauerwas, Stanley. "A Christian Critique of Christian America (1986)." In *The Hauerwas Reader*, edited by John Berkman and Michael Cartwright, 459–480. Durham, NC: Duke University Press Books, 2001.

———. "The Church and Liberal Democracy: The Moral Limits of a Secular Polity." In *A Community of Character: Toward a Constructive Christian Social Ethic*, chapter 4. 1st edition. Notre Dame, IN: University of Notre Dame Press, 1991. Kindle.

Hauerwas, Stanley, and William H. Willimon. *Resident Aliens: Life in the Christian Colony*. Expanded, anniversary edition. Nashville, TN: Abingdon, 2014. Kindle.

Heng, Pek Koon. "Chinese Responses to Malay Hegemony in Peninsular Malaysia 1957–96." *Southeast Asian Studies* 34, no. 3 (1996): 500–523.

Hew, Wai Weng. "The Battle of Bangi: The Struggle for Political Islam in Urban Malaysia." In *Towards a New Malaysia?: The 2018 Election and Its Aftermath*, edited by Meredith L. Weiss and Faizal S. Hazis, 195–210. Singapore: National University of Singapore Press, 2020.

Hiebert, Paul G. *Anthropological Reflections on Missiological Issues*. Grand Rapids, MI: Baker Academic, 1994.

Hill, Harriet. "Incarnational Ministry: A Critical Examination." *Evangelical Missions Quarterly* 26, no. 2 (1990). https://missionexus.org/incarnational-ministry-a-critical-examination/.

Ho, Wah Foon. "Feature: Spotlight on Jawi Issue." *The Star Online*, 22 December 2019. https://www.thestar.com.my/news/focus/2019/12/22/feature-spotlight-on-jawi-issue.

Hong, Bede. "Outlaw Evangelicalism in Malaysia, Says Islamic Coalition." *The Malaysian Insight*, 15 June 2017. https://www.themalaysianinsight.com/s/5196/.

Hooker, Virginia Matheson. "Reconfiguring Malay and Islam in Contemporary Malaysia." In *Contesting Malayness: Malay Identity across Boundaries*, edited by Timothy P. Barnard, 149–167. Singapore: NUS Press, 2004.

Hosne, Ana Carolina. "Friendship among Literati. Matteo Ricci SJ (1552–1610) in Late Ming China." *Transcultural Studies* 1 (2014): 190–214.

Hunsberger, George R. "Missional Vocation: Called and Sent to Represent the Reign of God." In *Missional Church: A Vision for the Sending of the Church in North America*, edited by Darrell L. Guder, 77–109. Grand Rapids, MI: Eerdmans, 1998.

Hunt, Robert. "Christian Theological Reflection and Education in the Muslim Societies of Malaysia and Indonesia." *Studies in World Christianity* 3, no. 2 (1997): 202–225.

Hussin Mutalib. *Islam in Malaysia: From Revivalism to Islamic State?* Singapore: NUS Press, 1993.

Hwa Yung. *Beyond AD 2000: A Call to Evangelical Faithfulness.* Kuala Lumpur: Kairos Research Centre, 1999.

———. "The Gospel and Nation-Building in Emergent Nations: An Evangelical Agenda." In *Mission in Context: Explorations Inspired by J. Andrew Kirk*, edited by John Corrie and Cathy Ross, Kindle location 2427–2789. Oxford: Routledge, 2016.

———. "Kingdom Identity in Christian Mission." *Mission Round Table* 4, no. 2 (December 2008): 2–12.

———. *Mangoes or Bananas?: The Quest for an Authentic Asian Christian Theology.* 2nd revised edition. Oxford: Regnum, 2014. Kindle.

"Internal Security Act (ISA) | HAKAM." *National Human Rights Society*. http://hakam.org.my/wp/tag/internal-security-act/.

Kamil, Maqsood. "Religious Extremism and Christian Response in Pakistan." *Evangelical Review of Theology* 42, no. 1 (2018): 41–56.

Keeble, Paul. *Mission with: Something Out of the Ordinary.* Watford, U.K.: Instant Apostle, 2017. Kindle.

Kessler, Clive. "The Dhimmi and an Old New 'Rationale.'" *New Mandala*, http://asiapacific.anu.edu.au/newmandala/2014/07/24/the-dhimmi-and-an-old-new-rationale/.

———. "Foreword: Where Malaysia Stands Today: A Personal Introduction to a Timely Collection of Essays." In *Misplaced Democracy: Malaysian Politics and People*, edited by Sophie Lemiere, vii–xv. Petaling Jaya, Malaysia: Strategic Information and Research Development Centre, 2014.

———. "UMNO, Then, Now and Always?" In *The End of UMNO?: Essays on Malaysia's Dominant Party*, edited by Bridget Welsh, 147–169. Petaling Jaya, Malaysia: Strategic Information and Research Development Centre, 2016.

Khairil Ashraf. "20 NGO Islam Ikrar Sokong Parti Lawan Sekularisme Pada PRU14." *Free Malaysia Today*, 3 March 2018. http://www.freemalaysiatoday.com/category/bahasa/2018/03/03/20-ngo-islam-ikrar-sokong-parti-lawan-sekularisme-pada-pru14/.

Khalif Muammar. "Islam dan Liberalisme." Institut Kajian Strategik Islam Malaysia (IKSIM). http://iksim.my/iksim/uploads/files/Makalah/Islam%20dan%20Liberalisme%20(Bahagian%20I).pdf.

Kharlamov, Vladimir. *Theosis: Deification in Christian Theology*, vol. 2. 1st edition. Cambridge: James Clarke & Co, 2012.

Khoo, Kay Keng, ed. *All Saints' Cathedral Parish Diamond Jubilee, 1911–1986*. Kota Kinabalu, Malaysia: Anglican Diocese of Sabah, 1986.

———, ed. *Diocese of Sabah Silver Jubilee, 1962–1987*. Kota Kinabalu, Malaysia: Anglican Diocese of Sabah, 1987.

Knitter, Paul F. "Inter-Religious Dialogue and Social Action." In *The Wiley-Blackwell Companion to Inter-Religious Dialogue*, edited by Catherine Cornille, 133–148. Chichester, UK: John Wiley & Sons, 2013.

Koo, Tuk Su, ed. *Diocese of Sabah 35th Anniversary, 1962–1997*. Kota Kinabalu, Malaysia: Anglican Diocese of Sabah, 1997.

Kostenberger, Andreas J. *The Missions of Jesus and the Disciples according to the Fourth Gospel: With Implications for the Fourth Gospel's Purpose and the Mission of the Conte*. Grand Rapids, MI: Wm. B. Eerdmans-Lightning Source, 1998.

Ladd, George Eldon. *A Theology of the New Testament*. Revised, subsequent edition. Grand Rapids, MI: Eerdmans, 1993.

Langmead, Ross. *The Word Made Flesh: Towards an Incarnational Missiology*. Lanham, MD: UPA, 2004.

Lau, Alwyn. "Intimating the Unconscious: Politics, Psychoanalysis and Theology in Malaysia." PhD diss., Monash University, 2016.

"The Lausanne Covenant." *Lausanne Movement*, 1 August 1974. https://www.lausanne.org/content/covenant/lausanne-covenant.

Lee, Julian C. H. *Islamization and Activism in Malaysia*. Singapore: Institute of Southeast Asian Studies, 2010.

Lee, Kam Hing. "Differing Perspectives on Integration and Nation-Building in Malaysia." In *Ethnic Relations and Nation-Building in Southeast Asia: The Case of the Ethnic Chinese*, edited by Leo Suryadinata, 82-108. Politics/Social Issues: Southeast Asia. Singapore: Institute of Southeast Asian Studies, 2004.

Lee, Raymond L. M., and Susan E. Ackerman. *Sacred Tensions: Modernity and Religious Transformation in Malaysia*. Columbia, SC: University of South Carolina Press, 1997.

Levy-Rubin, Milka. "Shurut Umar and Its Alternatives: The Legal Debate throughout the Eighth and Ninth Centuries over the Status of the Dhimmis." *Jerusalem Studies in Arabic and Islam* 30 (2005): 170–206.

Lim, Kit Siang. "Non-Muslim Malaysians as 'Kafir Zimmi'/"Kafir Harbi" – New Faultline in Nation-Building." *DAP*, 2003. https://dapmalaysia.org/all-archive/English/2003/oct03/lks/lks2716.htm.

Lim, P. G. "Towards National Integration: Of the Constitution, Governance and Ethnicity." *INSAF* 32, no. 1 (2003): 1–24.

Lim, Regina. "Islamization and Ethnicity in Sabah, Malaysia." In *Encountering Islam: The Politics of Religious Identities in Southeast Asia*, edited by Yew-Foong Hui, 158–190. Singapore: Institute of Southeast Asian Studies, 2012.

Liow, Joseph. *Religion and Nationalism in Southeast Asia*. Cambridge, UK: Cambridge University Press, 2016.

Liow, Joseph Chinyong. "Political Islam in Malaysia: Legitimacy, Hegemony and Resistance." In *Islamic Legitimacy in a Plural Asia*, edited by Anthony Reid and Michael Gilsenan, 167–187. New York: Routledge, 2008.

Loh, Francis Kok-Wah. "Developmentalism and the Limits of Democratic Discourse." In *Democracy in Malaysia: Discourses and Practices*, edited by Francis Kok-Wah Loh and Boo Teik Khoo, 19–50. Surrey, UK: Curzon Press, 2002.

"LOP 21 – Evangelism and Social Responsibility: An Evangelical Commitment." *Lausanne Movement*, 25 June 1982. https://www.lausanne.org/content/lop/lop-21.

Luping, Herman J. *Sabah's Dilemma: The Political History of Sabah, 1960–1994*. Ann Arbor, MI: Magnus Books, 1994.

Lutz, Jessie G., and Rolland Ray Lutz. "The Invisible China Missionaries: The Basel Mission's Chinese Evangelists, 1847–1866." *Mission Studies* 12, no. 1 (1995): 204–227.

Mahathir Mohamad. "Orang Melayu tidak percaya Anwar sebab tubuh Parti Liberal (Malays Distrust Anwar because He Establishes Liberal Party)." Interview by Baharom Mahusin, Badruldin Zakaria, Junhairi Alyasa, Mohd Fazli Zainul Abidin, Haslina Kamaluddin, and Nurul Riduan Norashaha. *Sinar Harian*, 12 March 2020. https://www.sinarharian.com.my/article/73526/BERITA/Nasional/Orang-Melayu-tidak-percaya-Anwar-sebab-tubuh-parti-liberal.

———. *The Malay Dilemma*. Singapore: Marshall Cavendish, 2008.

Majlis Agama Islam Selangor (Selangor Islamic Religious Council). *Pendedahan Agenda Kristian (Exposing the Christian Agenda)*. Shah Alam, Malaysia: Majlis Agama Islam Selangor, 2014. http://www.mais.gov.my/en/.

Malaysiakini. "Pengertian liberal menurut Anwar (The Definition of Liberal according to Anwar)." *Malaysiakini*, 2020. https://www.malaysiakini.com/news/520053.

Malaysia Human Development Report 2013. Edited by Jeffrey Hardy Quah. United Nations Development Programme, Malaysia, January 2014. http://www.mhdr.my/page/161/Download-MHDR-2013/.

"Malaysia's Lina Joy Loses Islam Conversion Case." *Reuters*, 30 May 2007. https://www.reuters.com/article/us-malaysia-religion-ruling-idUSSP20856820070530.

Marsden, George M. *Fundamentalism and American Culture*. 2nd edtion. New York: Oxford University Press, 2006.

Martin, Richard C. "From Dhimmis to Minorities: Shifting Constructions of the Non-Muslim Other from Early to Modern Islam." In *Nationalism and*

Minority Identities in Islamic Societies, edited by Maya Shatzmiller, 3–21. 1st edition. Montreal: McGill-Queen's University Press, 2005.

M. A. S. Abdel Haleem. "The Jizya Verse (Q.9:29): Tax Enforcement on Non-Muslims in the First Muslim State." *Journal of Qur'anic Studies* 14, no. 2 (2012): 72–89.

Maszlee Malik. "Rethinking the Role of Islam in Malaysian Politics: A Case Study of Parti Amanah Negara (AMANAH)." *Islam and Civilization Renewal Journal* 8, no. 4 (2017): 457–472.

———. "Salafism in Malaysia: Historical Account on Its Emergence and Motivations." *Sociology of Islam* 5, no. 4 (2017): 303–333.

Mauzy, Diane K. "United Malays National Organization." *The Oxford Encyclopedia of the Islamic World*. Oxford Islamic Studies Online. http://www.oxfordislamicstudies.com/article/opr/t236/e0824.

McConnell, Mez. "Why the Divine Incarnation of Jesus Is a Bad Model for Mission | 20schemes Equip." https://20schemesequip.com/why-the-divine-incarnation-of-jesus-is-a-bad-model-for-mission/.

Md. Asham Ahmad. "Debunking Multiculturalism." *The Star Online*, 22 August 2006. https://www.thestar.com.my/opinion/letters/2006/08/22/debunking-multiculturalism/.

Merdeka Center for Opinion Research. *Public Opinion Poll on Ethnic Relations: Experience, Perception & Expectations*. Bangi, Selangor, Malaysia: Merdeka Center for Opinion Research, March 21, 2006. https://merdeka.org/v2/download/public-opinion-poll-on-ethnic-relations-experience-perception-expectations-march-2006/.

Milner, Anthony. *The Invention of Politics in Colonial Malaya: Contesting Nationalism and the Expansion of the Public Sphere*. Cambridge: Cambridge University Press, 2002.

———. *The Malays*. Chichester, UK: Wiley-Blackwell, 2008.

Moffett, Samuel Hugh. *A History of Christianity in Asia Vol 1: Beginnings to 1500*. 2nd edition. Maryknoll, NY: Orbis Books, 1998.

———. *A History of Christianity in Asia Vol. 2: 1500–1900*. Maryknoll, NY: Orbis Books, 2005.

Mohamed Nawab Mohamed Osman. "The Islamic Conservative Turn in Malaysia: Impact and Future Trajectories." *Contemporary Islam* 11, no. 1 (2017): 1–20.

Mohamed Nawab Mohamed Osman and Edmund Terence Gomez. "Breaking Malay-Muslim Hegemony – Patronage, Factionalism and Feuds in the 14th Malaysian General Election." *The Round Table* 109, no. 2 (2020): 116–125.

Mohammad-Reza Djalili. Elizabeth Keller, and Matthew Gray. "Dār Al-Ḥarb." *The Oxford Encyclopedia of the Islamic World*. Oxford Islamic Studies Online. http://www.oxfordislamicstudies.com/opr/t236/e0177.

Monash, Paul. *Malay Supremacy: A Historical Overview of Malay Political Culture and an Assessment of Its Implication for the Non-Malays in Malaysia*. Auckland: Maygen Press, 2003.

Mondithoka, S. "Incarnation." *Dictionary of Mission Theology: Evangelical Foundations*, edited by John Corrie, 177–181. Downers Grove, IL: IVP Academic, 2007.

Moschella, Mary Clark. *Ethnography as a Pastoral Practice*. Cleveland, OH: Pilgrim Press, 2008.

"Mufti Anggap Tak Salah Rujuk Bukan Islam Sebagai 'Kafir' (Mufti Consider Referring Non-Muslims 'Kafir' Appropriate)." *MYNEWSHUB*, 5 March 2019. https://www.mynewshub.tv/utama-sensasi/mufti-anggap-tak-salah-rujuk-bukan-islam-sebagai-kafir/.

Muhammad Firdaus Zalani. "Kafir Harbi-Zimmi Perlu Difahami Dalam Kerangka Menyeluruh (Kafir Harbi-Dhimmi Needs to Be Understood in an Overarching Framework)." *Majlis Ulama ISMA*. https://muis.org.my/2019/10/kafir-harbi-zimmi-perlu-difahami-dalam-kerangka-menyeluruh/.

Muhammad Mujahid Ir Hj Mohammad Fadzil. "Liberalism Yang Terancang." *HarakahDaily*, 4 February 2020. https://harakahdaily.net/index.php/2020/02/04/liberalism-yang-terancang/.

Muhammed Abdul Khalid. *The Colour of Inequality: Ethnicity, Class, Income and Wealth in Malaysia*. Petaling Jaya, Malaysia: MPH Group Publishing, 2014.

Nagata, Judith. "Boundaries of Malayness: 'We Have Made Malaysia: Now It Is Time to (Re)Make the Malays but Who Interprets the History?'" In *Melayu: The Politics, Poetics and Paradoxes of Malayness*, edited by Maznah Mohamad and Syed Muhd Khairudin Aljunied, 366–1822. Singapore: NUS Press, 2013. Kindle.

Newbigin, Lesslie. "Church as Witness: A Meditation." *Reformed World* 35 (1978): 5–9.

———. *Foolishness to the Greeks: The Gospel and Western Culture*. Grand Rapids, MI: Eerdmans, 1986.

———. *The Gospel in a Pluralist Society*. Grand Rapids, MI: Eerdmans, 1989.

———. *The Open Secret: An Introduction to the Theology of Mission*. Revised edition. Grand Rapids, MI: Eerdmans, 1995.

Ng, Edmund. "A Post-Survey Analysis: Towards Greater Community Involvement." *Berita NECF*, 2002. http://www.necf.org.my/newsmaster.cfm?&menuid=2&action=view&retrieveid=77.

Ng, Kam Weng. "A Christian Social Vision for Nation Building." *Berita NEFC*, February 2008.

———. "Creating Social Space for Mission: Paradigm Shift in Mission in Malaysia." *Transformation* 20, no. 4 (2003): 222–225.

———. "The Dhimmi Syndrome: The Psychological Degradation of the Oppressed." *Krisis & Praxis*. http://www.krisispraxis.com/archives/2006/11/the-dhimmi-syndrome-the-psychological-degradation-of-the-oppressed/.

———. "Multiculturalism – How Can It Be Wrong?" *The Star Online*, 25 August 2006. https://www.thestar.com.my/news/nation/2006/08/25/multiculturalism--how-can-it-be-wrong/.

Ngeow, Yeok Meng. "Islamization and Ethnic Identity of the Chinese Minority in Malaysia." University of Malaya, 2011. http://eprints.um.edu.my/582/1/ICAS_of_NGEOW_YEOK_MENG%5B1%5D.pdf.

Nikolajsen, Jeppe Bach. *The Distinctive Identity of the Church: A Constructive Study of the Post-Christendom Theologies of Lesslie Newbigin and John Howard Yoder*. Eugene, OR: Pickwick, 2015.

Nur Hasliza Mohd Salleh. "Mujahid: Jangan Ada Lagi Gelaran Kafir Harbi, Zimmi (Mujahid – Don't Use the Terms 'Kafir Harbi, Dhimmi')." *Free Malaysia Today*, 24 July 2018. https://www.freemalaysiatoday.com/category/bahasa/2018/07/24/mujahid-jangan-ada-lagi-gelaran-kafir-harbi-zimmi/.

Oddie, Geoffrey A. "Indian Christians and National Identity, 1870–1947." *Journal of Religious History* 25, no. 3 (2002): 346–366.

O'Donovan, Oliver. *The Desire of the Nations: Rediscovering the Roots of Political Theology*. Cambridge, UK: Cambridge University Press, 1999.

Ongkili, James P. *The Borneo Response to Malaysia, 1961–1963*. Singapore: Donald Moore Press, 1967.

Opwis, Felicitas. "Maqāṣid Al-Sharīʿah." The [Oxford] Encyclopedia of Islam and Law. Oxford Islamic Studies Online., n.d. http://www.oxfordislamicstudies.com/opr/t349/e0113.

Ott, Craig, Stephen J. Strauss, and Timothy C. Tennent. *Encountering Theology of Mission: Biblical Foundations, Historical Developments, and Contemporary Issues*. Series editor, A. Scott Moreau. Grand Rapids, MI: Baker Academic, 2010.

Pannenberg, Wolfhart. *Jesus – God and Man*. Translated by Lewis L. Wilkins and Duane A. Priebe. 2nd edition. Philadelphia: Westminster John Knox Press, 1977.

Parekh, Bhikhu. *Rethinking Multiculturalism: Cultural Diversity and Political Theory*. Basingstoke, UK: Macmillan, 2000.

"Parti Keadilan Rakyat (PKR)." *Liberal International*. https://liberal-international.org/members/pkr_malaysia/.

Peleg, Ilan. *Democratizing the Hegemonic State: Political Transformation in the Age of Identity*. Cambridge, UK: Cambridge University Press, 2007.

Phillips, Elizabeth. *Political Theology: A Guide for the Perplexed*. London: Bloomsbury Academic, 2012. Kindle.

Poon, Michael Nai-Chiu, ed. *Pilgrims and Citizens: Christian Engagement in Asia Today*. Adelaide: ATF Press, 2006.

Population Distribution and Basic Demographic Characteristics. Population and Housing Census of Malaysia 2010. Putrajaya: Department of Statistic, Malaysia, 2011.

Poushter, Jacob. "In Nations with Significant Muslim Populations, Much Disdain for ISIS." *Pew Research Center*, 17 November 2015. http://www.pewresearch.org/fact-tank/2015/11/17/in-nations-with-significant-muslim-populations-much-disdain-for-isis/.

Povera, Adib, and Arfa Yunus. "Five Resolutions Presented at Malay Dignity Congress." *NST Online*. Shah Alam, Malaysia, 6 October 2019. https://www.nst.com.my/news/nation/2019/10/527514/five-resolutions-presented-malay-dignity-congress.

Pulcini, Theodore. "Review of Islam and Dhimmitude: Where Civilizations Collide." *Middle East Journal* 56, no. 4 (2002): 736–738.

Rajah, Ananda. "A 'Nation of Intent' in Burma: Karen Ethno-Nationalism, Nationalism and Narrations of Nation." *The Pacific Review* 15, no. 4 (2002): 517–537.

Ramasamy, P. "Civil Society in Malaysia: An Arena of Contestation?" In *Civil Society in Southeast Asia*, edited by Hock Guan Lee, 198–216. Singapore: Institute of Southeast Asian Studies, 2004.

Rauschenbusch, Walter. *A Theology for the Social Gospel*. Nashville, TN: Abingdon, 1990.

Riddell, Peter G. "Islamization, Civil Society, and Religious Minority in Malaysia." n *Islam in Southeast Asia: Political, Social and Strategic Challenges for the 21st Century*, edited by K. S. Nathan and Mohammad Hashim Kamali, 162–190. Singapore: Institute of Southeast Asian Studies, 2005.

Rowan, Peter. *Proclaiming the Peacemaker: The Malaysian Church as an Agent of Reconciliation in a Multicultural Society*. Oxford: Regnum Books International, 2012.

Roxburgh, Alan J., and M. Scott Boren. *Introducing the Missional Church: What It Is, Why It Matters, How to Become One*. Grand Rapids, MI: Baker Books, 2009.

Rutter, Owen. *British North Borneo: An Account of Its History, Resources and Native Tribes*. Kota Kinabalu: Opus Publications, 2008.

Sabah Council of Churches. "Press Statement by Sabah Council of Churches on Kelantan's Hudud Enactment." Press Release, 30 March 2015. http://www.majodi.org/v4/index.php/news/675-press-statement-by-sabah-council-of-churches-on-kelantan-s-hudud-enactment.

Sabah Statistics Yearbook 2015. Putrajaya, Malaysia: Department of Statistics, Malaysia, 2016.

Saeed, Abdullah. "Trends in Contemporary Islam: A Preliminary Attempt at a Classification." *The Muslim World* 97, no. 3 (2007): 395–404.

Samuel, Wilfred J. "Diakoinonia Spirituality: A Paradigm for Transformation and Empowerment in Practicing Redemptive Christian Social Action." In *Theology and Practice: Contextual Reflections from Asia*, edited by Weng Kit Cheong, 316–325. Kota Kinabalu, Malaysia: Sabah Theological Seminary, 2013.

"'Say No to RUU355 for Malaysia's Sake' – The Star." *The Star Online*. Kuala Lumpur, Malaysia, 7 May 2017. https://www.thestar.com.my/news/nation/2017/05/07/say-no-to-ruu355-for-malaysias-sake.

Schaff, Philip. *Creeds of Christendom Volume 1: The History of the Creeds – Enhanced Version*. Christian Classics Ethereal Library, 2009.

Schall, James V. "Matteo Ricci's 'Maxims' and Friends – Catholic World Report." *The Catholic World Report*, 19 June 2015. https://www.catholicworldreport.com/2015/06/19/matteo-riccis-maxims-and-friends/.

Scott, Peter, and William T. Cavanaugh, eds. *The Blackwell Companion to Political Theology*. 1st edition. Malden, MA: Wiley-Blackwell, 2004.

Shad Saleem Faruqi. "The Bedrock of Our Nation." *The Malaysian Bar*, 30 March 2007. http://www.malaysianbar.org.my/general_opinions/ comments/bedrock_of_our_nation.html.

Shaharuddin Maaruf. *Malay Ideas on Development: From Feudal Lord to Capitalist*. 2nd edition. Singapore: Strategic Information and Research Development Centre, 2014.

Shakila Yacob. "Political Culture and Nation Building: Whither Bangsa Malaysia?" *Malaysian Journal of Social Policy and Society* 3 (2006): 22-42.

Shamsul, A. B. "Identity Construction, Nation Formation, and Islamic Revivalism in Malaysia." In *Islam in an Era of Nation-States: Politics and Religious Renewal in Muslim Southeast Asia*, edited by Robert W. Hefner and Patricia Horvatich, 207–227. Honolulu, HI: University of Hawaii Press, 1997.

———. "Text and Collective Memories: The Construction of Chinese and Chineseness from the Perspective of a Malay." In *Ethnic Relations and Nation-Building in Southeast Asia: The Case of the Ethnic Chinese*, edited by Leo Suryadinata, 109–141. Politics/Social Issues: Southeast Asia. Singapore: Institute of Southeast Asian Studies, 2004.

Shamsul, A. B., and Sity Daud. "Nation, Ethnicity, and Contending Discourse in the Malaysian State," In *State Making in Asia*, edited by Richard Boyd and Ngo Tak-Wing, 134–143. London: Routledge, 2012.

Sheith Khidhir Abu Bakar. "Study Finds More Malay Youths Say They Are Muslims First." *FMT News*, 21 September 2017. https://www.freemalaysiatoday.com/category/nation/2017/09/21/study-finds-more-malay-youths-say-they-are-muslims-first/.

Shepard, William E., François Burgat, and Armando Salvatore. "Islamism." *The Oxford Encyclopedia of the Islamic World*. *Oxford Islamic Studies Online*.http://www.oxfordislamicstudies.com.fuller.idm.oclc.org/article/opr/t236/e0888.

Shorter, Aylward. *Toward a Theology of Inculturation*. Maryknoll, NY: Orbis Books, 1989.

Silver Jubilee of the Diocese of Kota Kinabalu 2002: Put Out into the Deep. Kota Kinabalu, Malaysia: The Diocese of Kota Kinabalu, 2002.

Singh, Ranjit. *The Making of Sabah, 1865–1941: The Dynamics of Indigenous Society*. Kota Kinabalu, Malaysia: Bahagian Kabinet dan Dasar, Jabatan Ketua Menteri, 2011.

Smith, Anthony D. *Nationalism: Theory, Ideology, History*. 2nd edition. Cambridge, UK: Polity, 2010.

Song, Robert. *Christianity and Liberal Society*. Oxford: Oxford University Press, 2006. Kindle.

Sta Maria, Bernard. *Peter J. Mojuntin, the Golden Son of the Kadazan*. Melaka, Malaysia: Sta Maria, 1978. https://koeln.ccc.de/media/pdf/TheGoldenSonOfTheKadazan(compact).pdf.

Sta Maria, Stephanie. "Harapan Komuniti Receives Death Threat." *Malaysia Today*, 27 August 2011. https://www.malaysia-today.net/2011/08/27/harapan-komuniti-receives-death-threat/.

Starke, John. "The Incarnation Is about a Person, Not a Mission." *The Gospel Coalition*, 16 May 2011. https://www.thegospelcoalition.org/article/the-incarnation-is-about-a-person-not-a-mission/.

Steensland, Brian, and Philip Goff, eds. *The New Evangelical Social Engagement*. New York, NY: Oxford University Press, 2013. Kindle.

Stetzer, Ed. "Monday Is for Missiology: What Is the Missional Church? – A New Series." *The Exchange* (blog), 12 October 2015. http://www.christianitytoday.com/edstetzer/2015/october/missional-church-and-its-manifesto.html.

———. *Planting Missional Churches*. Nashville, TN: B&H, 2006.

Stott, John. *Christian Mission in the Modern World*. Downers Grove, IL: IVP Books, 2009.

Suaedy, Ahmad. "Islam and Minorities: Managing Identity in Malaysia." *Al-Jami'ah: Journal of Islamic Studies* 48, no. 1 (2010): 1–44.

Sullivan, Anwar, and Patricia Regis. "Demography." In *Commemorative History of Sabah, 1881–1981*, edited by Anwar Sullivan and Cecilia Leong, 545–567. Kota Kinabalu, Malaysia: Sabah State Government, Centenary Publications Committee, 1981.

Sunquist, Scott W. *Understanding Christian Mission: Participation in Suffering and Glory*. Grand Rapids, MI: Baker Academic, 2013.

Suryani Awang, M. Maros, and N. Ibrahim. "Malay Values in Intercultural Communication." *International Journal of Social Science and Humanity* 2, no. 3 (2012): 201–205.

Swinton, John, and Harriet Mowat. *Practical Theology and Qualitative Research*. London: SCM Press, 2011. Kindle.

Tan, Chee-Beng. "Chinese Identities in Malaysia." In *Chinese Overseas*, 91–110. Comparative Cultural Issues. Hong Kong: Hong Kong University Press, 2004. http://www.jstor.org/stable/j.ctt2jbzp1.9.

———. "Ethnic Groups, Ethnogenesis and Ethnic Identities: Some Examples from Malaysia." *Identities* 6, no. 4 (1997): 441–480.

Tan, Kevin. "Malaysia a Fundamentalist Islamic Country, Says PM." *Malaysiakini*, 17 June 2002. https://www.malaysiakini.com/news/11804.

Tan, Liok Ee. *The Politics of Chinese Education in Malaya, 1945–1961*. Oxford University Press, 1997.

"Tawhid – Oxford Islamic Studies Online." http://www.oxfordislamicstudies.com.fuller.idm.oclc.org/article/opr/t243/e340?_hi=1&_pos=2.

Tay, Choon Neo. "The Role of Mission Schools in Nation Building: A Report for the Conference of Christian Mission Schools in Malaysia." *Pelita Methodist*, August 2009.

Taylor, Brian. *Elton Hill Diary: Story of the Founding of St. Michael's Church, Sandakan, Sabah, Malaysia*. Hong Kong: Lai Hing & Company, 1976.

———. "SPG and North Borneo." In *Diocese of Sabah Silver Jubilee, 1962–1987*, edited by Kay Keng Khoo, 16–21. Kota Kinabalu, Malaysia: Anglican Diocese of Sabah, 1987.

Teo, Cheng Wee. "More Malays Say They Are Muslim First: Malaysian Poll." *The Straits Times*. Kuala Lumpur, 12 August 2015. http://www.straitstimes.com/asia/se-asia/more-malays-say-they-are-muslim-first-malaysian-poll.

The Malaysian Insight. "G25's Book on Role of Islam in Malaysia Banned," 2017. https://www.themalaysianinsight.com/s/8837/.

The National Department for Culture and Arts. "National Culture Policy | JKKN." *Official Website of The National Department for Culture and Arts*. http://www.jkkn.gov.my/en/national-culture-policy.

Theology Working Group. "The Whole Church Taking the Whole Gospel to the Whole World." *Lausanne Movement*, 1 June 2010. https://www.lausanne.org/content/twg-three-wholes.

Thock, Ker Pong. "Discoursing Nation-Building and Civil Society Formation." In *Malaysian Chinese and Nation-Building: Before Merdeka and Fifty Years After*. Vol. 2, edited by Phin Keong Voon, 575–609. Kuala Lumpur: Centre for Malaysian Chinese Studies, 2008.

Thomas, M. M. *The Acknowledged Christ of the Indian Renaissance*. London: S.C.M. Press, 1969.

Thu, En Yu. *Ethnic Identity and Consciousness in Sabah: A Christian Perspective.* Kota Kinabalu, Malaysia: Sabah Theological Seminary, 2010.

Torrance, Thomas F. *Incarnation: The Person and Life of Christ.* Edited by Robert T. Walker. Milton Keynes, UK: Paternoster, 2008.

Tregonning, K. G. "American Activity in North Borneo, 1865–1881." *Pacific Historical Review* 23, no. 4 (1954): 357–372.

———. *A History of Modern Sabah, 1881–1963.* Kuala Lumpur: Published for the University of Singapore by the University of Malaya Press, 1965.

Tsen, Thomas Lip Tet, ed. *History of the Basel Christian Church of Malaysia (1882–2012).* Kota Kinabalu: Basel Christian Church of Malaysia, 2015.

———. "Pastoral Care amidst the Multicultural Context of a Lutheran Church – Basel Christian Church of Malaysia: A Proposal for a Theological Model of Contextual Pastoral Care in a Diverse Christian Community of Malaysia." PhD Dissertation. St. Paul, MN: Luther Seminary, 2006.

"The Unconstitutional Call – National Evangelical Christian Fellowship Malaysia." *Malay Mail Online*, 16 June 2017. http://www.themalaymailonline.com/what-you-think/article/the-unconstitutional-call-necf-malaysia.

UN Human Rights Office of the High Commissioner. "International Convention on the Elimination of All Forms of Racial Discrimination." *OHCHR.* https://www.ohchr.org/en/professionalinterest/pages/cerd.aspx.

Ursinus, M. O. H. "Millet." *The Encyclopaedia of Islam* 7:61–64. Leiden: Brill, 1993.

van Bruinessen, Martin. *Contemporary Developments in Indonesian Islam: Explaining the "Conservative Turn."* Singapore: Institute of Southeast Asian Studies, 2013.

Van den Toren-Lekkerkerker, Berdine, and Benno Van den Toren. "From Missionary Incarnate to Incarnational Guest: A Critical Reflection on Incarnation as a Model for Missionary Presence." *Transformation* 32, no. 2 (2015): 81–96.

Van Gelder, Craig, and Dwight J. Zscheile. *The Missional Church in Perspective: Mapping Trends and Shaping the Conversation.* Grand Rapids, MI: Baker Academic, 2011.

Vickers, Adrian. "'Malay Identity': Modernity, Invented Tradition and Forms of Knowledge." In *Contesting Malayness: Malay Identity Across Boundaries*, edited by Timothy P. Barnard, 25–55. Singapore: NUS Press, 2004.

Volf, Miroslav. *A Public Faith, How Followers of Christ Should Serve the Common Good.* Repr. edition. Grand Rapids, MI: Brazos Press, 2011.

von der Mehden, Fred R. "Islamic Movements in Malaysia." In *The Oxford Handbook of Islam and Politics*, edited by John L. Esposito and Emad El-Din Shahin, 587–599. Oxford: Oxford University Press, 2013. http://www.oxfordislamicstudies.com/article/opr/t9001/e005.

Voon, Phin Keong. "Whither the Malaysian Nation-State?" In *Malaysian Chinese and Nation-Building: Before Merdeka and Fifty Years After*. Vol. 2, edited by Phin Keong Voon, 25–55. Kuala Lumpur: Centre for Malaysian Chinese Studies, 2008.

Wahba, Tharwat. "Dialogues in Egypt: From the Elite to the Street." *Evangelical Interfaith Dialogue, Fuller Theological Seminary* (Fall 2014). http://cms.fuller.edu/EIFD/issues/Fall_2014/Dialogue_in_Egypt.aspx#sthash.Yh1OjPfM.dpuf.

Walker, Paul E., Reinhard Schulze, and Muhammad Khalid Masud. "Daʿwah." *The Oxford Encyclopedia of the Islamic World. Oxford Islamic Studies Online.* http://www.oxfordislamicstudies.com/opr/t236/e0182.

Walls, Andrew F. *The Missionary Movement in Christian History: Studies in the Transmission of Faith*. Maryknoll, NY: Orbis, 1996.

Wang, Gungwu. "Chinese Ethnicity in New Southeast Asia Nations." In *Ethnic Relations and Nation-Building in Southeast Asia: The Case of the Ethnic Chinese*, edited by Leo Suryadinata, 1–19. Politics/Social Issues: Southeast Asia. Singapore: Institute of Southeast Asian Studies, 2004.

Webster, John. *Word and Church: Essays in Christian Dogmatics*. Edinburgh: Bloomsbury T&T Clark, 2001.

Wells, Samuel. *A Nazareth Manifesto: Being with God*. 1st edition. Malden, MA: John Wiley & Sons, 2015. Kindle.

———. *Incarnational Ministry: Being with the Church*. Grand Rapids, MI: Eerdmans, 2017. Kindle.

———. *Incarnational Mission: Being with the World*. Grand Rapids, MI: Eerdmans, 2018.

Welsh, Bridget. "Umno's Reactionary GE13 'Victory,'" 2013. http://bridgetwelsh.com/2013/05/umnos-reactionary-ge13-victory/.

"Why Malaysia Backpedalled on ICERD Ratification." *NST Online*, 2018. https://www.nst.com.my/news/nation/2018/11/434078/why-malaysia-backpedalled-icerd-ratification.

William, John E. "Mission Strategy 1911–1985 with Particular Reference to the Period 1972–1985." In *All Saints' Cathedral Parish Diamond Jubilee, 1911–1986*, edited by Kay Keng Khoo, 22–24. Kota Kinabalu, Malaysia: Anglican Diocese of Sabah, 1986.

Wong, Danny. "A Hybrid Community in East Malaysia: The Sino-Kadazans of Sabah and Their Search for Identity." *Archipel* 84 (2012): 107–127.

Wong, Danny Tze-Ken. "The Basel Christian Church and 130 Years of the History of Sabah: A Survey." In *Sabah's Hakka Story*, edited by Delai Zhang, 77–98. Kota Kinabalu, Malaysia: Sabah Theological Seminary, 2015.

———. "Chinese Migration to Sabah before the Second World War." *Archipel* 58, no. 3 (1999): 131–158.

———. *Historical Sabah: The Chinese*. Kota Kinabalu, Malaysia: Natural History Publications, 2005.

———. *The Transformation of an Immigrant Society: A Study of the Chinese of Sabah*. London: Asean Academic, 1998.

Wong, Danny Tze-Ken, and Hui Ling Ho. "The Chinese in Sabah and Sarawak Politics: Ensuring a Role in Government." In *Malaysian Chinese and Nation-Building: Before Merdeka and Fifty Years After*. Vol. 2, edited by Phin Keong Voon, 525–552. Kuala Lumpur: Centre for Malaysian Chinese Studies, 2008.

Yapp, Eugene. "The 'Copyright' Controversy of 'Allah': Issues and Challenges of the Malaysian Church." *The Church in a Changing World: An Asian Response*, edited by Bruce J. Nicholls, Theresa R. Lua, and Julie Belding, 147–156. Quezon City: Asia Theological Association, 2010.

Yayasan Dakwah Islamiah Malaysia. "Tiada Lagi Gelaran Kafir Harbi, Zimmi Dalam Sistem Kewarganegaraan (No More Kafir Harbi, Dhimmi Titles in System of Citizenship)." *Yayasan Dakwah Islamiah Malaysia*, 3 October 2019. http://www.yadim.com.my/v2/tiada-lagi-gelaran-kafir-harbi-zimmi-dalam-sistem-kewarganegaraan/.

Ye'or, Bat. *The Decline of Eastern Christianity Under Islam: From Jihad to Dhimmitude: Seventh-Twentieth Century*. Translated by Miriam Kochan and David G. Littman. Madison, NJ: Fairleigh Dickinson University Press, 1996.

———. "Jews and Christians under Islam: Dhimmitude and Marcionism." Translated by Nidra Poller. *Commentaire* 97 (2002): 105–116.

Ye'or, Bat, and Jacques Ellul. *The Dhimmi: Jews & Christians under Islam*. Translated by David Maisel. Rev. enl. edition. Vancouver, Canada: Fairleigh Dickinson University Press, 1985.

Yoder, John Howard. *The Politics of Jesus*. 2nd edition. Grand Rapids, MI: Eerdmans, 1994.

Yong, Ping Chung. "Message from Bishop of Sabah." In *Diocese of Sabah 35th Anniversary, 1962–1997*, edited by Tuk Su Koo, 5. Kota Kinabalu, Malaysia: Anglican Diocese of Sabah, 1997.

Yow, Chuen Hoe. "The Chinese in Sabah and Sarawak Politics: Ensuring a Role in Government." In *Malaysian Chinese and Nation-Building: Before Merdeka and Fifty Years After*. Vol. 2, edited by Phin Keong Voon, 553–574. Kuala Lumpur: Centre for Malaysian Chinese Studies, 2008.

Zhang, Delai. *The Hakkas of Sabah: A Survey of Their Impact on the Modernization of the Bornean Malaysian State*. Kota Kinabalu, Malaysia: Sabah Theological Seminary, 2002.

———. "The History of Early Hakka Migration in Sabah." *Malaysian Journal of Humanities and Social Sciences* 3, no. 1 (2014): 1–9.

———, ed. *The Hakka Experiment in Sabah*. Kota Kinabalu, Malaysia: Sabah Theological Seminary, 2007.

———, ed. *Sabah's Hakka Story*. Kota Kinabalu: Sabah Theological Seminary, 2015.

Zuliza Mohd. Kusrin, Zaini Nasohah, Mohd. al-Adib Samuri, and Mat Noor Mat Zain. "Legal Provisions and Restrictions on the Propagation of Non-Islamic Religions among Muslims in Malaysia." *Kajian Malaysia, USM* 31, no. 2 (2013): 1–18.

Zurairi A. R. "Claiming 'Christian' DAP in Control of Dr M, Umno Man Plans Parliament Protest." *Malay Mail*. Kuala Lumpur, Malaysia, 12 July 2018. https://www.malaymail.com/news/malaysia/2018/07/12/claiming-christian-dap-in-control-of-dr-m-umno-man-plans-parliament-protest/1651529.

Langham Literature, with its publishing work, is a ministry of Langham Partnership.

Langham Partnership is a global fellowship working in pursuit of the vision God entrusted to its founder John Stott –

> *to facilitate the growth of the church in maturity and Christ-likeness through raising the standards of biblical preaching and teaching.*

Our vision is to see churches in the Majority World equipped for mission and growing to maturity in Christ through the ministry of pastors and leaders who believe, teach and live by the word of God.

Our mission is to strengthen the ministry of the word of God through:
- nurturing national movements for biblical preaching
- fostering the creation and distribution of evangelical literature
- enhancing evangelical theological education

especially in countries where churches are under-resourced.

Our ministry

Langham Preaching partners with national leaders to nurture indigenous biblical preaching movements for pastors and lay preachers all around the world. With the support of a team of trainers from many countries, a multi-level programme of seminars provides practical training, and is followed by a programme for training local facilitators. Local preachers' groups and national and regional networks ensure continuity and ongoing development, seeking to build vigorous movements committed to Bible exposition.

Langham Literature provides Majority World preachers, scholars and seminary libraries with evangelical books and electronic resources through publishing and distribution, grants and discounts. The programme also fosters the creation of indigenous evangelical books in many languages, through writer's grants, strengthening local evangelical publishing houses, and investment in major regional literature projects, such as one volume Bible commentaries like the *Africa Bible Commentary* and the *South Asia Bible Commentary*.

Langham Scholars provides financial support for evangelical doctoral students from the Majority World so that, when they return home, they may train pastors and other Christian leaders with sound, biblical and theological teaching. This programme equips those who equip others. Langham Scholars also works in partnership with Majority World seminaries in strengthening evangelical theological education. A growing number of Langham Scholars study in high quality doctoral programmes in the Majority World itself. As well as teaching the next generation of pastors, graduated Langham Scholars exercise significant influence through their writing and leadership.

To learn more about Langham Partnership and the work we do visit **langham.org**

www.ingramcontent.com/pod-product-compliance
Lightning Source LLC
Chambersburg PA
CBHW070804230426
43665CB00017B/2484